MANUAL OF
MODEL
STEAM LOCOMOTIVE
CONSTRUCTION

MANUAL OF MODEL STEAM LOCOMOTIVE CONSTRUCTION

MARTIN EVANS

MODEL & ALLIED PUBLICATIONS
ARGUS BOOKS LIMITED
14 St James Road, Watford,
Hertfordshire, England

Model and Allied Publications,
Argus Books Limited
14 St James Road, Watford,
Hertfordshire, England

First Published 1960
Second Edition 1962
Third Edition 1967
Second Impression 1969
Third Impression 1970
Fourth Impression 1972
Fifth Impression 1974
Sixth Impression 1976
Fourth Edition 1978

© Model and Allied Publications Limited 1967
© Argus Books Ltd and Martin Evans, 1976
ISBN 0 85242 161 3

All rights reserved. No part of this book may be reproduced in any form without the permission of the publisher.

Printed in Great Britain by A. Wheaton & Co. Ltd., Exeter

Contents

Chapter		Page
1	THE CHOICE OF GAUGE AND SCALE	1
2	TYPES OF LOCOMOTIVE	6
3	GENERAL PRINCIPLES OF DESIGN	12
4	MAINFRAMES, STRETCHERS, AXLEBOXES AND HORNS	20
5	WHEELS AND AXLES, CRANK AXLES, CRANK-PINS	29
6	BOGIES, PONY AND RADIAL TRUCKS	41
7	CYLINDERS AND DETAILS	50
8	CROSSHEADS AND MOTION DETAILS	63
9	VALVE GEARS: LINK MOTIONS	79
10	VALVE GEARS: RADIAL GEARS	88
11	BOILERS	109
12	BOILER FITTINGS	121
13	LUBRICATION, PUMPS, INJECTORS, BRAKES	139
14	PLATEWORK, TENDERS, TANKS AND FITTINGS	155
15	FUELS, RAISING STEAM AND DRIVING	163
	INDEX	169

Author's Preface

IN SPITE of the disappearance of steam traction from Britain's railways, in fact the almost total demise of steam in any country, the popularity of the model steam locomotive continues unabated.

It seems to me that there are an ever increasing number of steam enthusiasts wishing to try their hand at the construction of a working model steam locomotive, especially one large enough and powerful enough to haul "live" passengers. Thus it is hardly surprising that there are endless queries on the subject, especially on such important matters as valve gears and boiler design and construction.

It seems to me most important that the beginner in model locomotive work should make the right decision as to the scale and gauge he wishes to build to, and of course that he makes the right choice of prototype, of which there are an enormous number to choose from. The first two chapters, therefore, deal with these important matters, while later chapters deal with design and construction, both of the locomotive itself and of the great variety of fittings associated with it.

In the preparation of this book, which was originally written in 1959, I have drawn on the works of many well-known experts in the model locomotive world, both past and present, and I should like to mention the late C. M. Keiller in this connection, also the late L. Lawrence (better known under the initials L.B.S.C.), the late J. N. Maskelyne, the late G. S. Willoughby, the late K. N. Harris, and D. E. (Laurie) Lawrence, who happily is still with us.

I am indebted to the proprietors of the magazine *Model Engineer* for the majority of the photographs.

My sincere wish is that the book will prove of some assistance to all those who follow this most fascinating hobby.

Eydon, Nr. Daventry. MARTIN EVANS
1978.

Foreword

MODEL ENGINEERING IN GENERAL appeals to the mechanically-minded amateur as an absorbing hobby and its accomplishment gives deep satisfaction in the development of the necessary skill and the pride of craftsmanship which arises. Of the many subjects which can be taken for modelling none is more popular than the steam locomotive. It has a fascination all its own and our ancestors very aptly dubbed it the "Iron Horse". It has its parallels in the Derby Winners, the also-rans and the smart carriage horses, those patient beasts drawing heavy carts, the slow-moving plough or the narrow boats on the canals. There were willing horses, those needing the touch of the whip and the jibbers. Breeding played its part just as design does in a locomotive in its performance and suitability in service. Like a musical instrument the steam locomotive is influenced by the enginemen; some are better performers than others.

The naming of locomotives added interest and gave individuality to each of them. In the earliest days the "high-brows" were in the ascendant and drew the nomenclature from mythology, the classics and the heavens. What a lovely and imaginative selection of names followed on the old London and North Western with its haphazard numbering. Look up the eighty names of Dean's 7 ft. 8 in. single wheelers and try to imagine these wonderful creations of Swindon gliding almost silently at speed along Brunel's track of bridge rails on longitudinal sleepers as then reduced to standard gauge.

Regimentation of names and numbers began on the G.W.R. with Churchward, when blocks of numbers were issued for "Saints", "Stars" and "Counties".

Grouping subsequently extinguished a good deal of the romance attaching to the little railways absorbed. Pooling of locomotives led to indifference and neglect and it remained for Nationalisation to reduce the steam locomotive to its nadir in dirt and ugliness.

Only those at the present day who are sixty-five or over can recall such things as the glamour of Stroudley's engines on the old Brighton line, the thrill on first sighting an eight-footer on the Great Northern or a distant view of Caledonian blue streaking across country like a Kingfisher in flight.

The model engineer can turn away from the dirt and depression of the present day and try to recapture some of the charm of the past by looking back over some 150 years and alighting upon some design of bygone days which takes his fancy. A beginner could select some simple and straightforward design yet aesthetically pleasing in possessing beauty of line. The more ambitious can pick on a Webb compound, cross the Atlantic for a Pennsylvania design, adopt a Garratt from overseas or select that Rolls-Royce of the locomotive world, the Southern's "Lord Nelson".

Models can be divided into two branches, the static and dynamic. Examples of the former can be seen in the Science Museum, South Kensington, and other such places. These are scaled-down replicas of some actual locomotive and every detail is faithfully reproduced by working to a large number of drawings of the original.

Such a job is beyond the resources of the amateur, but something smaller and lacking the finer points in detail can be attempted by working to a general arrangement drawing and scaling it for dimensions of parts. The finished product may perhaps stand on a mantelpiece under a glass case as an exhibition of craftsmanship, but it would not survive the rough and tumble of operating on a track under its own steam.

Such an objective satisfies few. Most want something dynamic, a small locomotive which will steam well and pull loads on rails. To accomplish that, modifications are necessary, especially as regards boiler heating surface and superheater, smokebox layout and ashpan arrangement, while cab fittings may be somewhat out of scale if they are to be workable. Nevertheless, the exterior may be made to reproduce very closely that of the full-size locomotive which it represents to a reduced scale. It is actually a real locomotive in miniature rather than a model as strictly defined.

Present-day methods of construction are the outcome of patient development in producing a code of practice which anyone who possesses a small metal turning lathe and the necessary hand tools can follow the directions given, confident that the completion will produce a locomotive which will give the performance expected of it.

The most noted of the pioneers in the evolution of reducing the complex to the simple is Lawrence of Purley Oaks, and his serial articles in the *Model Engineer* have been an important feature for very many years under the magical initials of L.B.S.C. His peculiar genius has brought him world-wide fame and has resulted in chief mechanical engineers and other "high-ups" in the railway world, besides notabilities in other fields interested in his work, coming to his modest establishment in Purley Oaks to see and admire. Top link drivers have called round to try their hand on his multi-gauge track at operating the Lilliputian for a change.

Time moves relentlessly on and the original contributions of L.B.S.C. have come to an end leaving a deep sense of indebtedness in his followers for what has gone before.

The task of carrying on the good work in the *Model Engineer* has been entrusted to Martin Evans and he has continued by selecting some particular class of locomotive and following it through by descriptive matter and drawings of details derived from actually constructing the model himself.

Now we have his book and this opens up a much wider field for the adventurous. They can decide on some actual locomotive which they fancy or indulge in a free-lance design and find all the data to assist them in a veritable glossary, descriptive of all parts of their varieties which go together to form a working locomotive. They can take one of those delightful outline drawings by J. N. Maskelyne which appear from time to time in the *Model Engineer* and bring it to life with flesh, bones and "innards".

On being invited to contribute a Foreword to this book, I readily agreed, for although not a practising model-maker myself I have always taken a great interest in the subject generally. My contribution has hitherto been confined to making drawings for special parts on request, such as the valve gear of the famous *Tugboat Annie* and others. Of late I have furnished a complete set of drawings for the construction of a new locomotive having some novel features, just to keep my hand in after some fifty years spent on the job.   H. HOLCROFT, M.I.LOCO.E.

CHAPTER ONE

The Choice of Gauge and Scale

OF ALL THE MACHINES invented by man, the Steam Railway Locomotive probably commands our greatest interest and affection, and though its days on our main lines may now be numbered, the construction and operation of the model steam locomotive show no sign of slackening, indeed more and more model engineers all over the world are discovering the fascination of building and driving them.

The reason for all this is not so difficult to understand when we consider the power and grace and almost human qualities of the locomotive, and the endless variety of types and designs available to us.

A great deal has been and is being written in the technical press regarding the design, construction and running of small steam locomotives; in spite of this, however, there would appear to be a definite need, which this present volume attempts to meet, for a textbook covering the subject thoroughly and in an up-to-date fashion, so that those model engineers with little or no experience and modest equipment, will be able to produce a working model of good appearance and satisfactory performance.

As in other fields of model engineering, a great deal of progress has been made in the design of the small locomotive, and today it is quite common to see a $3\frac{1}{2}$ inch gauge engine of scale proportions hauling over ten times its own weight behind the tender and making non-stop runs of an hour or more. Even small 0-4-0 "industrial" type tank locomotives can be seen hauling live passengers with comparative ease.

The beginner in model locomotive work would be wise to choose first a simple type of engine, rather than a large express type with three or four cylinders. It is important to remember that the construction of a steam locomotive, even a small tank engine, is necessarily a long job for one person, and therefore the amateur of little experience and with limited workshop equipment would be well advised to tackle something simple at the outset, ensuring the completion of the job and the gaining of the confidence required for building a large express engine.

Gauges and Scales

The sizes of locomotive with which it is proposed to deal in this volume will be limited to those within the scope of the average amateur engineer. When it is realised that the driving wheels of a 15 inch gauge express passenger engine may be as much as 20 in. diameter, it will be understood that the equipment required to construct such a locomotive is really quite heavy, and beyond the great majority of model engineers.

The $10\frac{1}{4}$ inch gauge has a certain following and is employed for passenger carrying railways in pleasure parks, private estates and seaside resorts. This size gives a thoroughly stable engine and passenger car, while the boiler is large enough to steam for long periods without attention.

$9\frac{1}{2}$ inch gauge does not seem quite so popular as it was, possibly because it is in the way of being a half-way house between $10\frac{1}{4}$ inch and $7\frac{1}{4}$ inch, the latter gauge being nearer to the average amateur's resources. Locomotives built for this gauge are usually made to 2 inch scale, and as they may weigh anything up to 12 cwt. they are still a heavy job for the model engineer to tackle.

Coming now to $7\frac{1}{4}$ inch gauge, generally associated with $1\frac{1}{2}$ inch scale, this is an excellent size for the amateur who is well equipped, and provides a powerful locomotive for use on ground-level track. As a guide to the equipment required for constructing a $7\frac{1}{4}$ inch gauge engine, it may be said that a modern 6 inch centre lathe (12 inch swing) will handle the turning work necessary, the average driving wheel likely to be met with in this scale coming out at about 10 inch diameter. A small $7\frac{1}{4}$ inch gauge locomotive will negotiate a curve of about 30 feet radius, but for high speed running 60 feet is recommended. It must however be remembered that even a $7\frac{1}{4}$ inch gauge engine (except for the very small tank types) is too heavy to be lifted by one person, so that some form of lifting tackle is recommended for locomotives of this size.

The next smaller gauge in general use in this country is the 5 inch gauge, and models built for this gauge are generally made to a scale of $1\frac{1}{16}$ inch to 1 foot. In the U.S.A. the $4\frac{3}{4}$ inch gauge is used, together with 1 inch scale. This gauge is becoming increasingly popular, as it provides a locomotive powerful enough to haul 15 to 20 passengers, either on a ground-level or a raised track, while the equipment required for its construction is not beyond many model engineers. It may be said as a guide that a small 5 inch gauge tank engine can be lifted on to the track by one person, while two can handle a large express engine fairly comfortably.

$3\frac{1}{2}$ in. gauge, $\frac{3}{4}$ in. scale has today become the most popular size of all, and thousands of locomotives built to this scale are now running on club and private tracks. The reason for the popularity of this size is the fact that the model can be built using the typical 3 to $3\frac{1}{2}$ inch centre model engineer's lathe, while the boiler can be brazed up with an ordinary paraffin brazing lamp.

Given a minimum radius of curved track of about 30 feet, this size of locomotive can be driven at full speed and will haul from 2 to 15 passengers according to the type and size of engine. Even a large $3\frac{1}{2}$ inch gauge locomotive can be handled onto the track by one person, though a big American type might require the services of an assistant.

The next gauge to be considered is the $2\frac{1}{2}$ inch. Originally models for this gauge were built to a scale of $\frac{1}{2}$ inch to the foot. Nowadays however the scale used is $\frac{17}{32}$ inch which gives a slightly larger and more powerful locomotive. A large type of engine on the $2\frac{1}{2}$ inch gauge should be capable of hauling two or three "live" passengers, while curves for high-speed running should be 18–20 feet radius. Although coal firing is by far the more popular today, successful models to this scale have been built for methylated spirit or paraffin firing.

TABLE I
STANDARDS FOR THE DIFFERENT GAUGES

Gauge	Scale	Buffer height from rail	Weight of an average express loco.	Average train weight	Average speed	Loading gauge	Minimum radius of curves	Recommended radius for curves
1¼ ins.	7 mm.	24·2 mm.	7 lbs.	30 lbs.	2 m.p.h.	63 × 94½ mm.	4 ft.	6 ft.
1¾ ins.	10 mm.	34·6 mm.	20 lbs.	80 lbs.	3½ m.p.h.	90 × 135 mm.	5 ft.	10 ft.
2½ ins.	$\frac{17}{32}$ in.	$1\frac{27}{32}$ ins.	50 lbs.	2 cwt.	5 m.p.h.	4¾ × 7⅛ ins.	8 ft.	16 ft.
3½ ins.	¾ in.	$2\frac{19}{32}$ ins.	100 lbs.	9 cwt.	7 m.p.h.	6¾ × 10⅛ ins.	14 ft.	30 ft.
5 ins.	1$\frac{1}{16}$ in.	$3\frac{21}{32}$ ins.	2½ cwt.	18 cwt.	10 m.p.h.	9$\frac{9}{16}$ × 14⅜ ins.	18 ft.	35 ft.
7¼ ins.	1½ ins.	5$\frac{3}{16}$ ins.	6 cwt.	2½ tons	12 m.p.h.	13½ × 20¼ ins.	30 ft.	60 ft.
9½ ins.	2 ins.	6⅞ ins.	10 cwt.	4 tons	15 m.p.h.	18 × 27 ins.	40 ft.	100 ft.
10¼ ins.	2¼ ins.	7¾ ins.	17 cwt.	5 tons	17 m.p.h.	20¼ × 30¼ ins.	50 ft.	150 ft.

TABLE II

RECOMMENDED WHEEL STANDARDS

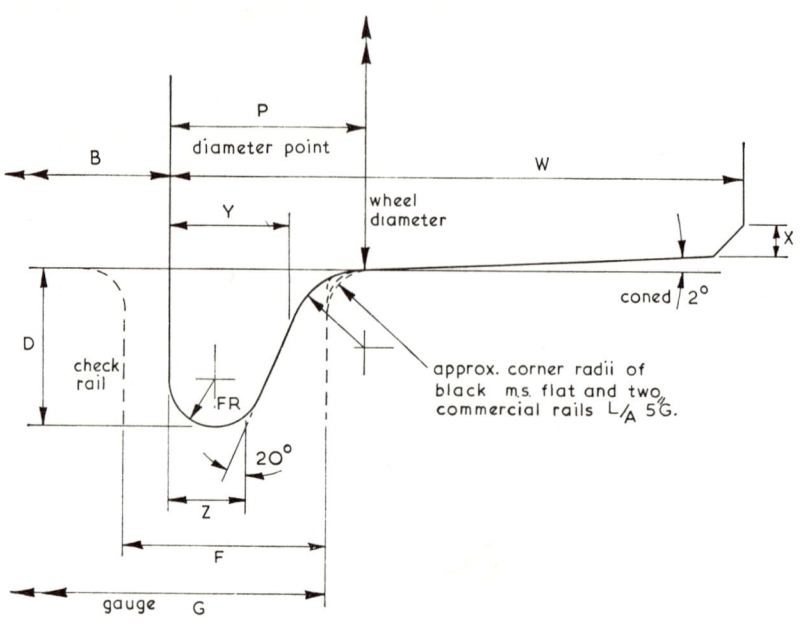

GAUGE	BACK TO BACK	TYRE WIDTH	FLANGE DEPTH	ROOT RADIUS	FLANGE RADIUS	CHAMFER	TREAD DIAMETER POINT	M/C^g DIMENSION	M/C^g DIMENSION	FLANGE WAY
G	B	W	D	RR	FR	X	P	Y	Z	F
2½"	2·281	0·268	0·085	0·035	0·020	0·015	0·090	0·055	0·034	0·093
63·5 m/m	58	6·8	2·2	0·9	·50	·40	2·3	1·4	0·90	2·3
3½"	3·281	0·375	0·110	0·050	0·030	0·020	0·126	0·076	0·051	0·130
89 m/m	83	9·5	2·8	1·3	·75	·50	3·2	1·9	1·3	3·3
5"	4·687	0·535	0·140	0·070	0·045	0·030	0·176	0·106	0·077	0·190
127 m/m	119	13·6	3·6	1·8	1·2	·80	4·5	2·7	1·95	4·8
7¼"	6·800	0·776	0·203	0·100	0·065	0·040	0·254	0·154	0·110	0·270
184 m/m	172	19·7	5·2	2·5	1·7	1·00	6·4	3·9	2·8	6·9
9½"	8·900	1·017	0·266	0·133	0·086	0·050	0·336	0·203	0·146	0·350
241 m/m	225	25·8	6·8	3·4	2·2	1·30	8·5	5·15	3·7	8·9
10¼"	9·600	1·097	0·287	0·144	0·093	0·060	0·363	0·219	0·158	0·380
260 m/m	244	27·8	8·0	3·7	2·4	1·50	9·2	5·55	4·0	9·7

Descending the scale once more, we come to the 1¾ inch gauge or gauge I associated with 10 mms. to the foot scale. This size of model is normally built for use on "scenic" model railways and both methylated spirit and paraffin firing is common, though solid fuel is sometimes used. For fast running, the minimum radius of curved track should be around 10 feet.

Models for Gauge "O" or 1¼ inch gauge are usually built to a scale of 7 mms. to the foot and are used on indoor or outdoor scenic railways. Spirit firing is the generally accepted method, though successful paraffin and even coal-fired models of this size have been built. The trouble with the coal-fired model in this scale is the tiny size of the furnace; unless the level of the coal and the blower are watched with the greatest care, the furnace will die down. A gauge "O" steam locomotive has been known to haul a live passenger, but this should only be regarded as a stunt rather than a serious model engineering proposition! Working steam models have been built for "OO" gauge and even for "OOO" gauge (⅜ inch) but this "watch-making" will not appeal to many enthusiasts.

Loading Gauges

Many model engineers, in order to gain greater power, or to obtain more clearance for outside cylinders and valve gears, increase the loading gauge beyond the normal accepted limit. There is no objection to this provided it is not carried so far as to spoil the external proportions of the locomotive. Another way to achieve the same result is to follow "narrow gauge" practice, and with this in mind several fine models have been built of the Lynton and Barnstaple engines and of Dominion and Colonial locomotives of the 3 ft. or 3 ft. 6 in. gauge.

The old broad gauge of the G.W.R. is also useful in this respect, to those whose interests lie towards the older locomotives. Such engines would have exceptional stability for their size.

A comparison between the average British loading gauge and that of the U.S.A. is interesting, the former measuring 9 ft. by 13 ft. 6 in., the latter 10 ft. 6 in. by 15 ft. It will be appreciated therefore that a model of the typical American locomotive is likely to be very much larger than its British counterpart.

CHAPTER TWO

Types of Locomotive

ONE OF THE GREATEST charms of the steam locomotive is the enormous variety of types, classes and designs available to us. Before deciding on the type of locomotive he intends to model, the amateur engineer should consider very carefully the pros and cons of the various full-size designs and their suitability or otherwise as prototypes. Generally speaking, the beginner or less-experienced model engineer should choose a fairly simple locomotive with cylinders outside the frames. If a full valve gear is essential, it will be found that there is little to choose between Joy's, Stephenson's, Walschaerts' or Baker's as regards difficulty of manufacture, provided that the detail design of the individual parts does not exactly follow the full-sized article. In fact it is in achieving great fidelity to the prototype locomotive that real skill is required.

Locomotives can be classified under four main headings: Express Passenger engines, Mixed-traffic locomotives, Goods or Mineral engines, and Tank engines; so let us now consider the various types available to us under these headings.

Express Passenger Engines

4-6-2 TYPE

The "Pacific" or 4-6-2 type locomotive is one which is very popular in this country and was at one time much used in America and most other overseas countries. In Great Britain today we have the well known British Railways "Britannia" class and classes 6 and 8, the various Gresley, Thompson and Peppercorn types of the ex-L.N.E.R., the Stanier "Pacifics" of the old L.M.S. Railway and the Bulleid streamlined "Pacifics" of the S.R., and their rebuilds.

The "Pacific" type of engine makes an excellent model, its only real drawback being the fact that a fairly large radius of curved track is necessary owing to the long wheelbase. In larger gauges, the length of tender makes the locomotive a little difficult to reach for driving purposes (unless the driver is able to sit on the tender) while the majority of this type of engine have inside cylinders in addition to outside cylinders introducing a certain amount of complication.

4-6-0 TYPE

This type is still very popular in Great Britain, but abroad its use is rapidly declining, although this is more due to the increased use of the Diesel-Electric rather than to any short-coming of this particular wheel arrangement.

As far as British railways are concerned, the 4-6-0 type gives us many excellent prototypes, both outside and inside cylinder. It is in fact a very good wheel arrangement for a medium-sized model, combining power with good flexibility, though some 4-6-0's, such as the ex-G.W.R. "Kings", "Castles", and "Stars" may prove rather troublesome as regards the latter quality owing to the proximity of the cylinders to the bogie wheels.

4-4-2 Type

The 4-4-2 or "Atlantic" type also makes a very good prototype for a model locomotive, particularly the old G.N.R. "Large Atlantic" and the S.R. "Atlantics" which had round-topped wide fireboxes, a type of firebox which is comparatively easy to build. Nearly all the "pre-group" railway companies designed 4-4-2 engines. The short rigid wheelbase of the "Atlantic" makes it suitable for rather sharp curves, while the size of the boiler allows good steam capabilities.

4-4-0 Type

At one time the 4-4-0 wheel arrangement was the most popular of all for express work in this country, and every major railway company possessed several varieties. Though the classic British 4-4-0 was an inside-cylinder machine, some engines of this type were built with outside cylinders such as the L.S.W.R. Adams express locomotives, while in more recent years some 3 cylinder 4-4-0's have been built such as the ex-L.N.E.R. "Shire" and "Hunt" classes and the S.R. "Schools".

Although at first sight the 4-4-0 wheel arrangement may appear a good one for model work, it suffers from the disadvantage that it usually makes a "front-heavy" engine. In the case of a S.R. "Schools" class locomotive, the weight of the three cylinders is concentrated over the middle of the bogie, and a good deal of adhesion weight is lost as a result.

2-4-0 Type

The 2-4-0 wheel arrangement was used to some extent towards the end of the 19th century, particularly on the old Great Eastern and London and North Western Railways.

Although not particularly flexible, this type can make quite a successful light express engine for model work, and several examples have been built in recent years particularly in $3\frac{1}{2}$ inch gauge.

2-2-2 and 4-2-2 Types

Many years have gone by since the "Single-Wheelers" were seen on our railways, yet several of the more successful designs have undoubted attractions for the model engineer. The famous Dean 4-2-2's of the old Great Western Railway were considered by many enthusiasts the most handsome locomotives ever built, while their performance on light trains was as good as their looks. Other "Singles" of beautiful proportions were the Johnson types of the ex-Midland Railway, the Caledonian No. 123 built for the railway races of the late 19th century and the outside cylinder Stirling "eight-footers" of the Great Northern.

From a model engineering point of view, the "Singles" make very interesting prototypes, though they cannot really be recommended to the beginner. It is most important that "scale" be closely adhered to, otherwise the proportions of a "Single" are spoilt. Although the type in full-size practice suffered from insufficient adhesion weight, this is not quite such a drawback in a model as might be expected as a relatively higher proportion of the total weight may be carried by the driving wheels. Several successful passenger-haulers have been built even on such a small gauge as $3\frac{1}{2}$ inch.

Mixed Traffic Engines

2-6-2 Type

This is a comparatively new wheel arrangement in this country, though it has been known in America and other overseas countries for some time.

The type is a useful one for model locomotives as it combines a large boiler, usually with wide firebox, and a wheelbase little more than a 4-6-0.

The "Green Arrows" of the ex-L.N.E.R. will be known to most readers as a very successful type of engine with this wheel arrangement.

2-6-0 Type

The "Mogul" type has been popular in many countries and all the old "Big Four" possessed several designs. Perhaps the largest and most imposing was the L.N.E.R. Gresley K.3 class, a three-cylinder machine with very large diameter boiler. The wheel arrangement is an excellent one for a model locomotive, being powerful and very compact and able to negotiate quite small radius curves, especially where the cylinders are not mounted too close to the leading wheels.

Though most of the British "Moguls" had outside Walschaerts' valve gear, the G.W.R. 2-6-0's had inside Stephenson's gear, the motion being transferred to the outside cylinders by rocking shafts.

4-6-0 Type

Originally the 4-6-0 type was designed as a goods engine, it was then developed almost exclusively for express work, finally, in more recent years, several 4-6-0's have appeared with medium-sized driving wheels for mixed-traffic work. Well known examples of the latter are the G.W.R. "Halls", "Granges" and "Manors", the L.M.S. Stanier 5P5F class, and the L.N.E.R. Thompson B.1 type.

All these locomotives make very good prototypes for passenger hauling models. For those who require a powerful locomotive which is not difficult to build, but which has a good reserve of power, the 2 cylinder mixed-traffic type is ideal.

Goods or Mineral Engines

0-6-0 Type

As far as this country is concerned, the 0-6-0 wheel arrangement was at one time the most numerous of all. It is certainly a typical British type. Almost every railway possessed some goods engines with this wheel arrangement, the driving wheels ranging from 4 feet diameter to the 5 ft. 8 in. of the Ivatt (G.N.R.) engines.

An advantage of the type is the great compactness and the fact that the whole weight of the locomotive is available for adhesion. Perhaps the most imposing of all the British 0-6-0's were the ex-G.E.R. engines designed by Mr. A. J. Hill and built at the Stratford works; these were classified as J.20 by the L.N.E.R.

0-8-0 Type

Several of the British railways had locomotives of this type, the Fowler design for the old Midland Railway, and the Webb and Bowen-Cooke designs for the London and North Western being well known. As with the 0-6-0 type, the 0-8-0 allows the whole of the weight of the engine to be used for adhesion. It is not quite so compact as the 0-6-0 and normally requires a larger radius of curved track for successful operation.

2-8-0 Type

The 2-8-0 or "Consolidation" wheel arrangement originated in the U.S.A. and also achieved great success in this country. The ex-Great Western had two distinct types which were very good engines, while the Somerset and Dorset, Great Northern, Great Central and L.M.S. Railways all built locomotives with this wheel arrangement. Both in the 1914-18 war and the 1939-45 war, this type of engine was chosen by the War department and built in large numbers.

From a model point of view, the 2-8-0 wheel arrangement is a good one provided the radii of curved track are adequate. On some models, greater flexibility is achieved by removing one or more pairs of flanges from the driving wheels, but this policy is not recommended where wheels are sprung owing to the danger of the wheels falling between the rails on model tracks. As a matter of fact this minor disaster has not been unknown in full-size practice! A better way is to allow additional end-play to the driving and coupled axles, particularly the trailing coupled axle.

2-8-2 Type

This type was fairly common in America until recent years, and on the L.N.E.R. in this country two engines with this wheel arrangement were built for mineral traffic. Later a few engines of similar wheel arrangement were built for heavy express passenger work in Scotland. Neither type had a long life.

The trailing wheels permit of a wide firebox and provided curves are adequate, the 2-8-2 type is suitable for a powerful model.

Tank Locomotives

Although tank locomotives have never been much favoured overseas, owing to limited fuel and water capacity, they have always been popular in this country, and are still used for semi-fast passenger trains, suburban trains, short distance goods trains and for shunting.

The main advantage of the tank engine in model form is that the whole locomotive is self contained, avoiding all flexible connections between engine and tender. On the other hand, most of the smaller tank locomotives are rather inaccessible from the driver's point of view, due to the back of the cab and the bunker preventing access to the firedoor and backhead fittings. For this reason many model engines of this type are built with part of the bunker and cab roof easily removable for driving purposes.

For those wishing to build a powerful locomotive quickly and without meeting too many technical difficulties, there is a lot to be said for an 0-6-0 outside cylinder engine such as the ex-L.M.S. Fowler 2F class. The complication of a crank-axle is avoided while there are no loose carrying wheels to bother about. Many industrial and narrow gauge locomotives have been built with this wheel and cylinder arrangement and these too make excellent prototypes for models.

For the larger tank engine model the 2-6-4 and 4-6-4 wheel arrangement should be considered. The former L.M.S. Railway had several fine examples of these two types, while the ex-L.N.E.R. and S.R. had 2-6-4 tank locomotives. The famous L.B.S.C. "Baltics", though later rebuilt as tender engines, will be known to many.

A point in favour of the larger tank locomotive as a prototype is the greater distance between the backhead and the back of the bunker, which greatly assists accessibility and ease of driving, while plenty of space is available for cab fittings and controls and for fuel and water.

Articulated Locomotives

Under this heading we have the "Mallet", at one time very popular in the U.S.A., the "Garratt" type, the "Fairlie", the "Shay" and "Heisler" geared locomotives and many other special purpose types.

A feature of the "Mallet" is the large boiler supplying two sets of cylinders, motion and driving wheels, each set of which can swing in relation to the other, thus providing greater flexibility. Generally these locomotives are built as compounds, the leading cylinders working on low pressure steam and the rear cylinders on high pressure.

The "Garratt" type generally consists of two complete "chassis", the leading chassis carrying a water container, the rear supporting a second "tender" of fuel, or fuel and water, the two units being bridged by a large boiler and cab mounted on a girder framework. This type of locomotive is proving very popular in South and East Africa, and is built for running on both standard and narrow gauge track.

The "Fairlie", "Shay" and "Heisler" are all special types of locomotive built for particularly sharp curves or for lines of indifferent level and stability. These locomotives, together with the "Mallet" and "Garratt", make fine prototypes for the more experienced model engineer who requires something out of the ordinary.

Free-Lance Designs

Many model engineers prefer not to build exact replicas of the full-size locomotives, but design their own, embodying the features which most appeal to them. This might at first sight appear an easier task than copying a prototype locomotive, but if the free-lance model is to be of good proportions and to have a first-class performance this is not necessarily so. However, the working out of the design and the proportioning of the various components will be found a most interesting and absorbing occupation.

CHAPTER THREE

General Principles of Design

IN ATTEMPTING THE DESIGN of a model steam locomotive, the model engineer should beware of relying too much on accepted data and formulae which have been adopted for the full-size engine. This is not to say that some formulae are not useful, they are, but many of the well-known principles of 4 ft. 8½ ins. design do not apply when we are dealing with 2½ in. or 3½ in. gauge.

As an example of this point of view we may consider the diameter of the driving and coupled wheels of locomotives. In full-size practice wheels of the order of 6 ft. 6 ins. to 6 ft. 9 ins. are general for high-speed passenger work, while wheels of 4 ft. diameter would only be regarded as suitable for shunting and slow goods traffic. On 3½ in. gauge however, it will be found that a locomotive with small driving wheels will attain a very high speed, and the limitation to its speed may well be the question of keeping the model on the track rather than the size of its driving wheels.

In designing his own locomotive, the amateur is usually compelled to think in terms of the capacity of his workshop, but suitable proportions of cylinders and boiler will be one of his first problems so it is now proposed to say a few words on this subject.

Tractive Effort

In determining the theoretical tractive effort of a model locomotive, it is most important to arrange for this to be in proportion to the weight available for adhesion. Obviously it would be no good putting very large cylinders on a locomotive of small adhesive weight, even if the boiler was capable of steaming those cylinders.

At one time it was accepted that the tractive effort of a model locomotive should not exceed ¼ of its adhesive weight, but recent experience has shown that it can be higher than this and successful engines have been built where the tractive effort was ⅓ or even ½ of the weight available for adhesion.

The formula generally employed for estimating the tractive effort of a locomotive with 2 cylinders is as follows.

$$\text{Tractive Effort} = \frac{B^2 \times S \times P}{W} \text{ lb.}$$

Where B is the diameter of cylinders in inches.
S is the stroke of cylinders in inches.
P is the effective steam pressure in lb. per sq. in.
W is the diameter of driving wheels in inches.

In full-size practice it is customary to use 85 per cent. of the boiler working pressure as the effective steam pressure (P) but a smaller figure is generally considered nearer to the mark, owing to the (comparatively) smaller steam pipes and passages usually employed.

For 3 cylinder simple locomotives, the above formula would be multiplied by $\frac{3}{2}$ and for 4 cylinder engines, by 2.

For 2 cylinder compound engines, the following formula (Von Borries) may be used:—

$$\text{T.E.} = \frac{D^2 \times S \times P}{4 \times W}$$

Where D is the diameter of the low pressure cylinder, and where the ratio between the high and low pressure piston areas is between 1: 2·1 and 1: 2·3.

For 4 cylinder compounds, the following formula (Baldwin) is generally used:—

$$\text{T.E.} = \frac{2B^2 \times S \times P}{3 \times W} + \frac{D^2 \times S \times P}{4 \times W}$$

Where D is the diameter of the low pressure cylinder
and B is the diameter of the high pressure cylinder.

As an example of the working of this formula, let us take a typical 3½ in. gauge mixed traffic 4-6-0 locomotive. The cylinders (two) might be 1⅛ in. bore × 1¾ in. stroke. The driving wheel diameter 4½ in. and the boiler working pressure 80 lb. per sq. in.

$$\text{Then T.E.} = \frac{1\tfrac{1}{8}^2 \times 1\tfrac{3}{4} \times 80}{4\tfrac{1}{2}} \times \frac{70}{100} \text{ lb.}$$

$$= 27\cdot15 \text{ lb.}$$

In estimating the load which a model locomotive can be expected to haul, the tractive effort formula will only give us an approximation as there are so many other factors of variable influence which have a bearing on the matter. Among these we may mention the adhesive weight of the engine itself, the actual area of contact between the wheels of the locomotive and the rails, the material and the condition of the rails themselves, the internal friction of the locomotive and the rolling resistance of the train being hauled. However, as a rough guide it may be said that in a model locomotive, 1 lb. of drawbar pull will haul a train of 30 lb. weight on level track.

Size of Cylinders

Although the formula for tractive effort given previously gives us some idea as to the size of cylinders required for a certain duty, it will be appreciated that unless the boiler can provide sufficient steam for them, the chosen size of cylinders may well prove useless. But here again it is difficult to give a suitable formula to enable the amateur designer to arrange for a boiler of the steam-producing capacity desired for the particular cylinders he has in mind. The steam producing capacity of a boiler depends on many factors, and there are too many "variables" to enable one to arrive at a reliable formula.

In boiler design, good proportion is all important; a huge boiler with inadequate grate area, with tubes of too small or too large a diameter or with badly proportioned firebox, might produce much less steam than a boiler of quite moderate overall dimensions, but where the barrel, tubes, firebox and grate were in good proportion to one another. As a very rough guide, it may be said that in a medium sized model, the grate area should be about 1/25 of the heating surface.

The working pressure of the boiler is another value which should be decided early on. Generally speaking, the larger the scale of the model, the higher the working pressure, and a table is given below showing recommended working pressures for different sizes of models.

TABLE III

RECOMMENDED WORKING PRESSURES

Gauge in.	Pressure lb. per sq. in.
1¼	45
1¾	60
2½	70
3½	80
5	90
7¼	100
9½	120
10¼	130

The advantages of a high steam pressure are as follows: less liability to "prime", higher tractive effort for a given size of cylinders, higher thermal efficiency in the cylinders themselves, improved draught for the furnace. The disadvantages are: a heavier and stronger boiler is required, leakage of steam past pistons, valves and glands more likely, lubrication more critical due to the higher temperature of the steam particularly where superheating is used.

As regards the overall dimensions of the boiler, the author's opinion, borne out by many practical examples, is that one cannot do better than to scale down the dimensions of the prototype, provided only that the prototype chosen is one that has been thoroughly successful in practice. The internal arrangement of the model boiler must of course be very different, and although it is not possible to give a formula from which one could calculate suitable proportions of barrel, firebox, grate, etc., the author has worked out the following table from actual examples of successful model locomotives in three gauges.

The figures given for firebox heating surface are only approximate, no allowance having been made for side stays, but it is hoped that the table will prove interesting and helpful to those designing their own boilers.

Table IV
Locomotive Boiler Proportions

Gauge of locomotive	Type of locomotive	Boiler barrel diameter	Barrel length	Tube heating surface	Superheater flue heating surface	Combustion chamber heating surface	Firebox heating surface	Grate area
1¾ ins.	2-cyl. Pacific	2¼ ins.	8¼ ins.	28 sq. in.	11 sq. in.	18 sq. in.	23 sq. in.	7½ sq. in.
2½ ins.	2-cyl. 2-8-0	3½ ins.	7 ins.	66 sq. in.	33 sq. in.	—	40 sq. in.	9½ sq. in.
3½ ins.	2-cyl. 4-4-0	4¼ ins.	9 ins.	115 sq. in.	43 sq. in.	—	79 sq. in.	12 sq. in.
3½ ins.	2-cyl. 0-8-0	3¾ ins.	11 ins.	155 sq. in.	81 sq. in.	—	76 sq. in.	10 sq. in.
3½ ins.	3-cyl. Pacific	4½ ins.	16 ins.	216 sq. in.	103 sq. in.	68 sq. in.	81 sq. in.	23 sq. in.
5 ins.	2-cyl. 0-6-0T	5 ins.	11½ ins.	284 sq. in.	126 sq. in.	—	83 sq. in.	13½ sq. in.
5 ins.	2-cyl. 4-4-0	5 ins.	13 ins.	275 sq. in.	123 sq. in.	—	118 sq. in.	17 sq. in.
5 ins.	2-cyl. 0-8-0	5½ ins.	16 ins.	377 sq. in.	150 sq. in.	—	101 sq. in.	19½ sq. in.

Boiler Tubes and Flues

Another important point in boiler design is the diameter of the tubes and superheater flues. Dealing with the former first, full-size British locomotive boilers have tubes from 1⅝ in. to 2⅜ in. outside diameter. By comparing the diameter of the tubes with their overall length, it soon becomes apparent that there is a definite relationship between the two. From actual examples the ratio $L/D^2 = 50$ to 70 would appear to be correct for almost any loco. type boiler, where L = the overall length of tube in inches, and D = the inside diameter of the tube.

Coming now to the flues housing the superheater elements, the elements themselves must be of sufficient size and of sufficient number to allow the live steam to pass through without any suspicion of "wire-drawing", and at the same time the internal diameter of the flues must be sufficient to ensure that the temperature of the steam is considerably increased. On the other hand, if the superheater flues are made too large in relation to the diameter of the tubes, too much heat will pass through and be lost up the chimney.

In practice it has been found that the outside diameter of the flues in the smaller model boilers should be twice the outside diameter of the tubes, or a little less, and the superheater elements should be approximately one third the diameter of the flues. For example, in a 3½ in. gauge engine, the tubes might be ⅜ in. outside diameter, the flues ¾ in. diameter and the superheater elements ¼ in. diameter. As regards the number of flues to be employed, this would depend to some extent on the overall dimensions of the boiler and the size of the main steam pipe, in order that the total cross-sectional area of the superheater elements shall be somewhat greater than the cross-sectional area of the main steam pipe. To take an example again, if the main steam pipe is 5/16 in. internal diameter, and the superheater elements are ¼ in. outside diameter × 20 s.w.g. thick, there would have to be 3 superheater flues of ¾ in. diameter to fulfil the above conditions.

Combustion Chambers

Boilers having very long barrels may often be improved by fitting a combustion chamber. This is in effect an extension of the firebox towards the front end of the boiler, thus shortening the tubes and flues and increasing the effective volume of the firebox without altering the grate area. This device has been employed in some full-size boilers, generally of the wide firebox type, with every success, and its use in model boilers too can often be recommended.

The length of the combustion chamber can be anything from ¼ to 1¼ times the length of the firebox, according to the barrel length and the general proportions of the boiler, while its cross-sectional area will follow the existing layout of the tubes and flues. For this reason it is not normally possible to make the chamber truly circular, so that unless it is made of rather heavy material, cross-staying becomes necessary. As an alternative to the usual rod stays, water tubes may be used. These should be of fairly large diameter, about ½ in. diameter in a ¾ in. scale boiler, and arranged at an angle to the vertical. Their position should be watched in relation to the position of the regulator steam-collecting pipe and to the position of the safety valves. These water tubes improve the water circulation of the boiler in addition to increasing the total heating surface.

Superheating

The economy of superheated steam has now been proved conclusively in full-size locomotive practice, and practically all modern locomotives are fitted with superheating apparatus.

Steam is said to be superheated when its temperature has been raised above that of the water from which it is formed. The term saturated is applied to steam when in contact with the water in the boiler, under which conditions its temperature cannot be raised without a corresponding increase of pressure. With modern piston valves and metallic packings, a superheated steam temperature of 700° F. is common, and the advantages gained are as follows: Larger production of steam, as a given volume of saturated steam increases in volume when superheated; Reduction of losses from cylinder condensation; More efficient expansive behaviour of the steam in the cylinders.

At one time superheating was not regarded as necessary on model steam locomotives, but when the results obtained from full-size practice are considered, it soon becomes apparent that similar results should apply to models, and in fact recent experience has shown this to be the case. On models with cast-iron cylinders fitted with proper rings and with adequate and reliable lubrication, quite a high degree of superheat can be used with every advantage, but where gunmetal cylinders with soft packings are in use, the superheating must not be overdone.

As regards the type of superheater to be used, the smokebox or "grid-iron" type is not to be recommended. Its heating value is doubtful, while it takes up too much room in the smokebox, making access to the various steam pipes, blower, etc., somewhat difficult. A better plan is to adopt the flue-tube type, sometimes called the "spearhead" type. With this type one or more elements are run from the smokebox "header", through one of the flue tubes nearly as far as the firebox and then back again to the "hot" header and so to the cylinders.

In most $2\frac{1}{2}$ in. gauge models, one or possibly two such flues and elements are used, in $3\frac{1}{2}$ in. gauge any number from two to five may be used according to the size of the boiler, while in the large models, the number of flues may go up to twelve or more.

The superheater elements should be made of copper or rustless steel of somewhat thicker gauge than that used for the ordinary boiler tubes, while the end of the element nearest to the furnace should preferably be built up by welding or a special fitting used to protect the element at this vital point. In addition the elements should be designed so that they can be easily removed should renewal be required at any time.

Blast Pipes and Orifices

The shape and size of a locomotive's blast pipe and orifice together with its chimney and petticoat pipe are very important matters in both full-size and model practice. In fact it is true to say that only in the last few years has this matter received the attention it deserves.

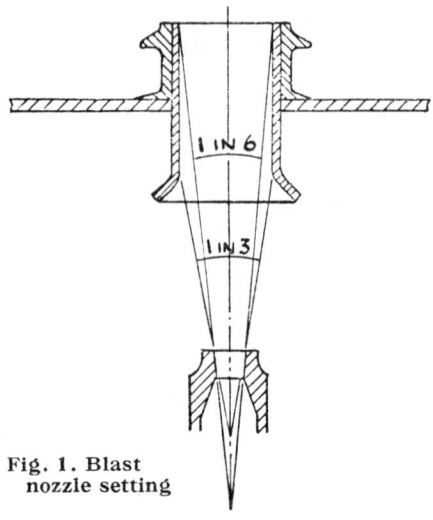

Fig. 1. Blast nozzle setting

The size of the exhaust orifice should always be finally determined by practical experiment, the blast nozzle being made removable for the purpose, but as a rough guide, for a 2 cylinder simple engine, the orifice can be made $1/7 \times$ the diameter of the cylinders. The orifice must be located in its correct position below the chimney, and on its vertical centre-line, the alignment of the pipe being checked by means of a broach or by a rod with a centring washer fitted in the chimney of the locomotive. The vertical position of the blast nozzle can be decided fairly accurately by the use of two coned templates, one being of 1 in 3 angle, the other of 1 to 6. The effective length of the petticoat pipe below the chimney can be decided by means of the 1 in 3 template, while the 1 in 6 template fixes the position in relation to the top of the chimney.

It is also important, especially with coal-fired boilers, that the smokebox door should be close fitting. Any leakage here or around the steam and exhaust pipes where they pass through the smokebox, will destroy the smokebox vacuum and result in poor steaming.

Compounding

As far as the smaller gauge of locomotive is concerned, it is very doubtful whether compounding increases efficiency very much. In full-size practice, where economy of fuel is so important, it is a different matter, and many different methods have been tried both in this country and abroad. The well-known Midland compounds proved very successful, while in France, the Chapelon 4-6-2 and 4-8-0 compound express engines were probably the most efficient steam locomotives ever built.

In model practice, the three or four cylinder system gives the best chance of success; the working steam pressure should be made fairly high, while the cut off in the high pressure cylinders should not be made too late. Compounding is certainly a most interesting field for the adventurous model engineer, who is prepared to try out his ideas and to spend some time experimenting before he achieves success.

Flash Steam Boilers

In an attempt to simplify the somewhat elaborate locomotive type boiler, a few model engineers have experimented with the flash steam system. The basis of this system is a closely coiled length of tube enclosed in an insulated casing, the tube being heated by either a coal fire or an oil burner. The water supply is carried in the tender and is pumped through this tube by means of one or two axle-driven pumps or by crosshead pumps. On meeting the heated part of the tube, the water is rapidly converted into steam at high temperature and pressure. From the first series of coils, the steam passes to the regulator, then through a secondary series of coils and finally to the cylinders. To start the boiler, it is of course necessary to use some form of hand-pump, but once steam is raised, the locomotive's own pumps take over.

While a powerful locomotive can be produced in this way, the flash system cannot be recommended as there is too little control over either the pressure or temperature attained, neither is there any reserve upon which the cylinders may draw when required. In any case, the number of controls needed for this system become too many and complicated for the average driver to handle with safety.

CHAPTER FOUR

Main Frames, Stretchers, Axleboxes and Horns

IN BUILDING A MODEL steam locomotive, the most usual practice is to make a start on the mainframes, and follow these with the buffer and drag beams, hornblocks, main axleboxes and frame stretchers. On the 4 ft. 8½ in. gauge engine, the mainframes are generally made of mild steel, which may be of 1 in. to 1¼ in. thickness, and are made as deep as possible especially over the slots which are cut for the axleboxes.

It is a mistake to make the frame of a model to scale thickness, something a good deal heavier is required to stand up to hard work, and the table below gives suitable thickness of frame according to the scale of the model, and also the recommended distance between frames.

TABLE V
DETAILS OF MAINFRAMES

Gauge	Thickness of frame	Distance between frames
1¼ in.	1/16 in.	7/8 in.
1¾ in.	1/16 in.	1 5/16 in.
2½ in.	3/32 in.	1 15/16 in.
3½ in.	1/8 in.	2 7/8 in.
5 in.	5/32 in.	4 1/16 in.
7¼ in.	3/16 in.	6 1/16 in.
9½ in.	¼ in.	8 in.
10¼ in.	5/16 in.	8 3/8 in.

As regards the material to be used, the model engineer cannot do better than to use a good quality planished, bright or blue mild steel plate. Cast frames are sometimes employed, having the horns, angles and brackets all cast in one piece; it is very doubtful if these really save any time, and it is difficult to prevent warping, though they have their use for American prototypes to simulate the forged bar frames generally employed in the latter.

Before commencing the marking out of the main frames, it is advisable to clean the steel thoroughly and coat it with marking out fluid, or with a solution of copper sulphate. The latter will give the steel a reddish colouring against which the scribed lines will show up very clearly. Only one mainframe need be marked out, this can then be drilled in about four places and temporarily riveted to the second plate with copper rivets. Before marking out, it is essential to true up one edge of the frame, usually the bottom edge is chosen, as many of the dimensions as possible being taken from this as a datum. The centre line of the cylinders should be scribed clearly and also the vertical centre lines of all wheels. The position of as many holes as it is possible to determine at this stage should be marked out, and after the two frame plates have been riveted together, all these holes should be drilled. The frames can then be sawn out, and filed to shape.

The task of sawing out the mainframes will be found a great deal easier if the correct hacksaw blade is chosen, a 12 in. high-speed steel blade is well worth while and plenty of cutting oil should be used. On long "cuts" it may be necessary to turn the blade through 90° in the frame, so as to avoid the back of the frame fouling the job. To avoid the possibility of distortion, chiselling should not be resorted to, where concave curves are required, as for instance in the clearance arches for bogie or pony-truck wheels, a row of small holes can be drilled, just outside the scribed line and as close together as possible, the unwanted piece of metal being broken out.

Buffer and Drag Beams

The buffer-beam and drag-beam are generally cut from flat steel plate a little thicker than the material used for the mainframes, and these are attached to the frames by means of steel angles. In models up to $3\frac{1}{2}$ in. gauge, these angles are usually placed on the inside of the mainframes only being riveted to the buffer-beams, while screws are used to hold the frames to the angles. On larger models it is advisable to put these angles on the outside as well as on the inside of the frames for additional strength.

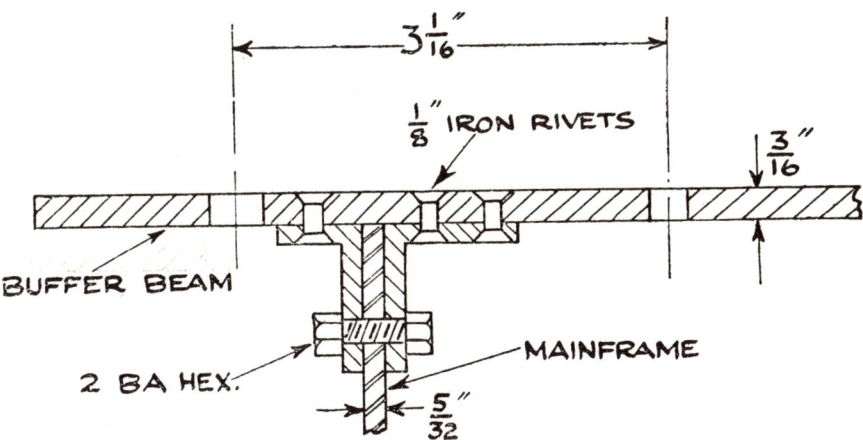

Fig. 2. Assembly of Buffer Beam for 5 in. gauge model

For models up to 1 in. scale, bright steel angle is often used for the buffer-beam itself, slots being cut in the top of the angle to receive the frames. This is a convenient method as the top of the angle provides a good "bed" for attachment of the footplates, however it is important to ensure that the angle chosen is really square as unfortunately a good deal of the commercial angle steel is definitely not so! Castings too are sometimes used for buffer-beams, especially for $2\frac{1}{2}$ in. gauge and 1 gauge models, in which case lugs are provided to receive the frames while guard irons are sometimes cast integral with the beams.

Some model engineers braze or weld the mainframes of the locomotives direct to the buffer-beams. This makes a very strong assembly but there are some disadvantages—it is impossible to separate the frames, an operation which might prove necessary at a later date for a variety of reasons; the frames are liable to distortion owing to the high temperature to which they are subjected; the brazing or welding operation generally leaves the metal in a discoloured and scale-covered state.

Frame Stretchers

It is most important that the mainframes of the locomotive are quite rigid and able to stand up to the severe stresses and strains to which they are subjected. The frame stretchers should therefore be sited with care and designed to absorb these stresses. In the case of inside cylinder locomotives, the motion plate which carries the outer ends of the slide bars, also acts as a strong frame stiffening. Plain round stretchers are quite satisfactory for models up to $2\frac{1}{2}$ in. gauge, and they have the advantage, if they are turned, drilled and tapped in the lathe, of ensuring that the frames are assembled quite square. For larger models, at least one of the frame stretchers should be rather more elaborate, and either a well-ribbed casting used, or a strong built-up construction employed.

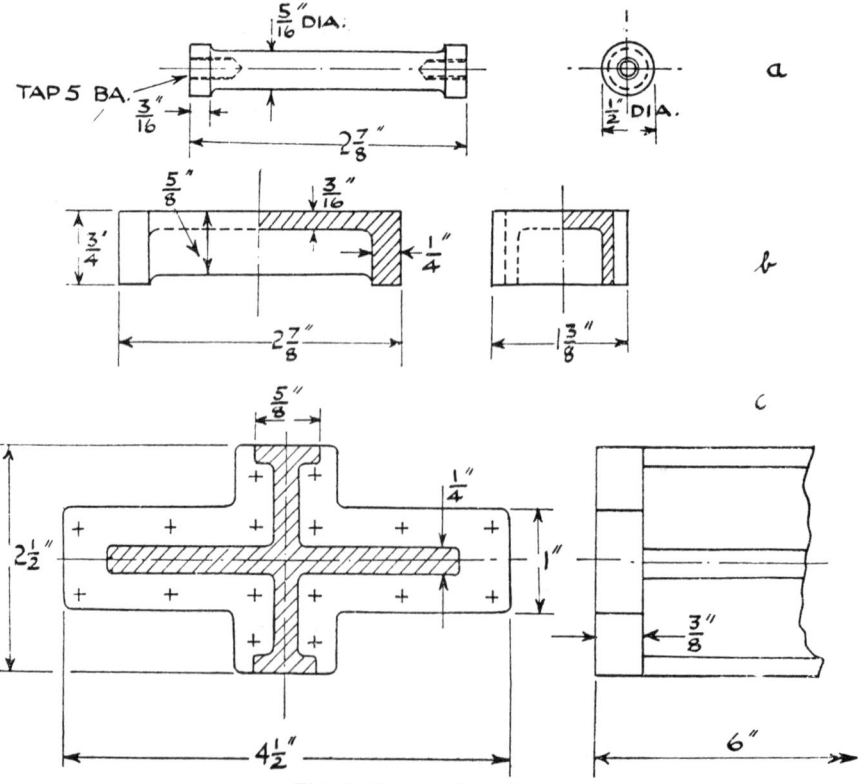

Fig. 3. Frame Stretchers
(a) Simple $3\frac{1}{2}$ in. gauge Stretcher. (b) Cast Stretcher. (c) A large cast Stretcher

Hornblocks

Before the mainframes can be erected, the hornblocks must be fitted and machined ready to take the main axleboxes. Hornblocks are essential on all except the smallest models, not only to provide greater working surface for the sides of the axleboxes but also to stiffen the frames themselves at their weakest point.

In Gauge "O" and "1" models, the main axlebox can bear directly against the frame, this practice will be found to give sufficient wear for most models. For $2\frac{1}{2}$ in. and $3\frac{1}{2}$ in. gauge, "hot-pressed" hornblocks are generally available, these will be found a great boon to the model engineer as they require practically no machining. For larger models gunmetal or iron castings are usually employed with steel hornstays. The inside face should first of all be filed, to remove sand and scale, the hornblocks can then be set up on a vertical slide in the lathe, and the bolting face machined by means of an end-mill held in the chuck or in a collet. After machining, the horns are riveted to the frames, using soft iron snaphead rivets, the heads being placed on the inside of the model, the outer ends being hammered into countersinks on the outsides of the frames.

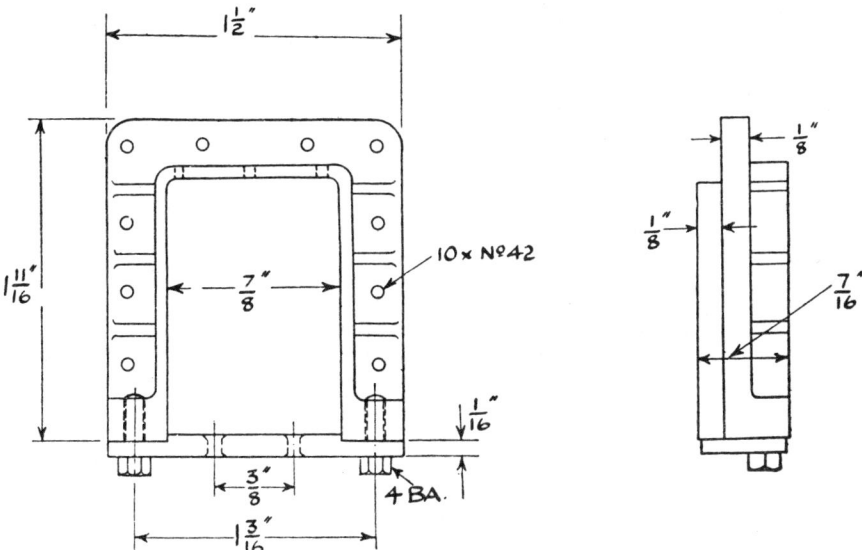

Fig. 4. Hornblocks for $3\frac{1}{2}$ in. gauge locomotives

Countersunk screws may also be used, instead of rivets, the nuts being placed on the inside, but care must be taken that they do not work loose in service. Separate horn checks are sometimes employed in models, but as these do not stiffen the frames appreciably, the one-piece hornblock is generally to be preferred. It is a good plan to drill holes in the top flange of the hornblock before assembly, so that lubrication pipes for the axle journal and the axlebox sides can be fitted at a later stage.

After the hornblocks are fitted to the frames, the latter must be bolted together back to back for the inside or working surfaces of the horns to be machined. Where a large lathe is available, it is sometimes possible to machine these surfaces with a large diameter side and face cutter the frames being clamped parallel to the lathe bed, and at centre height. Another method is to use a large end-mill in the lathe chuck, the frames being held across the lathe on an angle plate bolted to the vertical slide. Filing machines are also very useful for this operation, while if no mechanical method can be adopted, the horns can be hand filed using a steel bar of the appropriate width as a gauge.

Axleboxes

Locomotive main axleboxes may be made from iron or steel castings with gunmetal bearing "brasses", or from gunmetal castings, while on all types linings of white or anti-friction metal are provided on the upper half of the box. The latter

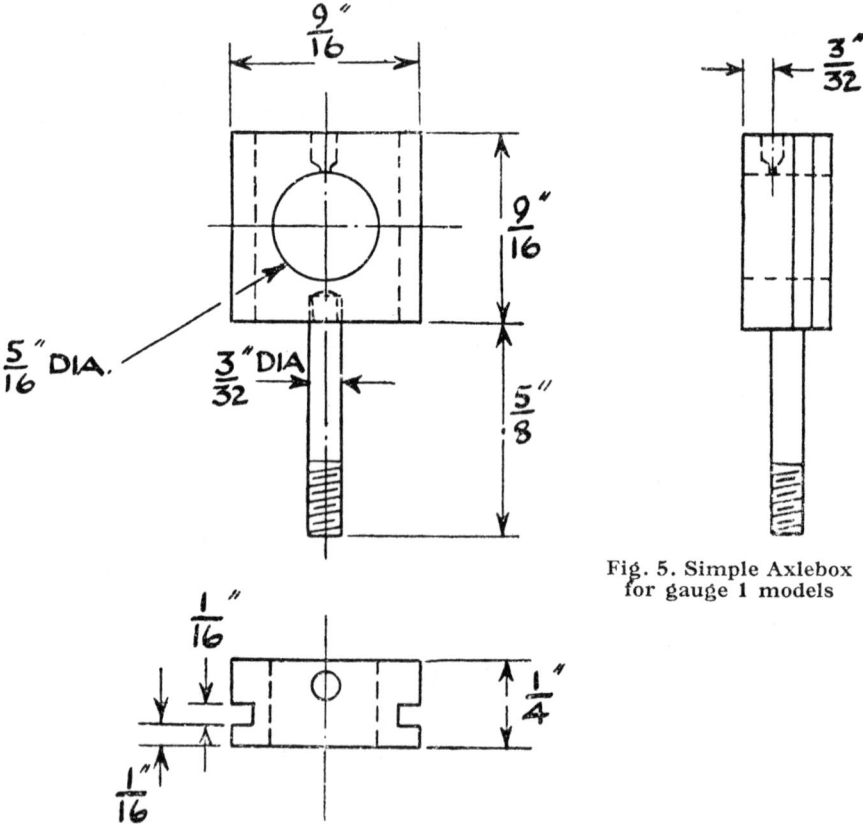

Fig. 5. Simple Axlebox for gauge 1 models

metal is employed for its smooth-running qualities and also because it does not damage the bearing should the axlebox run warm.

In model locomotive practice it is usual to adopt the one-piece rectangular cast gunmetal axlebox for engines up to $\frac{3}{4}$ in. scale. On larger models a separate keep is adopted while the axlebox itself may be either an iron or a gunmetal casting, the

MAINFRAMES, STRETCHERS, AXLEBOXES AND HORNS

former being provided with gunmetal "brasses". While not essential, models larger than 1½ in. scale may have white-metal inserts as in full size practice, and when these are fitted, serrations should be cut in the brasses to retain the white-metal in position.

A positive lubrication system is advised on larger gauge models, the oil being provided either by a mechanical lubricator mounted on the footplate, or from plain oil receptacles with hinged lids and separate pipes leading to each axlebox.

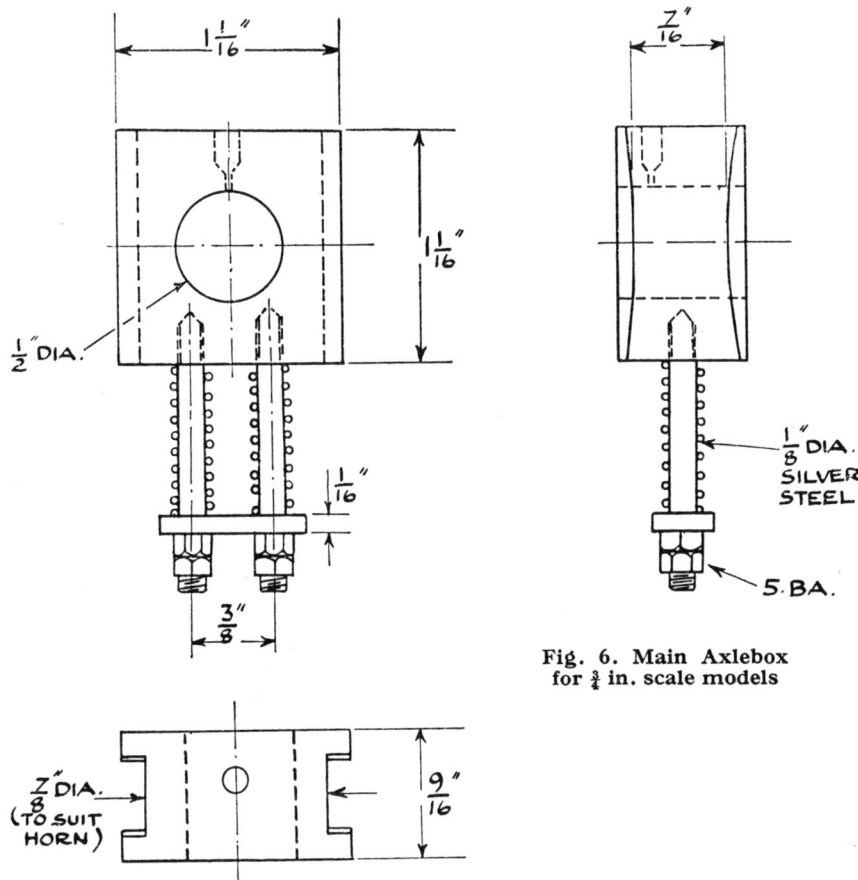

Fig. 6. Main Axlebox for ¾ in. scale models

Ball or roller races are sometimes adopted in models, where expense is not a consideration, and provided they are properly fitted, they definitely reduce friction and give longer wear if kept clean and lubricated. The double row self-aligning type ball races are probably the most convenient for the purpose; the needle roller type have also been used, particularly in America, but for these the axle journal must be hardened. In all cases, some lateral play between the axlebox and the horns should be allowed; this also applies to the plain type axlebox. It is advisable to round off the insides of the axlebox flanges so that there is no possibility of the axlebox jamming in the horns due to slight irregularities in the track.

26 MODEL STEAM LOCOMOTIVE CONSTRUCTION

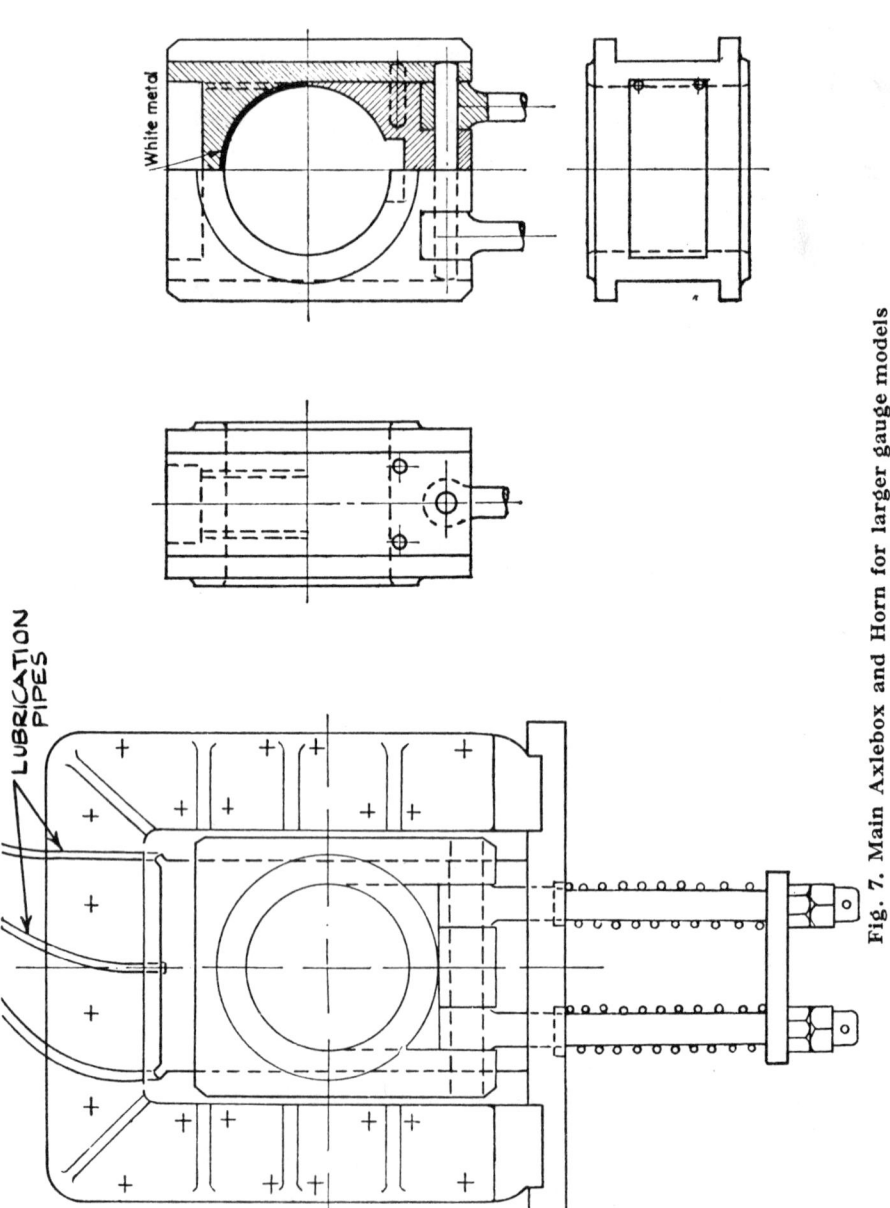

Fig. 7. Main Axlebox and Horn for larger gauge models

Springs for Axleboxes

Although laminated springs are now almost universal in full-size locomotive practice, they are not advised on small scale models as they do not provide sufficient deflection unless made of very light material. Where laminated springs are required, they should be made of proper spring steel, and to obtain greater flexibility, two thin leaves of each length may be employed rather than one of normal thickness. If each pair of such leaves are packed out at the centre, still more flexibility is obtained. Another point to note is that the spring leaves should not all lie at the same radius when not under load and before assembly. The shorter the leaf, the smaller its normal radius should be. As regards the radius or "camber" of laminated springs, it should be remembered that the more the "camber", the less the flexibility. Generally speaking, a laminated spring should be nearly flat when under full load, in order that it shall have plenty of flexibility.

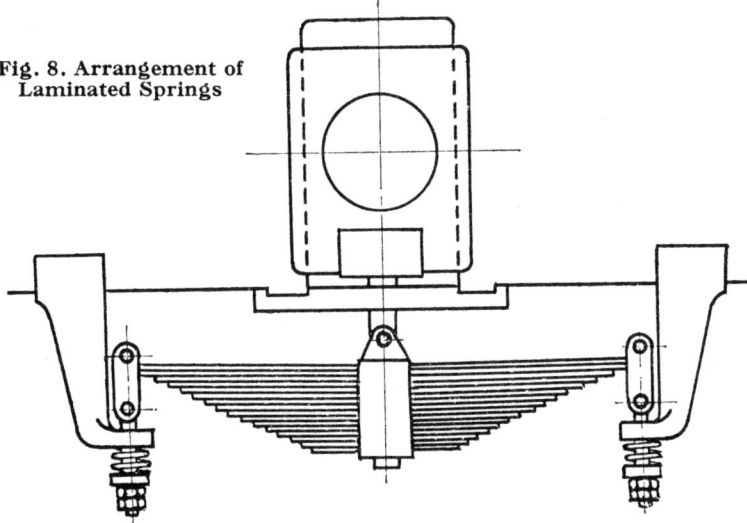

Fig. 8. Arrangement of Laminated Springs

Coil springs are very satisfactory on all models up to $10\frac{1}{4}$ in. gauge and except in the case of gauge "O" and "1" models, two springs should be provided for each axlebox. When the hornstays are of sufficient size it is a good plan to recess the stays to take the top ends of the springs, the bottom ends being similarly located by a stepped washer. This method keeps the spring central about its pin. Two nuts should be used, tightened against one another, to provide adjustment while ensuring security. The hornstays themselves should if possible be recessed into the gap of the hornblocks so that they take both compression and tensile stresses. The springs should have a bore rather more than the diameter of the spring pin. For a $3\frac{1}{2}$ in. gauge model, the spring pins may be of $\frac{1}{8}$ in. diameter, and the springs $\frac{5}{32}$ in. internal diameter and wound from 20 s.w.g. wire. For $\frac{1}{2}$ in. scale models, springs made from 22 s.w.g. wire will be found satisfactory in most cases. The holes in the hornstays through which the spring pins pass should be made a shade larger in diameter than the pin itself, otherwise the axlebox may tend to jam.

Machining of Axleboxes

Axleboxes for the smaller gauges are usually cast in the form of a "stick", or length sufficient for three or four boxes. These can be quickly machined where a horizontal milling machine is available, a side and face cutter doing most of the work. After machining the faces and the flanges and bearing surfaces, the "stick" is removed from the miller and the axleboxes parted off or sawn apart, the tops being faced off in the lathe. Where no milling machine is available, the baxes can be clamped in a machine vice on a vertical slide set up in the lathe and on end-mill held in the chuck or in a collet, used to machine the sides and faces. If the bar of axleboxes is very accurately centered, the same set-up can be used to drill and bore the axleboxes, but it is a good plan in any event to machine the bores a few "thou" undersize and to ream the axleboxes actually in position in the mainframe, the reamer being put right through each pair of boxes by hand.

Another method of drilling is to mark the axleboxes and then to clamp them in pairs by their working surfaces, when the drill can be run through both without shifting their relative position. After parting, the axleboxes can be mounted in the frames for drilling for the spring pins; in the case of the solid type axlebox, this can be done using the hornkeep as a guide for the drill. The position for the lubrication hole or holes can also be determined at this stage from the holes previously drilled in the hornblock.

CHAPTER FIVE

Wheels, Axles, Crank Axles, Crankpins

IN THE MODERN FULL-SIZE locomotive, the wheels are in two main parts; the centre, which is usually a steel casting toughened by annealing, comprising the boss, the spokes and the rim; and the tyres which are rolled in one piece from good quality open hearth or Bessemer steel. The tyres are turned all over and shrunk on, being additionally secured by studs or retaining rings. On some small goods engines and shunting engines the wheel centre may be an iron casting. The balance weights, essential to counterbalance the weight of the crankpins and motion, may be cast in, though modern practice appears to favour the fitting of separate balance weights which are held to the wheel by rivets and plates on the outside and inside of the spokes.

The wheels for all but the very largest models should be made as one-piece castings in a good quality grey iron, it is only on the larger scale locomotives that the extra trouble of fitting separate steel tyres is really justified. On the other hand there is good reason to believe that steel tyres give better adhesion than plain cast iron. In the smaller gauge of model care must be taken to avoid wheel castings which have been "chilled" in cooling in the mould. Such chilled wheels quickly spoil the ordinary type of lathe tool and in any case ruin the finish of the wheel itself.

Locomotive wheels are of five types:—driving wheels, coupled wheels, bogie trailing and tender wheels. The two former are almost identical except in size and disposition of the balance weights, though in some full-size engines the flanges of the driving wheels may be thinner. Bogie, trailing and tender wheels are generally of similar type, differing only in diameter and/or number of spokes.

Driving and coupled wheels generally have numbers of spokes as follows: shunting engines 8 to 14, goods engines 12 to 14, mixed traffic locomotives 14 to 18, and express engines 20 to 24. Bogie wheels have 9, 10 or 12 spokes, trailing and tender wheels 10 to 12, though on some older engines 14 is possible.

A few modern locomotives may have carrying wheels of the disc type, while some older engines had "Mansell" bogie and tender wheels. Some recent locomotives have been fitted with "B.F.B." type wheels, these have no spokes in the ordinary sense, but the wheel is lightened from the completely solid form by a symmetrical arrangement of alternate recesses, blind holes and through holes cast in all around the boss; such wheels are used in the S.R. "Bulleid" engines and extensively in America, and have been copied in model practice.

Patterns for Wheels

Patterns for model locomotive wheels should be made in Yellow Pine or Honduras Mahogany, or wood of similar quality. The rim and tyre and the front and back of the boss should be left a good deal thicker than the final dimension required, other parts being made finished size plus the usual shrinkage allowance. In the case of driving and coupled wheels, it is a good plan to first obtain a set of castings in brass, clean these up, add the correct balance weights, and then obtain the final castings in grey iron. In this case of course, double shrinkage allowance must be made.

Suitable proportions for treads and flanges are given in Table II. The question of whether the treads should be coned is a debatable one. Although this may not help to ease an engine around curves, as was at one time thought, the author's opinion is that it does help to centre the wheels upon the rails and may reduce friction slightly when the train is in motion; on the other hand unless the rails are well worn in to the same angle, the locomotive may be more inclined to slip than with wheels having parallel treads.

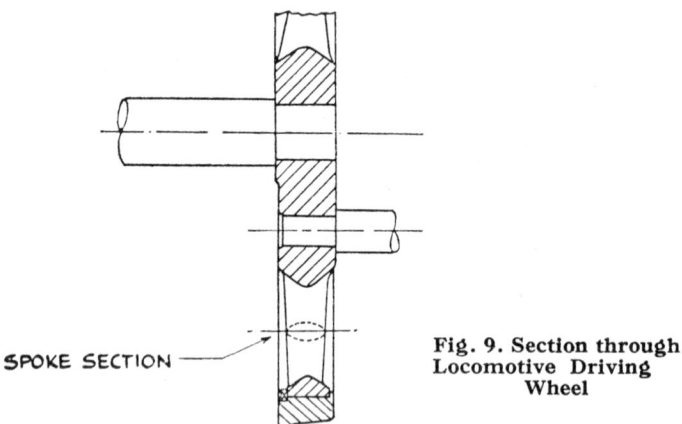

Fig. 9. Section through Locomotive Driving Wheel

Although the spokes of modern locomotive wheels should be oval or elliptical in section, in the smaller sizes of models the spokes are usually made flat on the back and evenly tapered towards the front of the wheel, this section being easier to mould in small wheels.

Turning Locomotive Wheels

All locomotive wheels under $1\frac{1}{2}$ in. scale should be turned in three distinct operations:

1. The casting should be chucked in the lathe in a three jaw (or four jaw) chuck by its tread, back outwards. Where no chuck large enough for this is available, the casting can be held to the faceplate by means of plates and bolts through the spokes, packing being provided to keep the wheel just clear of the faceplate. A round-nose tool can now be set cross-wise in the toolholder and the back of the wheel faced off, the wheels being then centred and drilled, using a small drill initially at high speed,

followed by a drill just under finished size at lower speed. A reamer should then be put through at lowest speed, the reamer being held in a tailstock chuck, or if too large for this, held hard against a centre in the tailstock. Wheels over ¾ in. scale should be bored before reaming. After reaming, the wheels should be lightly countersunk on the back. Before removing the wheel from the chuck, a cleaning cut should be taken over the outside of the flange.

2. In the second operation, the flange and tread can be turned. The easiest way to do this and at the same time to ensure that all wheels are exactly the same size is to use a fixture mounted in the chuck or on the faceplate.

A spare driving wheel casting or a chuck backplate casting is generally suitable for the fixture; this is turned to a slightly smaller overall diameter than that of the finished wheel. It is now faced up, drilled and tapped to take a pin of such a diameter that the pin can be turned down, in position, to an exact fit for the wheels in hand. The end of the pin is then threaded and fitted with a nut and washer. It is a good plan, before fitting this pin, to take a very light cut across the centre of the fixture so that the wheel, when mounted, bears on its outside only.

The wheels can now be mounted in turn for machining the flange, tread and rim The tool should be positioned so as to turn the flange to the correct profile and should be ground so as to leave a good radius between the flange and the tread. In smaller lathes, the tool may chatter as it reaches this radius and starts to cut the flange, the remedy is to reduce speed still further, or even to pull the lathe belt by hand for the last few "thou". By noting the readings on the dials of the top-slide and cross-slide, all wheels should come out exactly the same.

3. The third operation is to machine the bosses. For this the wheels can be chucked lightly by the flange, leaving the centre clear for the tool; this operation can also be done on the faceplate if a spigot is used to locate the wheel by its centre. The spigot must be of such a length that the facing tool clears it on its finishing cut. The chamfer on the front edge of the tread can also be put in at this setting and is best done with a tool ground for the purpose and run in to a definite reading.

As regards the final rounding off of the wheel flanges, a form tool can be used to ensure absolute uniformity, and such a tool should not be required to remove more metal than necessary. On small wheels, this rounding is often done with a file, a satisfactory method providing the file is handled with due care.

Except on the smallest lathes, tools of the cemented carbide type will be found to give remarkably good service on wheel turning, though their use may be made difficult unless the special grinding wheel or lap required for re-sharpening them is available.

Drilling for Crankpins

Care must be taken in drilling driving and coupled wheels for crankpins, to ensure truth and correct throw. The author recommends that a simple jig be made, which can be clamped to the wheel, the drilling bush being hardened if a number of wheels are being dealt with. If the jig is designed so that it can be bolted to the wheel, either the drilling machine or the lathe can be used for the drilling operation, a reamer being used for finishing.

32   MODEL STEAM LOCOMOTIVE CONSTRUCTION

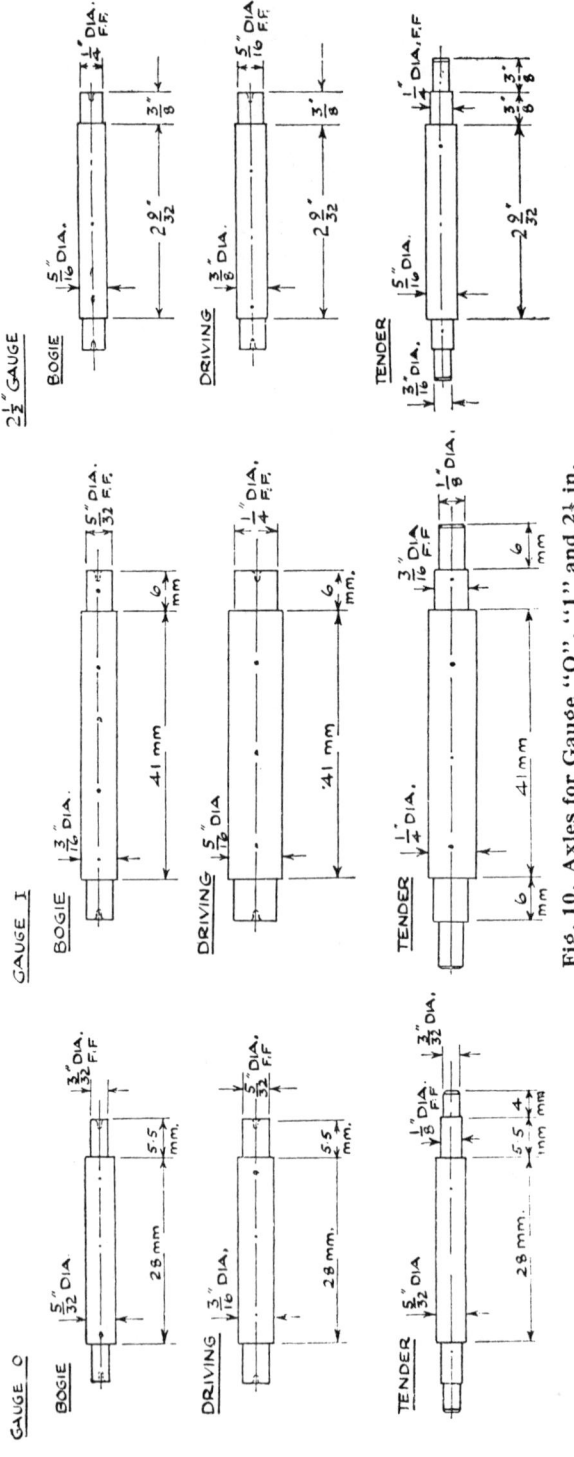

Fig. 10. Axles for Gauge "O", "1" and 2½ in.

WHEELS AND AXLES, CRANK AXLES, CRANKPINS

Axles

Axles for model locomotives may be made from a good quality mild steel. In the smaller sizes a mild steel with a ground finish is available, and as it is usually centreless ground it is generally very accurate. For large models an open-hearth or Bessemer steel should be specified.

Small axles can be turned in a collet, or even in a self-centring chuck, provided the latter is reasonably true. Larger axles should be turned between centres, but in

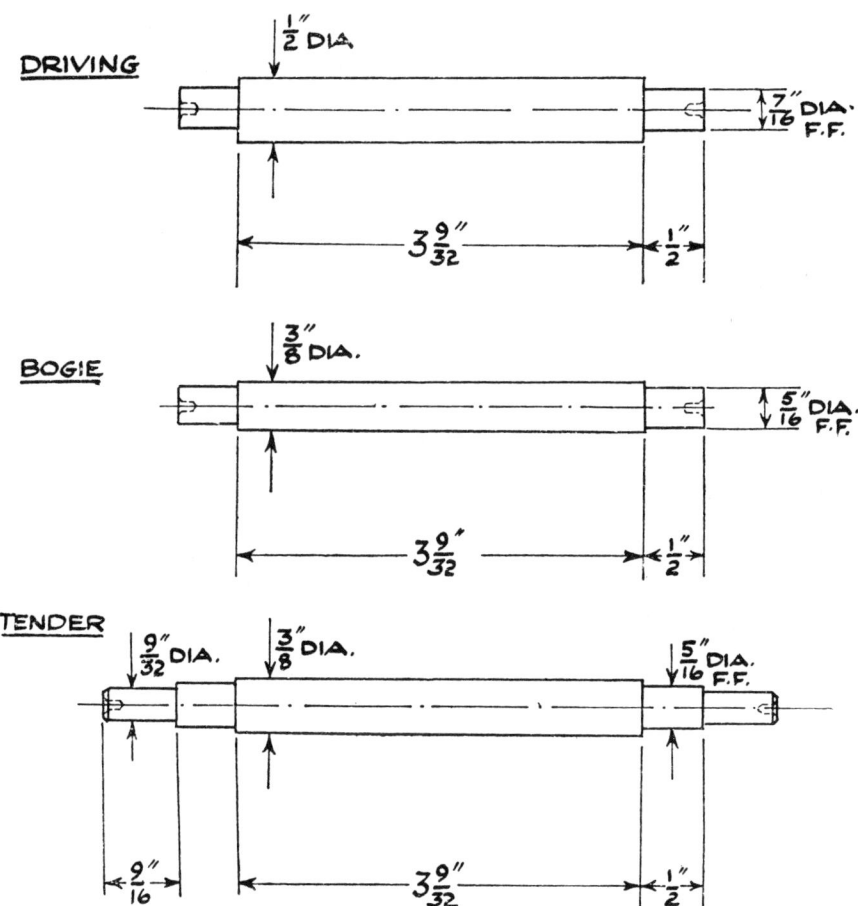

Fig. 11. Axles recommended for 3½ in. gauge

either case centres are always left in the ends of axles. The "wheel-seats" of axles are turned a press-fit into the wheels, and should be made 0·001 in. to 0·0025 in. larger than the bore of the wheel. The former figure is suitable for models up to

34   MODEL STEAM LOCOMOTIVE CONSTRUCTION

¾ in. scale, the latter figure for a 10¼ in. gauge model, other gauges between these being of course in proportion. In the case of driving, coupled and bogie wheels, the

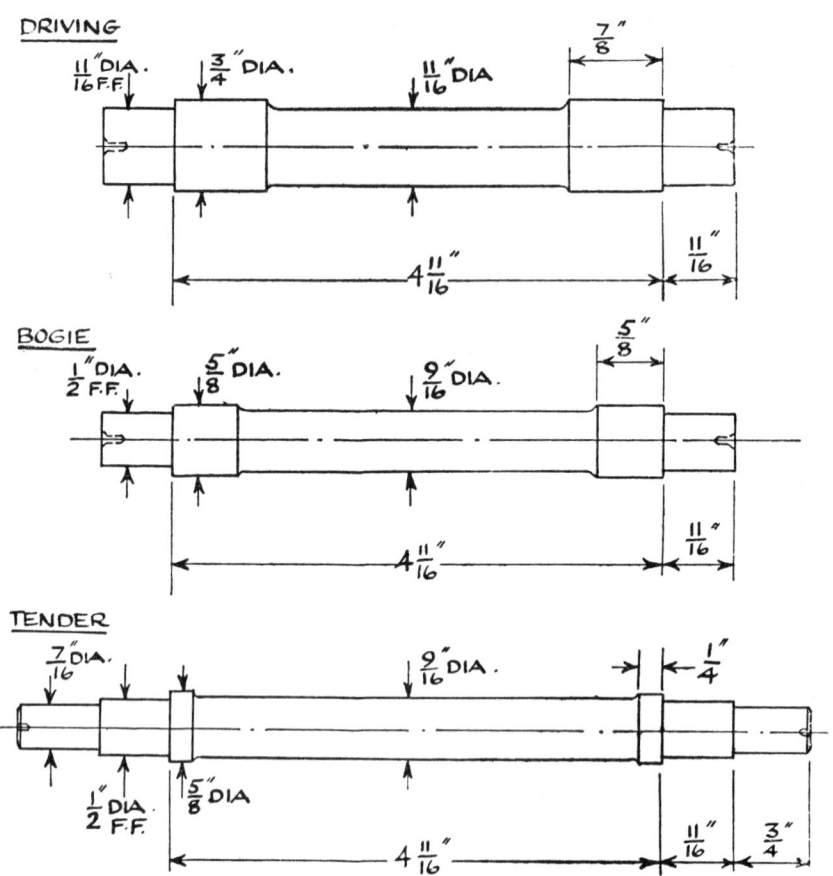

Fig. 12. Axles for 5 in. gauge locomotives

wheel seats should be a few "thou" longer than the thickness of the wheel upon them, so that the axle protrudes on the outside by that small amount.

It is advisable to turn wheel seats strictly parallel though it is permissible to slightly taper the extreme ends of the axle to help the wheel to "start". If a proper press is not available for forcing wheels on to their axles, the operation may be started in the lathe, and then transferred to a parallel bench vice for the final press home.

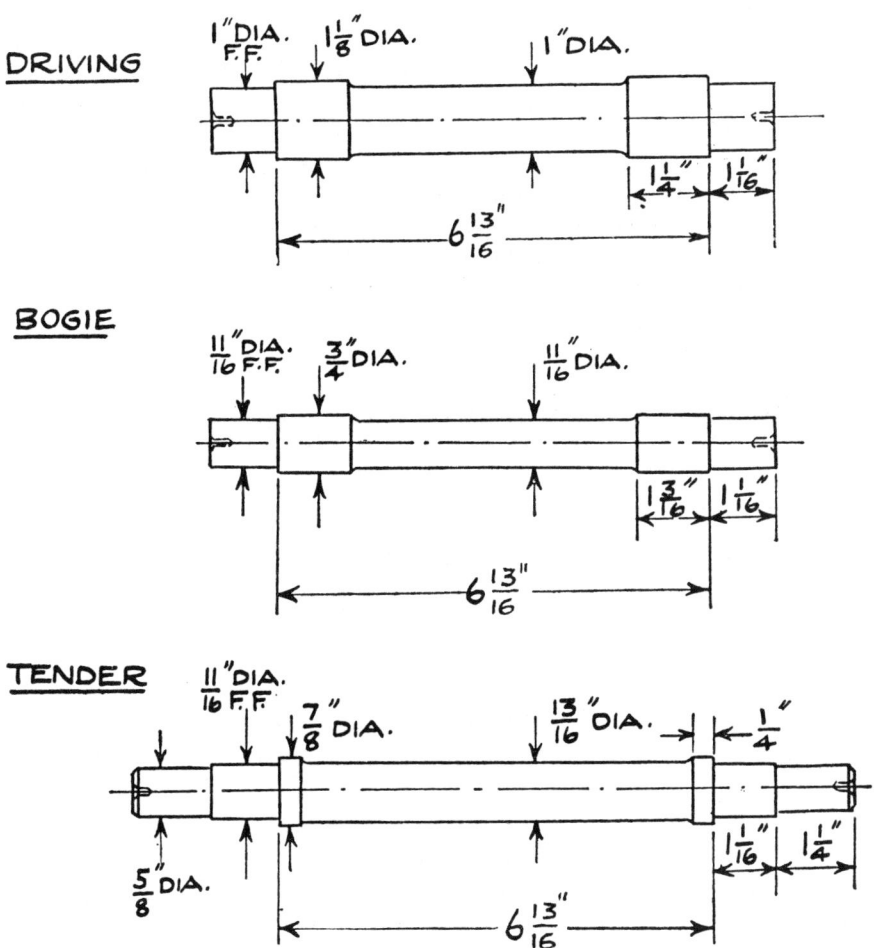

Fig. 13. Axles for 1½ in. scale locomotives

"Quartering" of Driving Wheels

Driving and coupled wheels must be "quartered" before pressing home. That is to say the wheels on one side of the locomotive must be set exactly at 90° to those on the other side (for a 2 cylinder engine, or 120° for a 3 cylinder). The usual practice is that the right-hand crank leads.

This question of "quartering" is most important and causes more trouble to beginners than practically any other operation; but if tackled on the right lines, is not really difficult. Perhaps the safest method is to make up a simple jig, consisting of two flat steel plates at least $\frac{1}{8}$ in. thick, on which are set out the locations of the crankpins on both sides of the locomotive and also the location of the axle centre, as accurately as possible. The plates are then clamped together and drilled and reamed to take the crankpins in use, an exact sliding fit. At the axle centres, accurately turned pegs, one end of each being coned at 60° are arranged, these being made a hand push fit in the plates and locate the axle accurately.

The wheels are started on their axles and turned approximately to their correct positions by eye, and the two plates, now separated and finished, are held together by means of four heavy turned and shouldered stretchers of suitable length. The crankpins on each side are allowed to pass through the holes in the plates prepared for them, thus "quartering" the wheels at the required angle. The wheels are now carefully pressed for a part of the way upon the axle, the unit being returned once again for checking. It must be remembered that even though the wheels have been pressed partly home, they may still twist slightly before being pressed right up to the shoulder of the axle, so that this second check is essential.

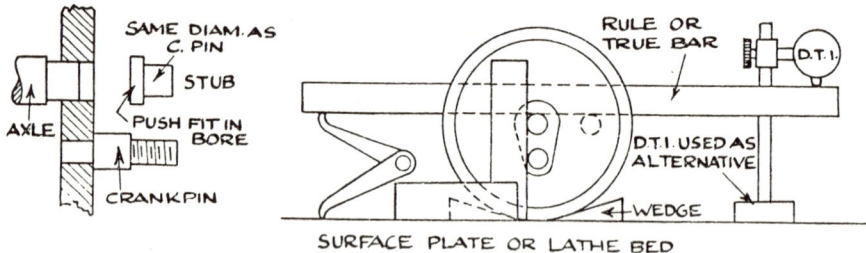

Fig. 14. Quartering Driving Wheels

Another method is shown in fig. 14. Small "stubs" are turned up in the lathe, the ends of which are made an exact hand push fit into the wheels, while the other ends are made exactly the same diameter as the crankpins. These are then put into the wheels, the latter being just started on their axles on each side. They are then placed on the surface plate or some other flat surface such as the lathe bed, a square being applied to one side as shown while on the other side a true flat bar is applied and is checked for level by means of a Dial Test Indicator (as on the right) which is applied at the extreme ends of the bar, or by means of a pair of inside calipers (as on the left), the former, in all but highly skilled hands, may be considered the more accurate.

Keying the Wheels

Driving and coupled wheels in all sizes above Gauge 1 should always be pinned or keyed to their axles. In models up to $1\frac{1}{2}$ in. scale a plain round pin of silver-steel pressed home half in the wheel and half in the axle will be found quite satisfactory. A screw cannot be recommended as it prevents the wheel from being removed from the axle without damage. On models larger than 1½ in., scale a standard rectangular flush key is generally adopted. It is of course important to ensure that the "quartering" of the wheels is correct before pinning.

Bogie, trailing and tender wheels do not require keying to their axles.

Crank Axles

Although crank axles can be turned from the solid, this method is not recommended to any except the highly experienced worker. The author has seen it advised that both the crank axle and the four eccentrics required for link valve gear should all be turned from the solid, but the difficulty of marking out the ends of the bar to sufficient accuracy should alone be enough to deter most model engineers from adopting this method.

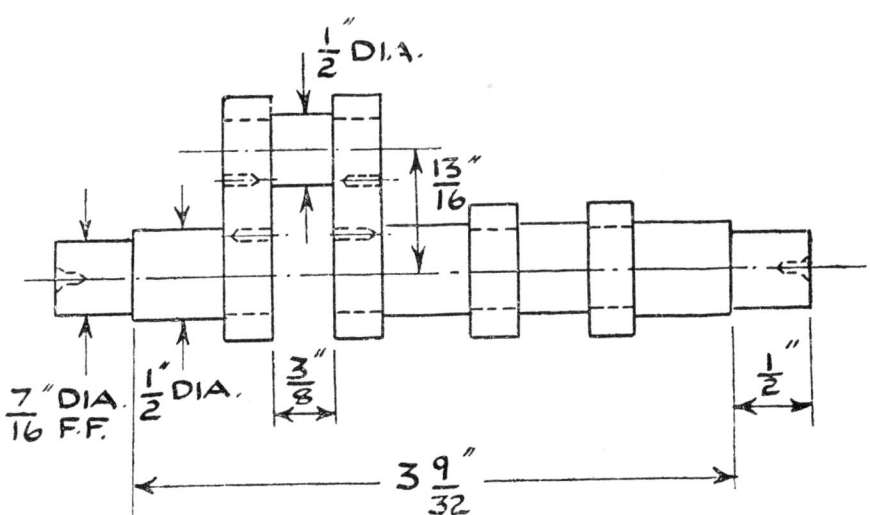

Fig. 15. Built-up Crank Axle, ¾ in. scale

The built-up crank axle is generally adopted in full-size practice and one advantage in following suit in models is that the webs can be easily cut to any shape required before assembly, avoiding the need for separate counterweights. A good quality mild steel should be used, and to ensure accuracy, all the webs may be set up in the lathe and bored and reamed together for the journals and crankpins. The services of a proper press should if possible be obtained for the assembly of the various parts and all parts must be pinned after assembly, the pins used being of silver steel, and given a very minute amount of taper to ease pressing home.

Another method of making crank axles is to braze the webs and crankpins to a plain axle, using ordinary brass wire. The webs are machined up in the usual way, but only a light press fit for the axle and crankpins; they should be lightly countersunk on each side. The crankpins, where they enter the webs, should be roughened with coarse emery cloth. These precautions assist the brazing material to penetrate properly. After brazing, the parts of the axle not required are sawn away. This method is not entirely satisfactory owing to the danger of the crank axle distorting after the sawing has been carried out.

As regards the settings of the cranks, on three and four cylinder locomotives, the inside cylinders usually drive the leading coupled axle, though on some three cylinder engines such as the Gresley designs for the ex L.N.E.R. the inside cylinder may be steeply inclined and drive on to the same axle as the outside cylinders. In this case the settings of the cranks must allow for the difference in angle between the inside and the outside cylinders.

Four cylinder engines usually have their cranks arranged at 90°, the commonest order of leading being:

1. Outside left
2. Inside right
3. Inside left
4. Outside right

A few four cylinder engines have their cranks set to give eight separate exhaust beats per revolution of the driving wheels; in this case there would be 90° between the outside right hand crank and the outside left and 45° between outside left and inside right, 90° between inside right and inside left, and 135° between inside left and outside right.

Crankpins

Crankpins are generally made from silver steel or from a high carbon steel, and where normal gunmetal or phos-bronze bushes are in use, there is really no need to harden them.

The design of crankpins for model locomotives must depend mainly on the scale of the model. On models larger than $\frac{1}{2}$ in., scale some positive means of keeping the retaining collar or nut on the end of the crankpin should be adopted. This usually takes the form of a split pin, though a small taper pin may also be used.

On outside cylinder locomotives, there is generally little clearance between the leading crankpin and the crosshead or slide bars. The solution here is to use a recessed type of retaining collar, taking a bearing partly inside the coupling rod boss, the crankpin itself being tapped to take a screw, the Allen type being very convenient in larger crankpins.

Crankpins are always made a press fit into the wheels, in larger sizes the hole in the back of the wheel may be countersunk and the crankpin hammered into this. Where crankpins carry return cranks for the operation of valve gears, it is a good plan to use a small pin, half in the crankpin and half in the wheel, pressed in from the back. This will effectively prevent any movement, which would of course be fatal to the valve setting of the engine.

WHEELS AND AXLES, CRANK AXLES, CRANKPINS

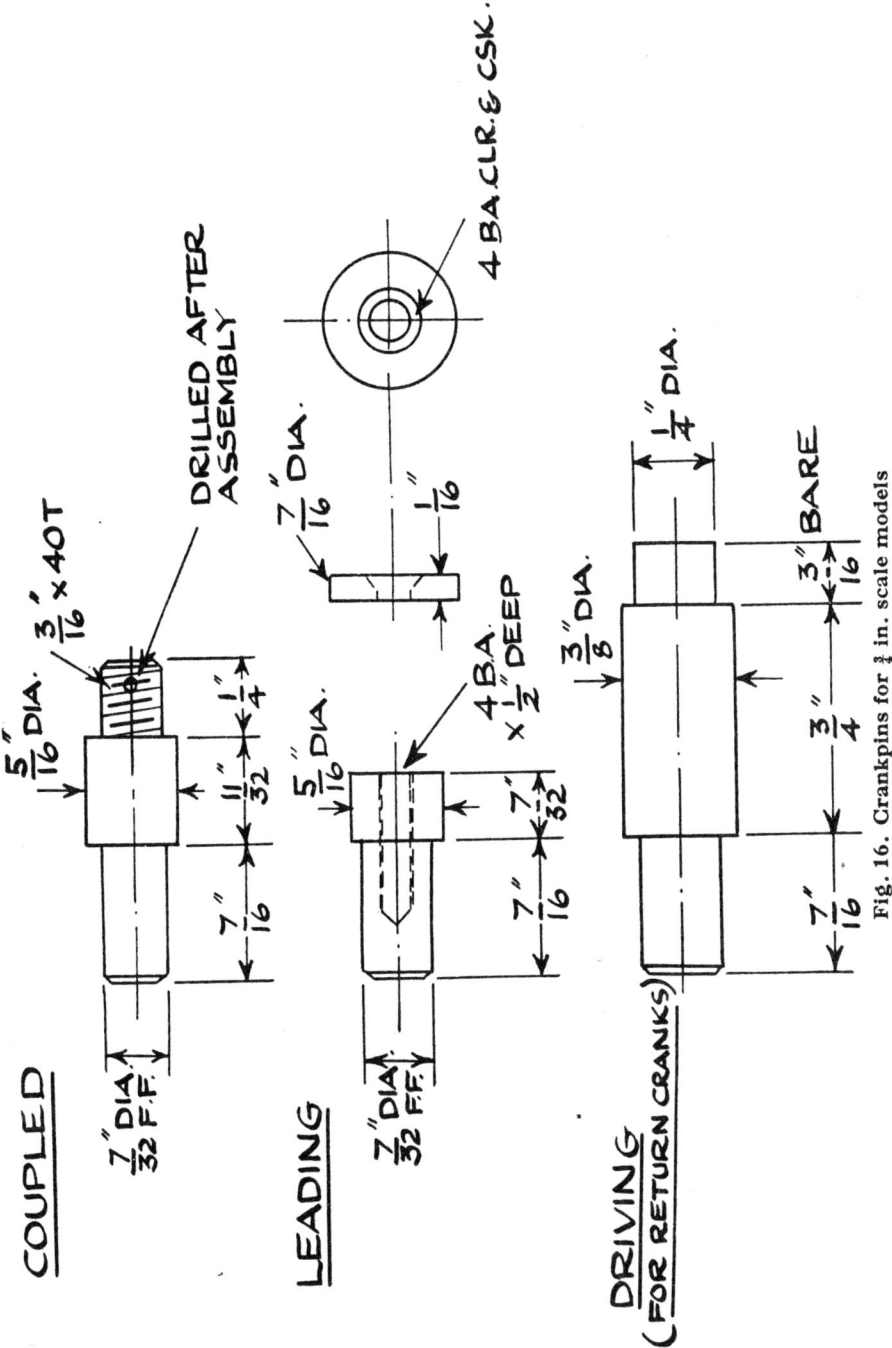

Fig. 16. Crankpins for ¾ in. scale models

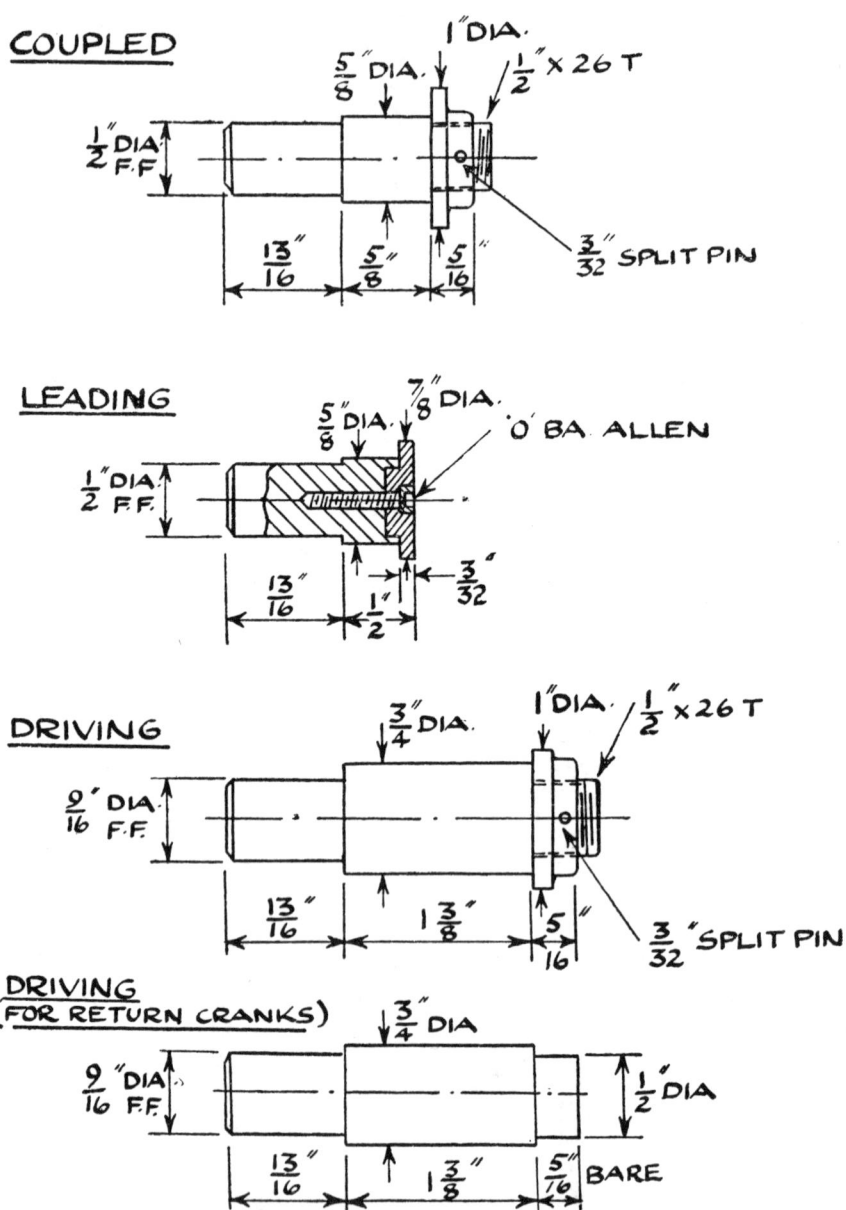

Fig. 17. Crankpins for 1½ in. scale

CHAPTER SIX

Bogies, Pony and Radial Trucks

Bogies

LOCOMOTIVE BOGIES ARE GENERALLY of the four wheel type, they are attached in such a way that they support some of the weight of the engine and at the same time help to guide it along the track. Thus a bogie makes a locomotive much more flexible, whether put before or behind the driving and coupled wheels, especially as its central pivot is given considerable side-play. The main types of four-wheel bogie in general use are the Adams type, the Swing-link type and the Bar frame type.

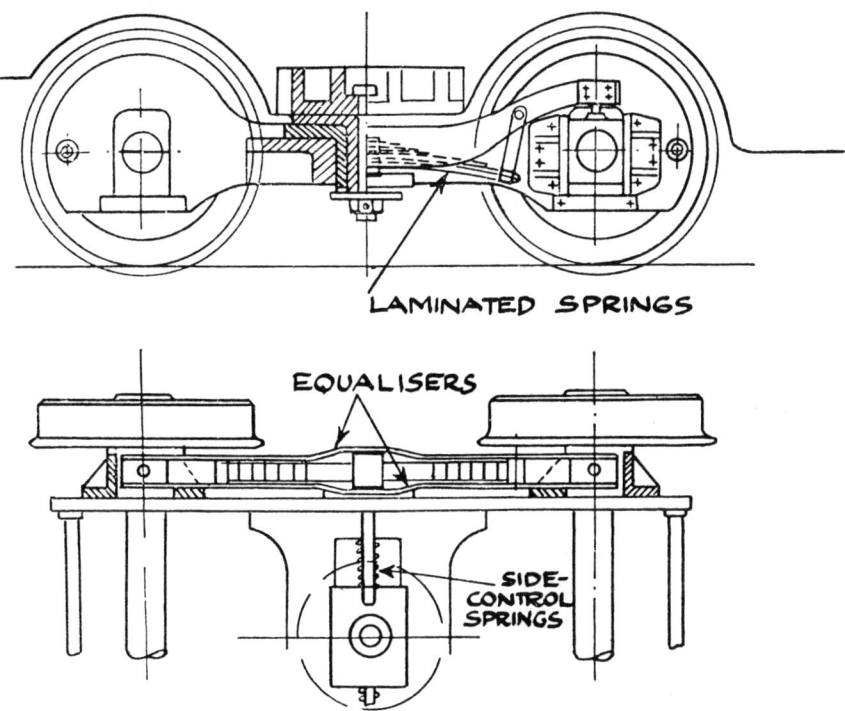

Fig. 18. The Adams type Bogie

The Adams type bogie is probably the best known in this country. In the basic design the four wheels are placed with the axleboxes working in pairs of horns rivetted or bolted to plate type frames. The frames are generally held apart at the correct spacing by a pair of castings and two or more turned framestays. A centre casting is then arranged in the centre of the bogie, free to slide either side of the longitudinal centre-line of the bogie and controlled by means of spiral or laminated springs.

The weight of the locomotive which is carried by the bogie is applied through inverted laminated springs on each side of the bogie frames and through the outer ends of these springs to a continuous equalising bar spanning the tops of the axleboxes.

The laminated springs may be outside or inside the bogie frames, while the equalisers are generally doubled, being placed on each side of the springs. The whole bogie is located under the locomotive mainframes by means of a special casting, usually called a saddle plate, which is secured by flanges at each end to the main frames. The underside of this saddle plate is circular, machined to form a smooth bearing contact with a bronze friction washer, and carries a spigot which passes down through the centre casting. The bogie is kept on by means of a long centre pin, fitted underneath with a nut, washer and locking pin.

The Adams type of bogie may allow for a total side-play of anything between 1 in. and 4 ins. Control of its swivelling movement on the vertical pin is not usually provided.

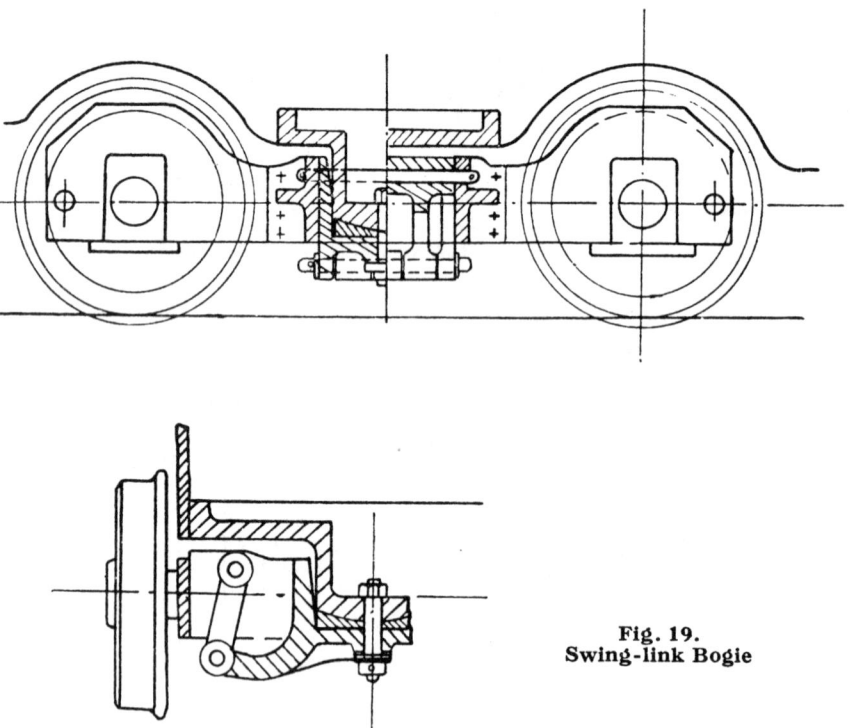

Fig. 19.
Swing-link Bogie

The Swing-link bogie, sometimes called the American type bogie, differs from the Adams in that the controlling gear is vertical instead of horizontal. The weight of the engine carried on the bogie is applied by means of a set of links connecting the

BOGIES, PONY AND RADIAL TRUCKS

bogie centre casting to the bogie frame. The links are arranged at an inclination to the vertical on each side of the bogie. A central pivot pin is used as before, but the lower surface of the saddle plate is dished, and its curvature is followed by an equivalent concave curvature on the bogie centre casting.

On curves, the outer rail tends to lift the engine and thus increases pressure on the outer wheels, and due to the inclination of the links, the bogie slides bodily to suit the radius of the curve.

Some bogies of the swing-link type have side-control springs of the laminated type in addition to the link arrangement.

The bar-frame bogie, used on many modern locomotives, may use the Adams type side control arrangement or the swing-link gear. The main longitudinal bars, which may be from 3 to 5 ins. thick, are bolted to vertical castings forming the guides for the axleboxes, and these are stiffened by tie bars along the underneath, connecting the castings together and acting as keeps for the axleboxes. The laminated springs lie underneath with equalising bars each side.

Sometimes the equalisers are dispensed with, and individual coil springs used to each axlebox.

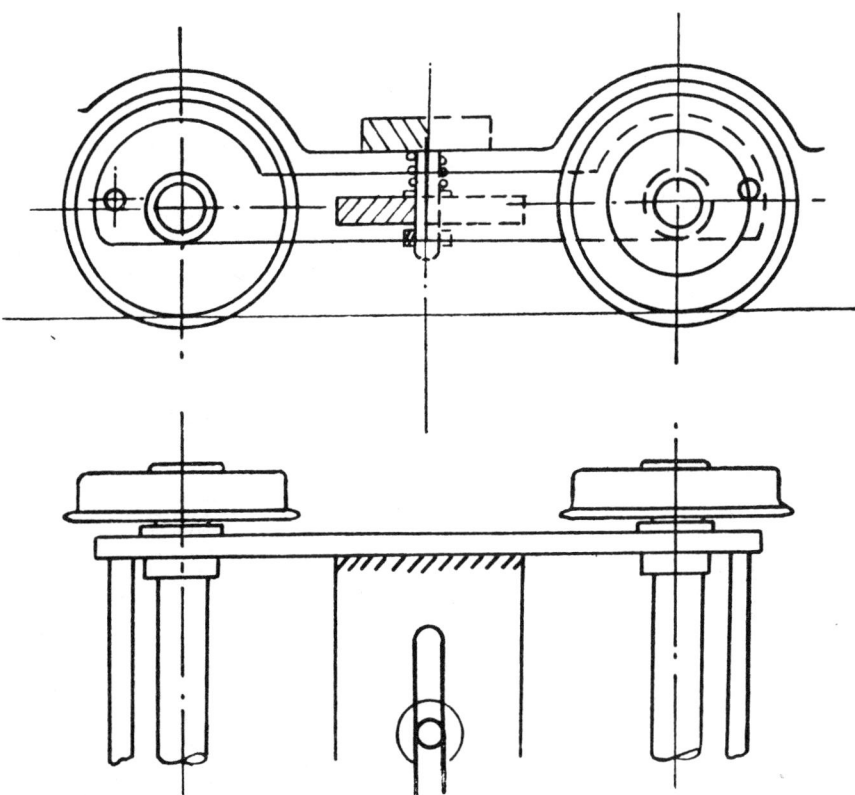

Fig. 20. Simple Bogie for Gauge "O"

44   MODEL STEAM LOCOMOTIVE CONSTRUCTION

A special type of bogie is used on the ex Great Western "King" class locomotives. As the inside cylinders are arranged above and behind the leading bogie wheels, the leading bogie axlebox horns and springs are arranged outside the frames, which are of the plate type and bent outwards from just forward of the rear bogie wheels so as to lie outside the front wheels. The side-control gear is based on the Adams type, but the controlling springs are carried right through the frames into deep receptacles. The weight of the locomotive is applied via hemi-spherical members on to pads above the frames fixed to the centre casting.

In models built for gauges of $2\frac{1}{2}$ in. and below, side-control springing is seldom used, while the main springing is generally much simplified. The most simple form used mainly on Gauge "O" models, consists of a plain vertical pivot pin attached to a cross-stretcher on the locomotive, passing through a transverse slot in the bogie centre, a coil spring and washer being inserted between the two. A better method is to dispense with the spring on the pivot pin and use separate axleboxes sliding direct in the frames, having a small coil spring immediately above each axlebox.

In the smaller gauges, the gap in the frames for the axleboxes need not be cut right through, thus doing away with the need for a separate keep.

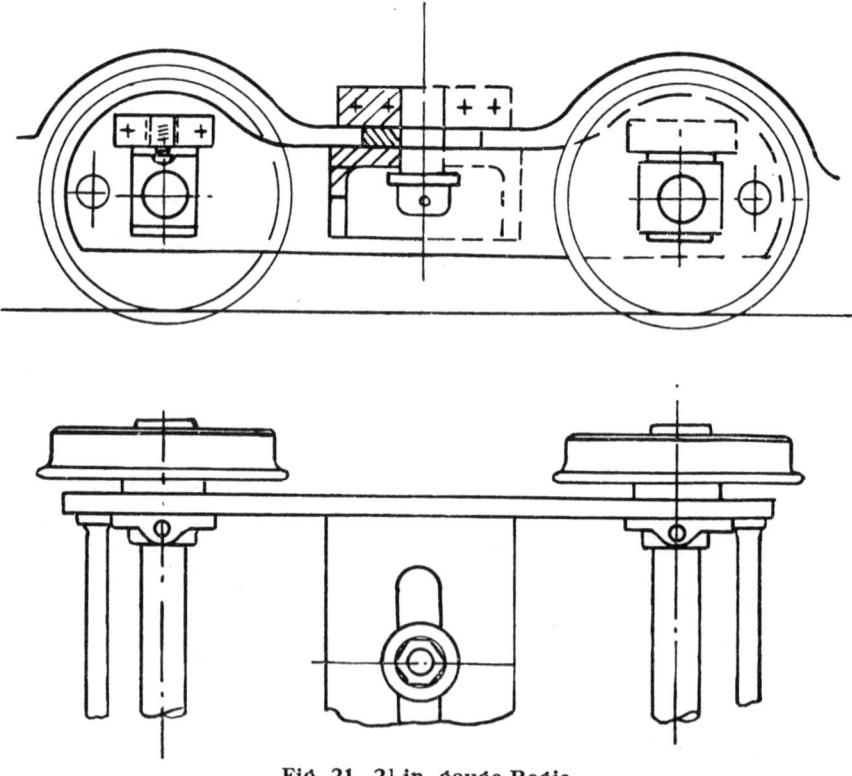

Fig. 21. $2\frac{1}{2}$ in. gauge Bogie

Bogies for $2\frac{1}{2}$ in. gauge models are generally built with gunmetal axleboxes sliding in horns, which may consist of lengths of ordinary angle brass or proper castings riveted to the frames. Springing may be individual, with one coil spring above each axlebox, or by equalisers, the equalising beams being slung on tension springs or arranged to bear against compression springs.

When we come to $\frac{3}{4}$ in. scale models, some form of side-control springing is desirable. Probably the simplest method of building a bogie with side-control is to adopt individual springing for the axleboxes, and use a deep bogie centre casting with a double-flanged sliding block, bored for the pivot pin, and arranged to slide transversely against coil springs on either side of it. If the centre casting is bored right through, the springs may be allowed to bear directly against the insides of the frames. The axleboxes in this scale should slide in proper horns riveted to the bogie frames, while either single coil springs may be used, housed in "pocket" castings above the axleboxes, or twin coil springs on either side of the axleboxes with a spring beam across the top.

Generally speaking, bogie frames may be made of the same thickness of metal as the main frames and they should be dealt with in much the same fashion as regards marking out, drilling and cutting. Gunmetal castings are generally used for the axleboxes, while the main frame or pivot stretcher casting and the bogie centre casting may be in gunmetal or iron.

On models below 1 in. scale, too much weight should not be carried on the bogie, otherwise the adhesion of the driving and coupled wheels may be impaired. The coil springs generally used in $\frac{3}{4}$ in. scale models are about 20 or 22 s.w.g. when one spring per axlebox is used, and around 24 s.w.g. when two are used, though this will of course depend to some extent on the diameter being employed.

Guard irons are often fitted to bogies and these may be represented by strips of mild steel a little thinner than the bogie frames. It will be found easier to temporarily bolt these to the frames before bending; after the bending is successfully accomplished, the bolts may be replaced by rivets. The guard irons should clear the rail by about $\frac{1}{8}$ in. in a $\frac{3}{4}$ in. scale model, and by about $\frac{3}{16}$ in. in a 1 in. scale engine.

Pony Trucks

A locomotive Bissel or Pony truck consists of a truck with two wheels only, pivoted at some point behind the wheels, in the case of a leading truck, or in front of the wheels in the case of a trailing truck. The wheels of leading pony trucks are generally made small enough to swing clear under the main frames, avoiding the necessity of narrowing the frames at this point; while the radius of the truck is made such that the axle is radial to the centre of an average curve.

In full-size practice many pony trucks are compensated with the leading coupled springs, by means of a long compensating beam pivoted near its centre from a bracket on the engine main frame. The radial arm pin is mounted on a cross-stretcher between the engine frames. The axleboxes are, as usual, arranged to work in horn-cheeks riveted to the pony truck frames and the vertical springs are situated above the axleboxes. The pony truck swings sideways on swing links to traverse curves.

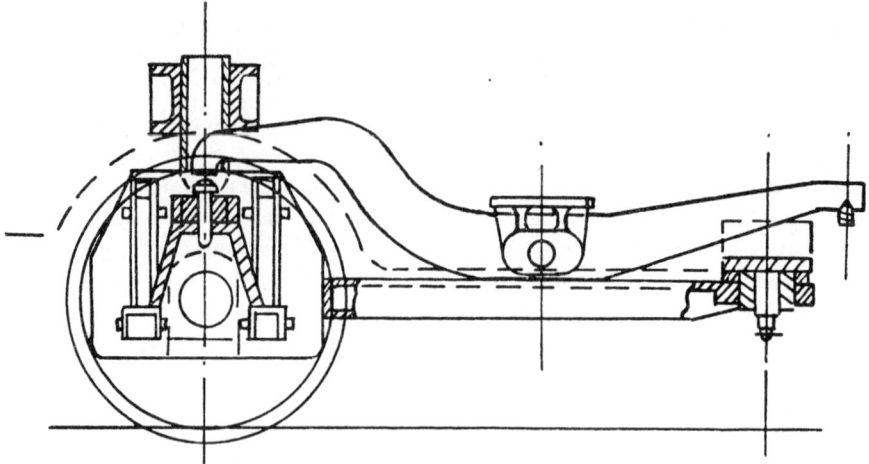

Fig. 22. Compensated Pony Truck

The compensated type pony truck is not an easy one to model, especially in the smaller scales, and it is doubtful whether it is as successful in model practice as it is in full size work.

Pony trucks for small gauge models are generally made up with quite a simple triangular shaped framework, the axleboxes being arranged between horns and having either a single coil spring directly above the axlebox or two coil springs on

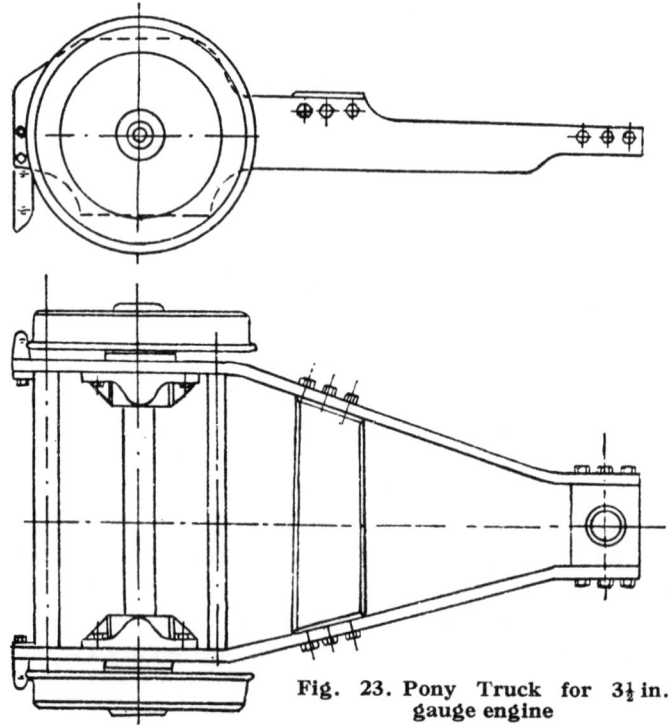

Fig. 23. Pony Truck for 3½ in. gauge engine

BOGIES, PONY AND RADIAL TRUCKS

each side of the axlebox with the usual spring beam above it. The weight of the engine is carried on a gunmetal pad fixed to a cross stretcher between the pony truck frames.

Side control springs are not usually considered essential in models below 1 in. scale. The problem which faces one in small models is the much greater angle of swing required as compared with full-size practice. Figure 24 gives a suggested arrangement for a ¾ in. scale model pony ruck.

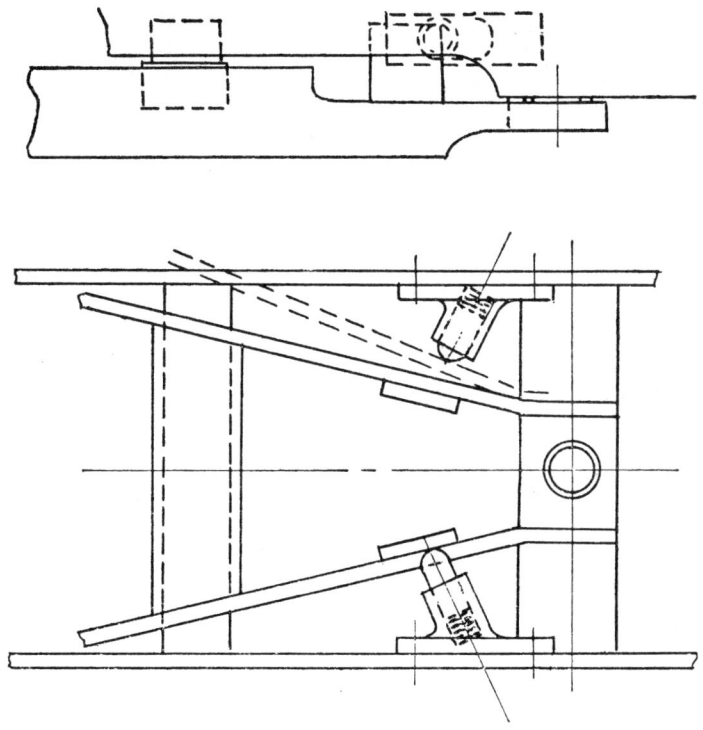

Fig. 24. Arrangement of Side Control Springs

Radial Axleboxes

Radial axleboxes are sometimes used in place of pony trucks, especially where less flexibility is required as for instance on 2-4-2 tank locomotives or for the trailing wheels of 0-6-2 and 2-6-2 tank engines.

The action of radial axleboxes is very similar to that of pony trucks. The axleboxes are generally mounted inside the frames, are tied together and guided by curved horns, or horns set at an angle to the normal arrangement.

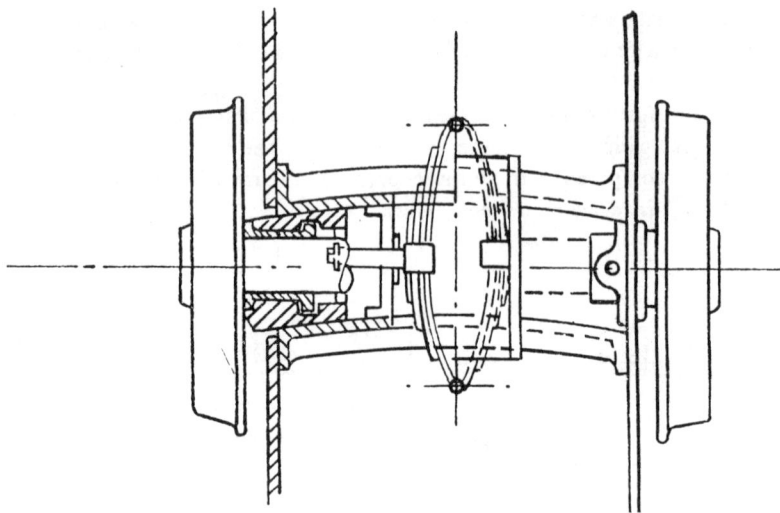

Fig. 25. Radial Axleboxes

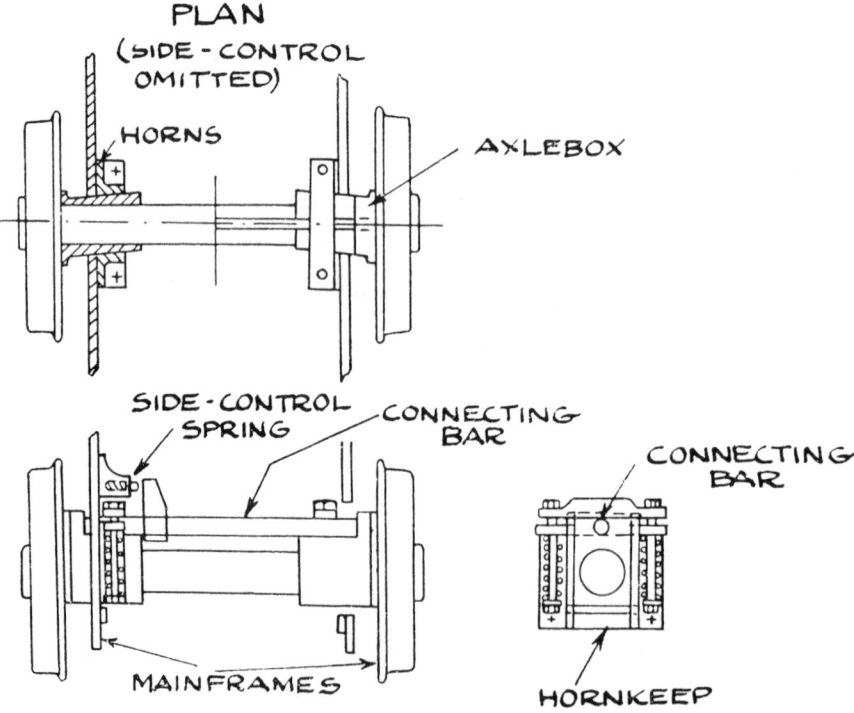

Fig. 26. Radial Axleboxes for small models

Radial axleboxes are rather awkward items of construction where models are concerned owing to the difficulty of machining the curved horns and the sides of the axleboxes, also the main frames require to be set in or recessed to provide the extra clearance required. One solution is to machine the axleboxes at an angle approximately tangential to the required radius, and to make the horns to suit. The axleboxes can be joined by a round bar across the top on which the spring beams can bear.

Side control springs can then be arranged above this bar by means of lugs fixed to the bar, on each of which bear spring plungers attached to the main frames. This method, which is suitable for models up to 1 in. scale, will be found easier to build than the type normally used in full-size work. The frames should be reduced in width to give the necessary extra clearance, and if difficulty is experienced in bending a frame which may be quite deep at this point, separate frame extensions may be used, rivetted to the mainframes with spacing pieces in between if required.

CHAPTER SEVEN

Cylinders and Details

Types of Cylinders

LOCOMOTIVE CYLINDERS MAY BE classified into five main groups:
1. Outside cylinders with valves on top.
2. Outside cylinders with valves between the frames.
3. Inside cylinders with valves on top.
4. Inside cylinders with valves underneath.
5. Inside cylinders with valves between the bores.

Cylinders may be further classified as either slide (or flat) valve, as piston valve or as poppet-valve type.

The advantages claimed for the arrangement of cylinders between the frames are greater rigidity to the whole structure as the cylinders act as a frame stay, while the motion being transmitted between the frames makes an engine steadier; the disadvantages are the cranked axle which is necessary, the difficulty of getting in large enough bores without cramping the steam chests, and the inaccessibility of the motion.

From the model point of view the disadvantages apply with even greater force, thus explaining the present popularity of outside cylinders though a 3 or 4 cylinder arrangement is quite often used in the larger types of model locomotive.

Outside Cylinders with valves on top

Most modern 2 cylinder locomotives have outside cylinders with piston valves on top, though the poppet valve has made some progress in recent years. This type of cylinder is probably the most convenient for the model engineer to adopt, though slide valves may be used without sacrificing either efficiency or external appearance to any extent. The great majority of locomotives with outside cylinders having valves on top also have outside valve gears, though Great Western practice was always to use inside valve gear, the motion being transmitted by means of a rocking shaft.

The question of whether to use piston valves or slide valves in model cylinders has always been a hotly disputed one. Piston valves have been used successfully in nearly all scales of models, and their use lightens the load carried by the valve gear, while generally allowing somewhat more direct paths for the live steam and the exhaust steam. The author's opinion is that the expert model engineer can undoubtedly achieve success by adopting piston valves, but to those of more average ability and experience the slide valve may well prove a better proposition. One advantage of slide valves is that when wear does develop, they will generally remain

A 3½ in. gauge model Baltimore and Ohio "Pacific" model built by Mr. H. J. Coventry of Baltimore

Plate 1

A free-lance "Pacific" model for $3\frac{1}{2}$ in. gauge

Another free-lance "Pacific" built by Mr. Rowlands

A $\frac{3}{4}$ in. scale "Britannia" class "Pacific" built by Mr. V. J. Bailey

Plate 2

A fine scale model of old L.S.W.R. "Paddlebox" by Mr. A. G. Mead

A ¾ in. scale large "Atlantic"

A modern type free-lance "Atlantic" by Mr. H. Philpot

Plate 3

A fine ¾ in. scale model G.N. "Single" by Mr. Buist

Plate 4

2-4-0 ex-G.E.R. express locomotive by Mr. K. Dean

An ex-G.E.R. mixed-traffic 2-4-0 model

4-6-4 tank locomotive for 5 in. gauge (unfinished)

Plate 5

4-6-0 L.M.S. type model in ¾ in. scale

L.M.S. 2-6-0 "Mogul" locomotive built by R. E. Lee

Another "Mogul" based on the S.R. type

A 5 in. gauge G.W.R. goods engine built by Mr. Baldwin for Mr. A. J. Maxwell

Plate 6

A large tank model, 7¼ in. gauge, ex-L.N.E.R. "L1" class, by Mr. A. Balmforth

A 0-6-0 tank locomotive designed by "L.B.S.C." and built by Mr. Burville

Plate 7

5 in. gauge tank locomotive built by Mr. Younghusband to a design by Mr. Austen-Walton

Plate 8

A prize-winning Beyer-Garratt locomotive for 3½ in. gauge by Mr. A. W. G. Tucker of Bramhall

Baltimore and Ohio R.R., ¾ in. scale, "D30" class, in course of construction

5 in. gauge "Switcher" built by Mr. A. Castle of Worcester

Plate 9

A 5 in. gauge L.S.W.R. "Britannia" built by Mr. F. Buckle of Ilford

L.M.S. "Pacific" for 2½ in. gauge by Mr. A. B. Mills

¾ in. scale L.M.S. "Royal Scot" by Mr. A. G. Peacock

A Caledonian "Dunalastair" in ¾ in. scale

Plate 10

Mr. G. C. Smith's 7¼ in. gauge mogul at work at Malden, Surrey

Mr. J. F. Banyard's fine 4 cyl. 4-6-4 tank engine for 3½ in. gauge

An unfinished 4-6-0 to the author's "Springbok" design by Mr. E. C. Dearman, of Hazelbrook, N.S.W.

Plate 11

A 2-4-0 well-tank engine for 3½ in. gauge by Mr. Gilbert Lindsey

The author's ¾ in. scale L.M.S. 2-6-4 tank engine approaching completion

K. E. Wilson's unfinished chassis of the famous G.W.R. "City of Truro"

Milling locomotive axleboxes in horizontal milling machine

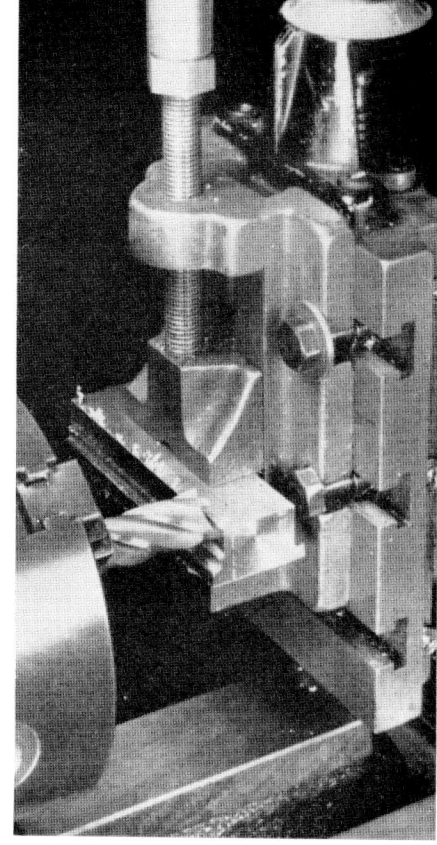

Milling axleboxes in the lathe

Machining front of driving wheel

Plate 13

End-milling the inside of the horns of a 5 in. gauge locomotive main frame

Boring driving wheel in lathe   Turning the face of a tender wheel held to a lathe faceplate

Plate 14

Underside view of ¾ in. scale bogie, showing side control springs

View of model "Britannia" bogie

Plate 15

Bogie with individual springing

L.N.E.R. type bogie with two springs per axlebox

Pony truck with individual springing

Plate 16

Cylinder block and steam chest, ¾ in. scale

Milling ports of slide valve cylinder in the lathe

Machining cylinder block in 4-jaw chuck

Drilling for cylinder studs

Plate 17

Lining up outside cylinders

Boring piston valve cylinder using boring-bar between centres

Two-bar crosshead with drop-link

Piston valve cylinders for a 5 in. gauge model showing pistons and covers

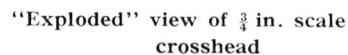

"Exploded" view of ¾ in. scale crosshead

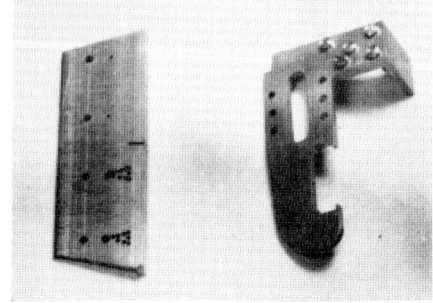

Stages in construction of motion bracket

Plate 18

Coupling and connecting rods, ¾ in. scale "Britannia"

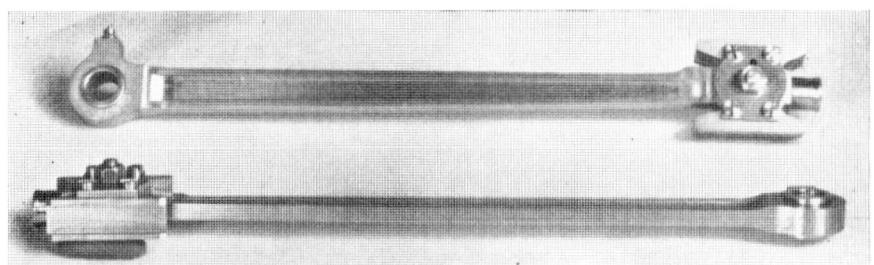

A pair of connecting rods and crossheads

Cutting a tapered flute in connecting rod

A Gauge 1 chassis with slip-eccentric valve gear

Outside Walschaerts' gear on a ¾ in. scale locomotive

Plate 20

CYLINDERS AND DETAILS 51

steam tight, whereas the piston valve, especially if no rings are used, must remain a close fit or they will leak to exhaust. Where piston valves are used with gunmetal cylinders, lubrication must be thoroughly reliable or the bores will quickly be scored.

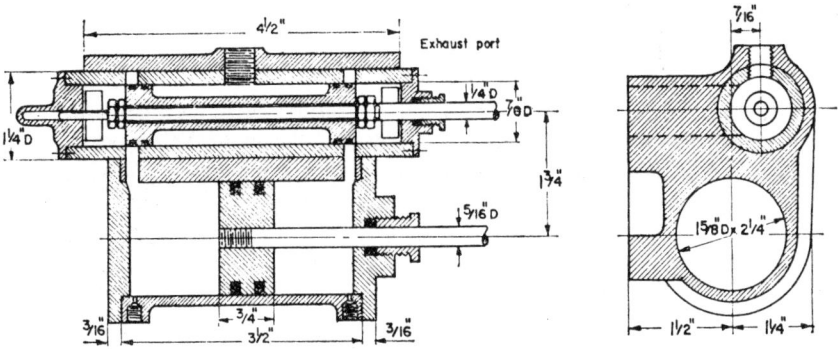

Fig. 27. Outside Piston Valve Cylinders, 1 in. scale

If slide valves are adopted, their presence can be disguised to some extent by providing large circular bosses on the steam chests. If outside Walschaerts' or Baker valve gear is required, the top joints of the combination lever will have to be reversed, altering the layout of the valve gear as compared with the inside admission piston valve arrangement.

Outside Cylinders with valves inside

Outside cylinders with steam chests between the frames were used a good deal in full-size practice at one time, particularly on the old Great Northern and Great Central Railway, the London and South Western and others.

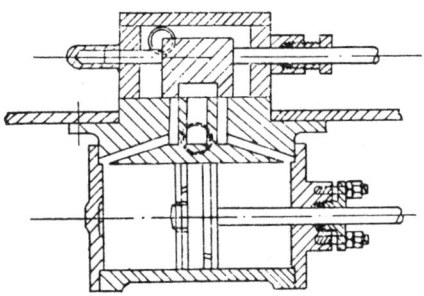

Fig. 28. Outside Cylinders with inside steam chests

This type of cylinder was generally arranged for use with Stephenson's valve gear with direct drive to the valve spindles, the steam chests passing through large gaps

M.M.S.L.—C

in the main frames. It is a type quite suitable for use in models, though "visual" valve setting is not quite so easy as with cylinders having the valves on top. The seam passageways between the ports and the bores are, of necessity, rather longer than in other types of cylinders.

Inside Cylinders, valves on top

The more modern locomotives with inside cylinders generally have the valves fitted above the cylinders. This position lends itself to the use of Walschaerts' or Joy's valve gear, the valve spindles being offset to suit the former type of valve gear.

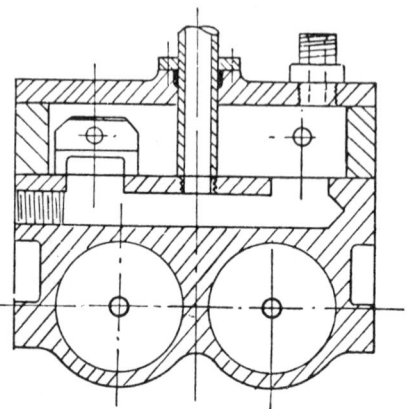

Fig. 29. Inside Cylinders with valves on top

In cylinders of this type, the steam connections are quite simple to arrange, the exhaust being led through the middle of the steam chest, a stuffing box being used on the top of the cover. The live steam is led straight into one of the front corners of the steam chest.

Four cylinder locomotives usually have the inside cylinders of this type, and as a bogie may lie rather close to the underside of these cylinders, it is advisable to arrange the bolting flanges as high up as possible to give additional clearance.

Inside Cylinders, valves underneath

This arrangement of inside cylinders has been used in full-size practice and is also very satisfactory in model locomotives especially where link motion is employed. When Stephenson's valve gear is adopted the port-face may be horizontal, the valve gear driving through rockers, or the port-face may be inclined, so that a direct drive can be used.

In this design of cylinders, the valves do not rest on the port-face when steam is shut off, while drainage is generally considered to be better than with other types.

CYLINDERS AND DETAILS

As far as model practice is concerned, the valves are very accessible for the purpose of valve setting, while the steam passages can be easily arranged by drilling from the side of the cylinder block and plugging the end. The blast pipe may be screwed directly into the block.

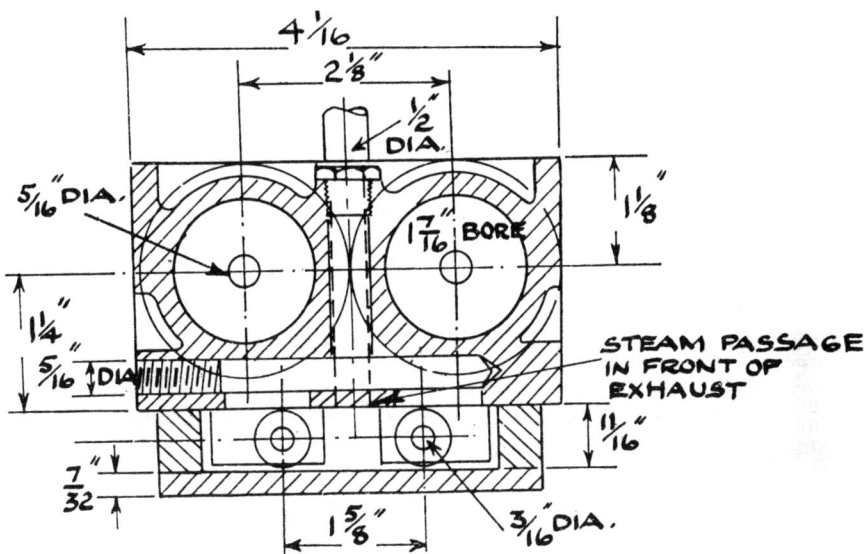

Fig. 30. Inside Cylinders with valves underneath for a 5 in. gauge model

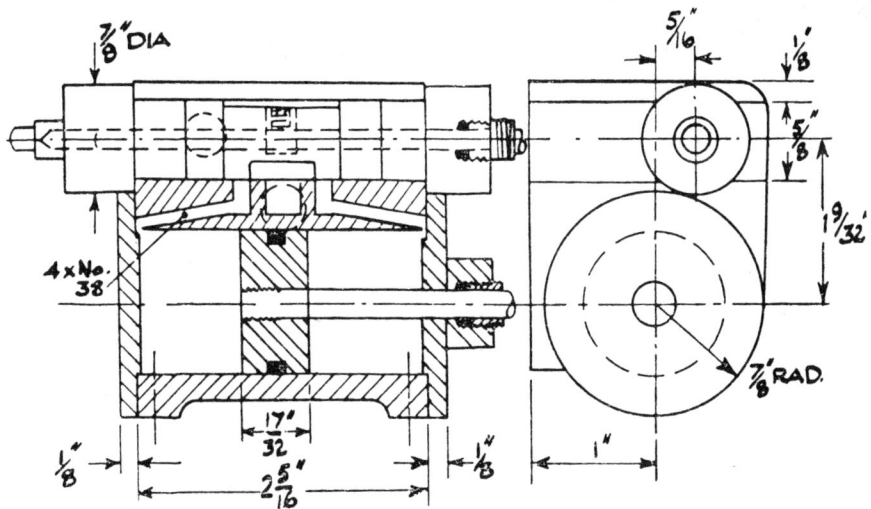

Fig. 31. Outside Cylinders for a 3½ in. gauge model

TABLE VI
Recommended Sizes of Cylinders and Ports

Gauge	Bore ins.	Stroke ins.	Steam ports ins.	Exhaust Ports ins.
1¼ in.	⅜	9/16 – 5/8	1/16 × 3/16	⅛ × 3/16
1¾ in.	7/16 – 9/16	¾ – 13/16	1/16 × 5/16	⅛ × 5/16
2½ in.	11/16 – ⅞	1 – 1¼	3/32 × ½	3/16 × ½
3½ in.	1 1/16 – 1¼	1⅝ – 1⅞	⅛ × 13/16	¼ × 13/16
5 in.	1⅜ – 1¾	2⅛ – 2½	3/16 × 1	⅜ × 1
7¼ in.	2⅛ – 2½	3¼ – 3¾	¼ × 1½	½ × 1½
9½ in.	2¾ – 3⅜	4⅜ – 5	5/16 × 1⅞	⅝ × 1⅞
10¼ in.	3 – 3⅞	5 – 5½	⅜ × 2¼	¾ × 2¼

NOTE: Port sizes above refer to slide valve cylinders.

Inside Cylinders with valves between

Before the advent of the piston valve, this arrangement was very common in full-size practice; the scheme cannot however be recommended to the model engineer as the cylinders are restricted by the space which has to be allotted to the steam chests, while the valves are rather inaccessible. Valve setting would have to be done under air or steam pressure.

Poppet Valve Cylinders

With the aim of increasing cylinder efficiency and the more economical use of the steam in the cylinders, various types of poppet valves have been tried and adopted in full-size practice. In the Caprotti system, separate means are employed for operating the inlet and exhaust valves, this makes it possible to maintain the periods of release and compression constant for any degree of cut-off, thus the dual advantage is secured of obtaining more work from the expansion of the steam, and enabling a reduction in clearance volume to be effected.

Very few attempts have been made to adopt poppet valves for model locomotives due to the complication involved. It remains, however, a very interesting field of experiment for the more experienced model engineer.

Material for Cylinders

Model locomotives that are not in regular use should have cylinders cast in a non-ferrous metal. A good quality gunmetal is the most suitable material; brass should not be used. Slide valves may be made in a grade of gunmetal slightly different from that of the cylinder block or a drawn phosphor-bronze section used. Piston valves are often made of ground rustless steel, the liners being in gunmetal which makes a good combination. Some model engineers make slide valves in two parts, the lower part which works on the port-face being of rustless steel, while the upper part is of brass or gunmetal, the two halves being silver-soldered together. One advantage of this method is that the "cavity" of the valve can be produced by drilling and filing, rather than by end-milling into the solid.

Locomotives above 1 in. scale usually have cylinders cast in iron, the pistons being also in iron with cast-iron or steel rings. Where slide valves are used in iron cylinders, these could be made in gunmetal, although iron is also quite satisfactory. Pistons made of non-ferrous metals should be fitted with one or more grooves into which may be packed graphited yarn. Piston and valve rods are nearly always made from rustless steel, though german-silver is sometimes used in very small models.

Valve Functions

Suitable dimensions for steam and exhaust ports in cylinders are given in Table VI, and the valves are proportioned from these.

The function of a valve, whether of the piston or slide type, is to control the inlet of steam to the cylinders, and the outlet of it into the blast pipe. There are four events which take place on each side of the piston during one revolution of the driving axle. These are:

1. Admission
2. Cut-off
3. Exhaust
4. Compression

In normal running, admission takes place slightly before the piston reaches the end of its previous stroke. A small amount of the exhaust steam is trapped in the cylinder at the point of compression, and between this point and the point of admission is the period of compression. Admission of live steam now takes place and raises the pressure in the cylinder to 80 or 85 per cent. of boiler pressure. Steam then continues to enter until the point of cut off is reached, as determined by the valve gear, after which the steam continues to do work by expanding. When the piston has nearly reached the end of its stroke, the valve opens to exhaust, and the period of exhaust takes place until the valve closes to exhaust, and the point of compression occurs.

Lap and Lead

During the early days of the steam locomotive, slide valves had no "lap", i.e., the valve just spanned the ports, thus at almost any position the valve was either open to live steam or to exhaust, and the steam was of course used most wastefully as it had no chance to expand. In modern engines, lap is added to the valve, giving smooth and economical running as described in the cycle of events previously. The **lap of a valve may be defined as the amount by which the valve overlaps the outside edge of the steam port when the valve is in its mid position.**

In a steam cylinder without "lead", when the piston is exactly on dead centre, the valve is just about to open the port to live steam at that end. If the valve opens to steam before the piston reaches dead centre, it is said to have lead. Lead may there-

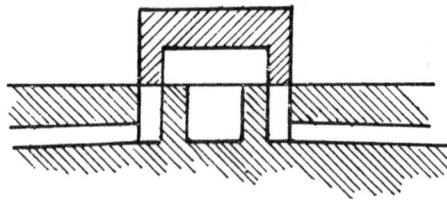

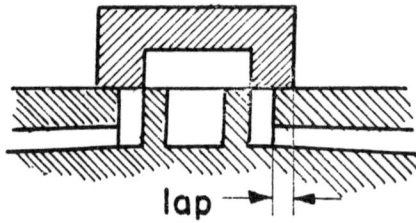

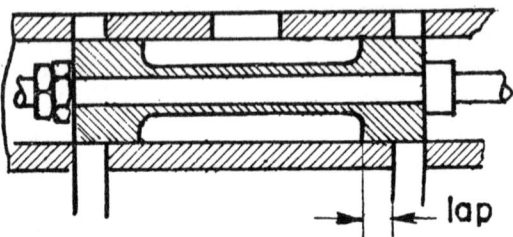

Fig. 32. Slide and Piston Valves.

fore be defined as the amount by which the valve is open to live steam when the crank is at dead centre.

In full-size locomotives, a certain amount of lead is essential for fast running, and in a model locomotive, it is necessary for both speed and rapid acceleration, though the amount depends on many other factors, such as the type of valve gear, the proportions of steam and exhaust pipes, and the proportions of ports and passageways in the cylinders themselves.

Generally speaking, the lap in model cylinders, with a valve gear such as Stephenson's, Walschaerts' or Baker's, should be made between $\frac{3}{4}$ and $1 \times$ the port width. The lead, in the case of constant lead valve gears such as Walschaerts' and Baker's, should be between 1/9th and 1/13th of the lap. Where Stephenson's valve gear is used, a variable lead is produced according to the position of cut off, but this will be discussed in a later chapter.

To assist a free exhaust, valves are sometimes given "Exhaust Clearance". Exhaust clearance can be defined as the amount by which the inside edges of the valve overlap the inside edges of the steam ports, or in other words, the amount by which the valve is open to exhaust when in its mid position.

The question as to whether exhaust clearance should be used or not in model valves is a highly controversial one. The author's opinion is that it can be useful in smaller models where the cross-sectional areas of steam and exhaust pipes and passageways may be comparatively small. The amount should in any case be small, generally $\frac{1}{2}$ to $\frac{3}{4}$ of the lead.

The steam passageways between the bores and the ports should be made of reasonable size; in large model locomotives with slide valves, the total cross-sectional area of the passageways may approach that of the steam ports, thus when an engine is being worked at short cut-off, there will be no throttling of the exhaust steam, for it must be remembered that the steam passageways also have to act as the exhaust ways.

Valve Travel

In a two-cylinder locomotive, the cut-off in full gear must not be too early, otherwise starting will be difficult, and at least 75 per cent. should be allowed for; in fact anything up to 85 per cent. is of advantage in starting. For a valve which opens the ports fully in full gear, the valve travel will be 2 (port width + lap) in full gear.

The cut off in full gear can be calculated as follows:

$$\text{Cut off} = \frac{\text{Port}^2 + 2\,(\text{port} \times \text{lap})}{(\text{Port} + \text{lap})^2} \times 100 \text{ per cent.}$$

To take an example, if the port width in a $\frac{3}{4}$ in. scale cylinder is say $\frac{1}{8}$ in. and the lap is $\frac{3}{32}$ in. Then:

$$\text{Cut off} = \frac{\frac{1}{8}^2 + 2\,(\frac{1}{8} \times \frac{3}{32})}{(\frac{1}{8} + \frac{3}{32})^2} \times 100 \text{ per cent.}$$

= 82 per cent. approx.

In the above formula, lead is neglected, but this would decrease the cut off point.

Machining Cylinders

When machining model cylinders, the block is generally dealt with first. If the lathe in use is large enough, the block may be held on an angle-plate on the face-plate, a Keat's Vee angle plate is very useful for the smaller sizes of cylinder. Another method is to use a large four-jaw chuck, though care should be taken to see that the jaws do not mark machined surfaces. In all cases the casting should be counter balanced to prevent vibration.

One end is now faced off and the boring carried out with a stiff tool, the cutting edge of which is set far enough out to enable it to run clear of the end of the bore. Self-act should be used and boring stopped at 4–8 "thou" below finished size, according to the size of the cylinders. The tool may then be put through once again without shifting the cross-slide, and the bores reamed.

If neither a solid parallel reamer is available, nor an adjustable reamer, the bores may be lapped; cast-iron cylinders can also be bored, but in either case, the lapping should only remove a very small amount, and great care should be taken to avoid the bore becoming "bell-mouthed". A very smooth bore that is not parallel is much worse than a parallel bore that is not quite smooth, as for instance when left after boring only in the lathe. After lapping, great care should be taken to get rid of all traces of the lapping compound used, by washing thoroughly in paraffin.

For inside cylinders, the block may now be lined up for the second bore by shifting the angle-plate; this also applies for boring a piston valve cylinder block for the valve liner. An outside slide valve cylinder would now be reversed for facing the other end. One way of tackling this operation is to turn up a brass mandrel, a tight push fit in the bore, and push the cylinder block on to this for facing the end.

Where cylinders are too large or heavy to be attached to the face-plate or held in a chuck, they may be bored by bolting them to the saddle or boring table of the lathe. The cylinder block is packed up so that the centre of the bore is exactly at lathe centre height; a boring head or a between centre boring bar may then be used. Care must be taken that the clamping bars used to hold the block down do not distort it.

After completing the bores, and facing both ends, the port face and the bolting face of the cylinder block may be dealt with. A large four jaw chuck can be used here, but great care should be taken to ensure that the block is held square. Alternatively the block could be bolted to an angle plate once again, by means of a long bolt through the bore, fitted with a nut and washer.

Cutting Ports

The steam and exhaust ports can be cut by "gang-milling" either in a milling machine or in the lathe. This method leaves the ports as a "$\frac{1}{4}$-moon" shape, which may cause difficulty when drilling the outer holes for the steam passageways, although in larger cylinders in which the ports are cored, this disadvantage would not apply. A very good method is to use an end-mill or slot drill. The latter can be obtained down to $\frac{1}{16}$ in. dia., which is small enough even for Gauge "O" cylinders. If a vertical slide is available for the lathe, the cylinder block can be bolted on an angle plate on this, facing the lathe mandrel, and the end-mill used in a collet or in the three jaw chuck. This is a convenient method where the lathe cross slide and leadscrew have graduated dials or hand-wheels, as the width and length of the ports as well as their depth, can be quickly read off from these, although the ports should be marked out beforehand as a precaution and as a check on one's figures.

CYLINDERS AND DETAILS

The passageways between the steam ports and the ends of the bores can then be drilled, if not already cored out. This is best done on a drilling machine, the exact angle required can be determined by "sighting" the drill against the side of the block before drilling. A depth stop should be used where possible. The position for the passageways should be chosen with due regard to the position of the steam chest and cylinder cover fixing studs.

Turning Pistons

Care should be taken when turning and fitting pistons. They need to be a good close fit without any sign of mechanical tightness. No amount of packing will make up for a piston which has been badly fitted in the first place. Figure 33 shows several methods of fitting pistons to their rods. The piston blanks should be turned a few "thou" over the finished size before mounting on the rods, and the grooves for packing put in with a parting tool. For the final machining, the piston rod may be held in a collet in the lathe. If no collet of suitable size is available a split bush could be made as it is essential that the piston rod should run absolutely true while the piston is given its final skim. It should not be necessary to lap pistons.

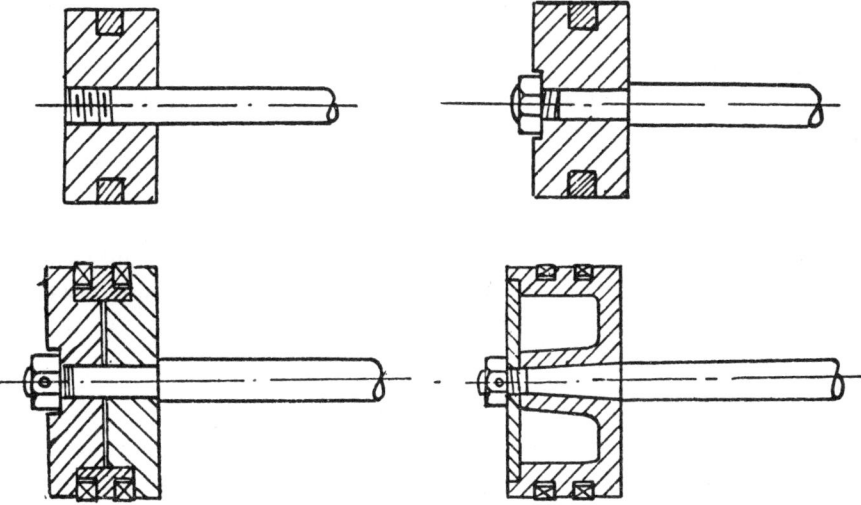

Fig. 33. Methods of fitting Pistons

When fitting piston rings, the ring should be turned slightly larger than the bore (about 0·0005 in. per ½ in. of bore). The slot can then be made from the inside at an angle of 45° by filing through with a knife-edge needle file, or by using a very fine metal fretsaw blade. When inserted in the cylinder, the gap should practically close. The slots in adjacent rings in the piston are arranged opposite to one another; on large models, the rings are arranged so that they cannot turn around in the cylinder, this being achieved by a small peg engaging a hole on the inside of the ring.

Piston rods are best made of rustless steel, and their diameter may be about 1/5 of cylinder bore up to 1 in. scale, or 1/6 of cylinder bore in larger models (to the nearest $\frac{1}{32}$ in.).

Machining Valves for Cylinders

Piston valve cylinders are generally fitted with separate liners which are pressed into the body of the cylinder, after cutting for steam ways; and reamed in position. Piston valves of the solid bobbin type may often be made from ground rustless steel as purchased, the liner being made to suit. In this way it is possible to avoid lapping altogether, though if lapping is used it is better to lap the liner internally to suit the piston valve, as the ground rustless steel is generally centre-less ground to fine limits.

Slide valves can be readily machined by end-milling, a $\frac{1}{16}$ in. dia. slot drill being used on Gauge "O" and "1" valves, or an $\frac{1}{8}$ in. dia. end-mill on valves for larger models. The outsides can also be milled, faced in a four jaw chuck, or even filed.

There are two ways in common use for driving a slide valve. In the first, a "buckle" completely surrounding the valve is used with bosses on the front and rear ends into which the valve spindle and the front extension of the valve spindle are screwed. The other method is to slot the top of the valve both longitudinally and transversely; the spindle, which is screwed with a fine thread, lying in the former slot, while a nut, usually made of square section gunmetal or bronze lies in the other slot. In either case adjustment is made by screwing the spindle in one direction or the other.

Another method, used by the author, is to adopt a plain valve spindle of rustless steel and a similar cross "nut", the nut in this case being reamed a close fit on the spindle and an Allen grub screw fitted through the top of the nut. This screw must only be tightened very lightly until valve setting has been completed, after which it can be tightened down for keeps. Provided there is sufficient depth of thread, this Allen screw is very unlikely to work loose in service.

Cylinder Covers and Steam Chests

Cylinder covers are generally cast with a spigot on the outside of the casting. In this case they can first be chucked by the outside, with the spigot running as truly as possible, the spigot is then given a cleaning cut when the casting can be reversed, chucked by the spigot, faced, drilled and reamed, the outside turned and the register for the cylinder bore turned an accurate fit for same. The other side can then be machined by holding the cover in a "split ring".

Steam chests of slide valve cylinders can generally be machined in the four-jaw chuck, though if large bosses are required, to represent piston valves, these can be separate turnings pressed into the steam chest. Care should be taken to drill and ream steam chests accurately for the valve spindles; to ensure this it is a good plan to set the steam chests up on the surface plate and mark the position for the spindle at both ends; the two positions are then deeply centred and a pilot hole drilled in

CYLINDERS AND DETAILS

the lathe, the drill being held in a chuck in the lathe mandrel, while the casting is supported against a centre in the tailstock. The steam chest is now reversed and the other end drilled. The pilot drill can now be put right through followed by one a little larger in diameter. If any inaccuracy is now observed, the incorrect hole can be drawn over with a round needle file before the final sizing drill or reamer is used.

Glands for stuffing boxes

The glands for the stuffing boxes for both the piston rods and the valve spindles may be either of the studded type or the plain screwed type. The former are generally used in full-size practice and models of 1 in. scale and above look better with them. Screwed glands are quite satisfactory for smaller models, but it is

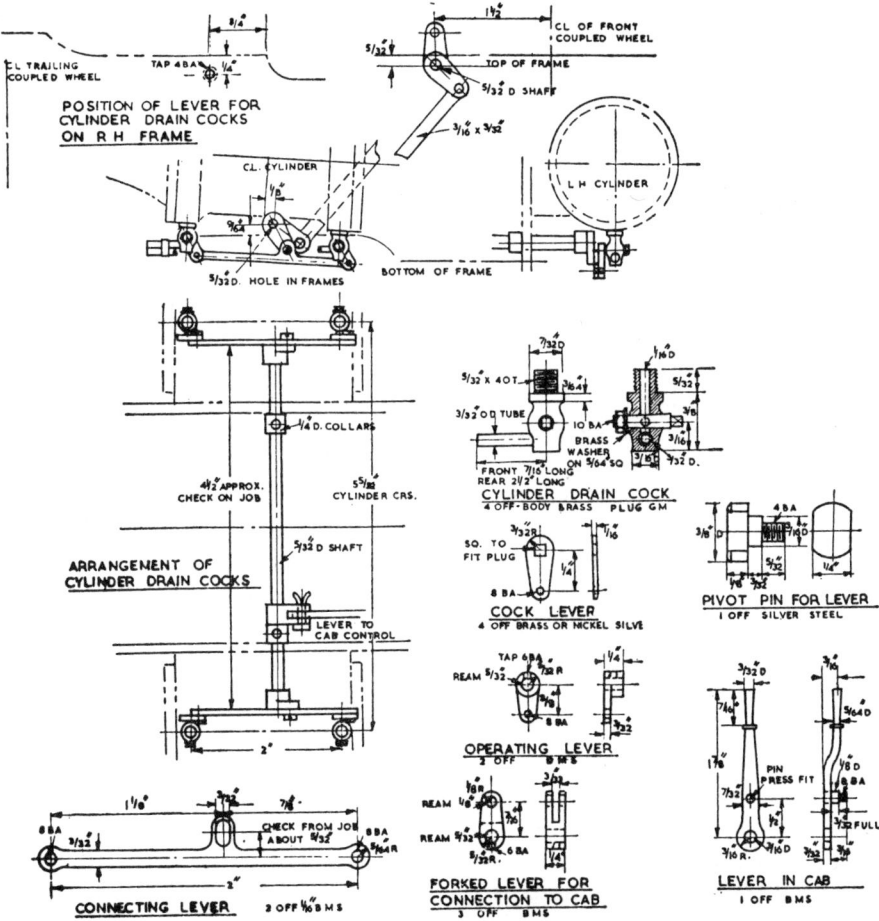

Fig. 34. Cylinder Drain Cocks for a ¾ in. scale locomotive

important that the threads are concentric otherwise a great deal of friction will be caused. The threads should be fairly tight or they may slacken off in service with disastrous results! The author generally uses a small lug attached to the bottom slide bar, which prevents the gland coming too far out.

Drain Cocks and Water-release Valves

All model locomotives above $\frac{1}{2}$ in. scale should be provided with cylinder drain cocks, preferably one at each end of the cylinder. They can be arranged for operation from the cab by means of rods and cranks or by adopting the use of a Bowden cable. Ordinary taper plug cocks give good service and do not dribble as do so many ball type cocks.

The piston valve cylinders of large models are usually fitted with automatic water-release valves situated above each valve head in order to prevent damage to covers due to trapped water. These may take the form of simple ball valves.

Lining up and fixing Cylinders

Cylinders should be carefully lined up with the driving axle before bolting to the main frames. A good method of doing this is to clamp the cylinder block temporarily to the frame with a large toolmaker's clamp; obtain a straight length of silver steel rather larger in diameter than the piston rod, and bore one end of this a nice push fit on the latter, the other end being turned to a point in the lathe. This rod is then pushed on to the end of the piston rod—which is pulled out to its fullest extent, the pointed end of the extension rod should then coincide with the centre of the driving axle, the axleboxes being jacked up to the correct running position.

The cylinder block itself is of course located in a "fore and aft" direction from the general arrangement drawing of the model. For inside cylinders the extension rod may be located rather more easily by dropping the driving axle and arranging a small diameter rod temporarily across the frames in the position normally occupied by the driving axle, this can be located from the bottom edge of the main frames.

Cylinders should be held to the frames by hexagon head screws or Allen screws from the inside, into tapped holes in the cylinder block, unless outside bolting flanges are provided, when hexagon screws should be put in from the outside with nuts on the inside.

Cylinders above $\frac{3}{4}$ in. scale may be provided with locating dowels or pins fitting reamed holes in the main frames for greater accuracy.

A good plan in smaller models is to insert "Hallite" washers between the cylinder block and the main frame; this avoids some loss of heat through conduction. The **outsides of outside cylinders** are generally lagged with asbestos covered by thin **steel sheet.**

CHAPTER EIGHT

Crossheads and Motion Details

Crossheads

LOCOMOTIVE CROSSHEADS MAY BE designed for one, two, three or four slide bars. The single-bar type is not much used today in full-size practice, though it was common on some railways such as the old Great Eastern and London and South Western; it is a useful design for model locomotive work. The two-bar crosshead, where the bars lie above and below the piston rod, is a very commonly used type and was used on most Great Western and L.M.S.R. locomotives and on many other railways; it makes a neat and nicely balanced crosshead for model work.

Most of the ex L.N.E.R. locomotives were fitted with the "Laird" three-bar crosshead, and British Railways have also adopted a similar type for many of their standard engines. It is rather more difficult to model satisfactorily, especially in the smaller sizes.

Crossheads for model locomotives are generally made in mild steel and the working surfaces case-hardened, though sometimes separate "slippers" made of

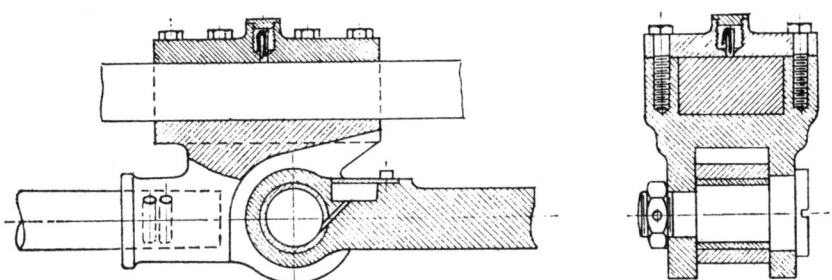

Fig. 35. Crosshead for single slide bar

bronze with or without white-metal linings are employed. For models up to ½ in. scale, a two-bar crosshead can be made from the solid, the boss for the piston rod being turned in the lathe (the blank being held in the four-jaw chuck) while the recess for the little end can be "pin-drilled" or counterbored from the back, the head of the gudgeon pin being made a close fit in this recess.

One disadvantage of this method of construction is the fact that the gudgeon pin can only be removed through the back of the crosshead, making it difficult to dismantle the connecting rod. In the author's design for 3½ in. gauge engines the

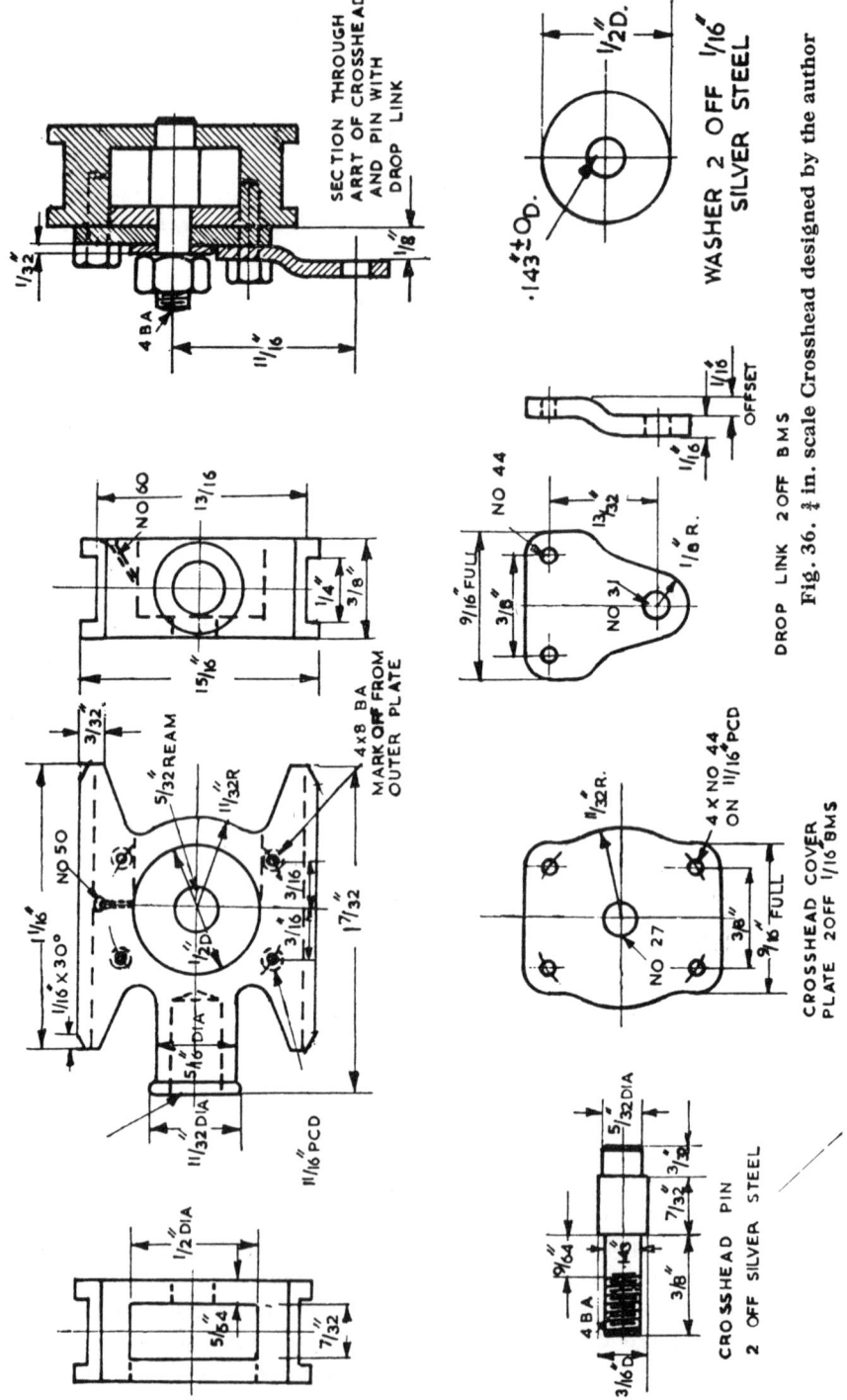

Fig. 36. ¾ in. scale Crosshead designed by the author

gudgeon pin is "loose" in the body of the crosshead, being clamped only by an outer plate which is itself bolted to the crosshead by four screws inserted from the outside. To avoid the thrust of the piston coming direct on these screws, a thin circular

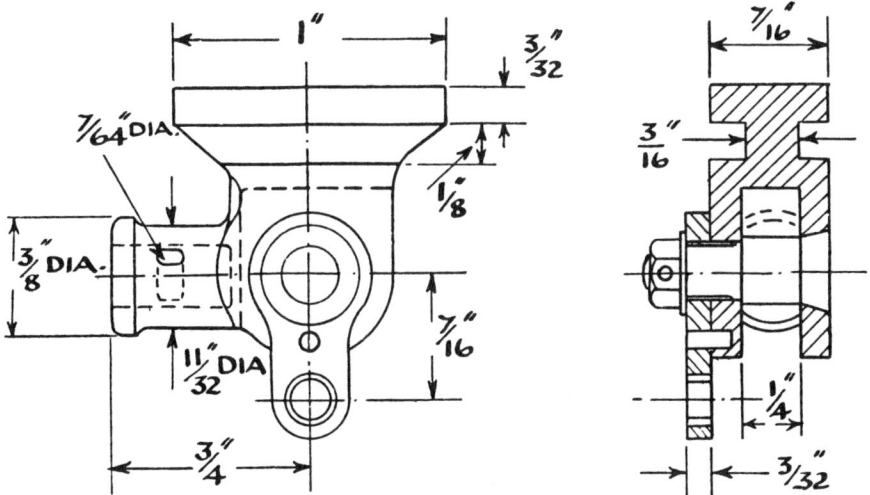

Fig. 37. L.N.E.R. type Crosshead, ¾ in. scale.

washer is inserted into the counterbored recess, which is opened out for the connecting rod by drilling and filing. If a drop arm is required for Walschaerts' valve gear, this can be held on by the two lower screws.

The grooves, top and bottom, of the two-bar crosshead can be formed by milling in a horizontal milling machine, a side and face cutter of the same width as the slide

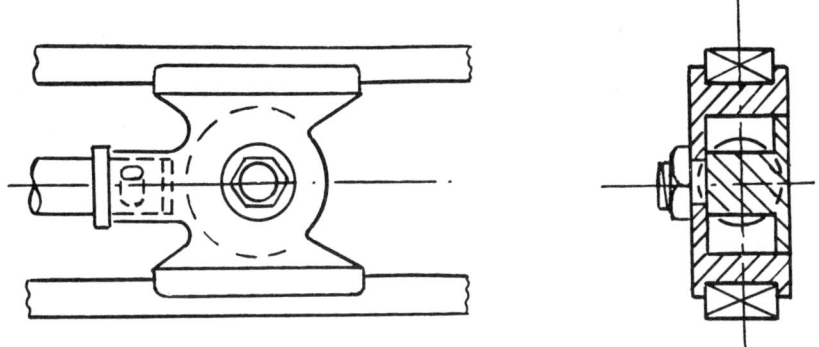

Fig. 38. Two-bar Crosshead for small models

bars being used. They can also be end-milled in the lathe, an end-mill of diameter equal to the width of the slide bars being employed. The crosshead blank can be clamped under the lathe toolholder at centre height for this operation.

Crosshead gudgeon pins are generally turned from silver steel, hardening not being essential where the small end bushes are made in phosphor-bronze. The fitting of the piston rod into the boss of the crosshead should be done carefully.

In large models, the end of the piston rod should be tapered, the crosshead boss being reamed to suit with a taper reamer, and a flat cotter used. A sound alternative to a flat cotter is the use of three small taper pins set in line and fairly close together. These may be put in at an angle of approximately 45° to the vertical and it is advisable to drill, ream and fit one pin at a time to ensure that each pin carries its correct proportion of the load.

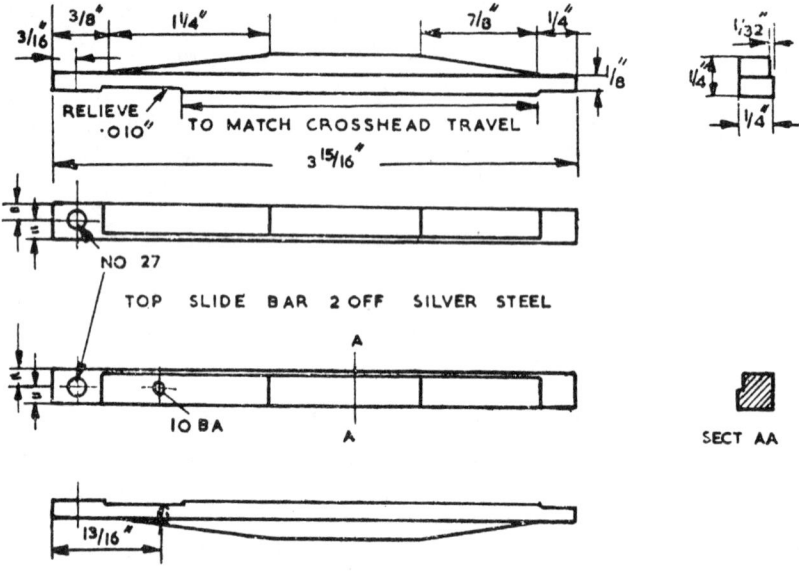

Fig. 39. L.M.S. type Slide Bars, ¾ in. scale.

In models of 1 in. scale, the end of the piston rod may be left parallel and the crosshead carefully reamed to a tight hand push fit, two taper pins being used for security, while in locomotives of ¾ in. scale and smaller, one pin only may be used provided it is of sufficient diameter.

Slide Bars

Slide bars are generally carried from the rear cylinder cover and supported at their outer ends by the motion plate. In small models the slide bars may be turned down at one end and threaded, being screwed into the rear cover above and below the piston rod. Where this method is adopted care must be taken to ensure that the slide bars are in line with the piston rod. When the size of the slide bars allows it, they may be drilled and hexagon head or Allen screws used to hold them down to a machined flange or step on the rear cover. This method permits the use of shims to adjust the fit of the slide bars upon the crosshead.

In larger models, the outer ends of slide bars are usually bolted to lugs cast on the motion plate, but on models below ¾ in. scale, a satisfactory arrangement is simply to put the ends through slots cut in the motion plates.

CROSSHEADS AND MOTION DETAILS

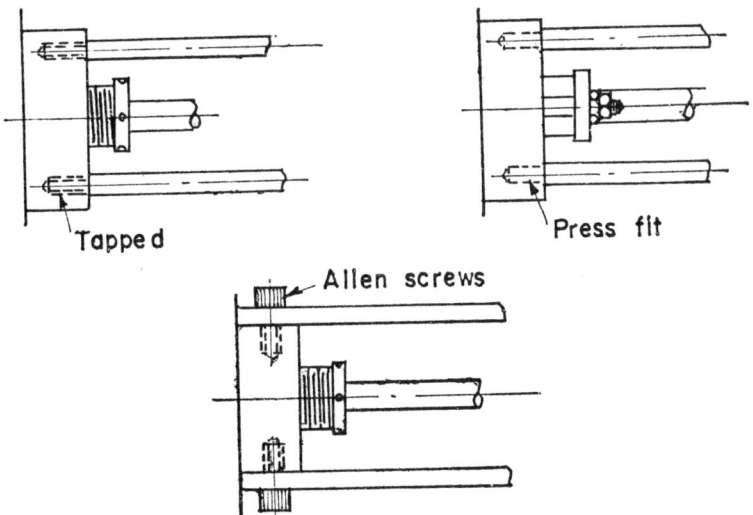

Fig. 40. Three methods of fitting Slide Bars

Slide bars should be made in silver steel or mild steel and hardening is not generally regarded as essential, for when wear does take place it is better to allow the slide bars to wear rather than the crossheads.

Motion Plates

The design of locomotive motion plates varies a great deal as it depends on the type and disposition of the valve gear and motion in use.

For models of G.W.R. engines gunmetal castings may be used, as the ribbing and beading used on the prototype can be easily arranged on the pattern. On some L.M.S. and L.N.E.R. locomotives the outside motion plates are combined with brackets to carry the expansion links of the Walschaerts' valve gear. When this type is used on model locomotives, they must be designed so that the expansion link, together with its radius rod, can be inserted or removed without difficulty.

Inside motion plates are generally castings, and may have slots to accommodate the ends of the slide bars, and clearance slots for the connecting rods and valve rods. On larger models the inside motion plates usually have lugs cast on for attachment of the slide bars, and on some engines, for fitting a crosshead pump. The machining of the bolting flanges of such motion plates can be done in the four-jaw chuck.

When fitting outside motion plates to the frames, the bolting flanges should be drilled beforehand; the motion plate may then be carefully lined up with the cylinders, the crosshead being pulled out to its fullest extent when the drill can be put through the bracket holes to make centres on the frames. In the case of inside motion plates, the process is reversed, the fixing holes being previously drilled in the frames.

When no castings are available, motion plates may be made from bright mild steel plate, the thickness of which should be at least equal to the thickness of the mainframes. The plate can be rivetted to steel angle for attachment to the frames.

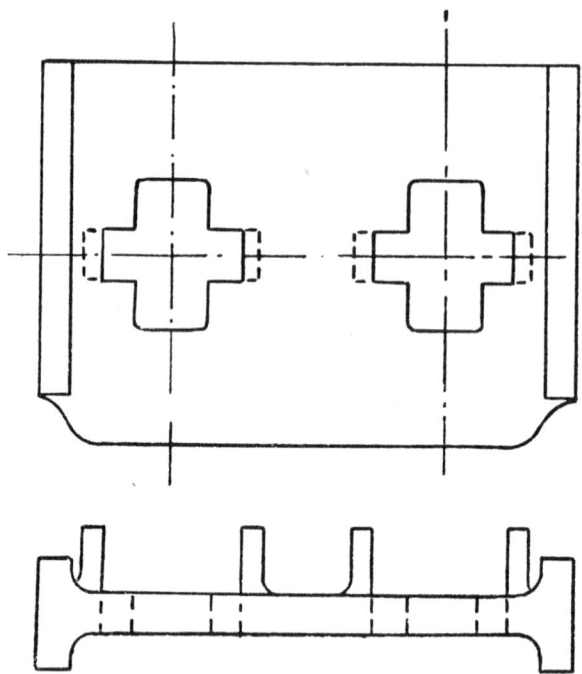

Fig. 41. Motion Plate for inside cylinders

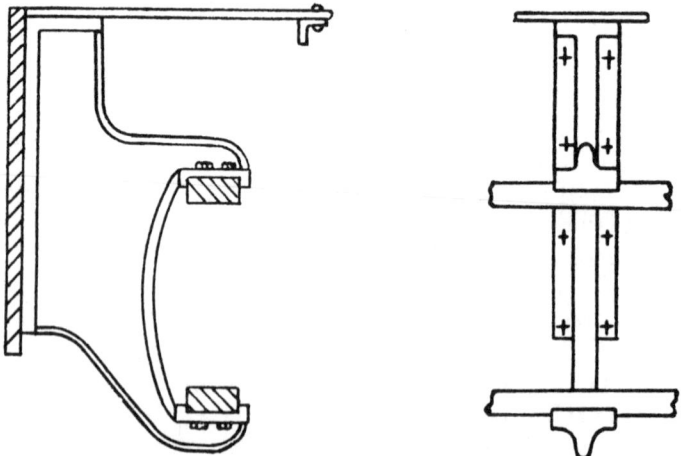

Fig. 42. G.W.R. type Outside Motion Plate

CROSSHEADS AND MOTION DETAILS 69

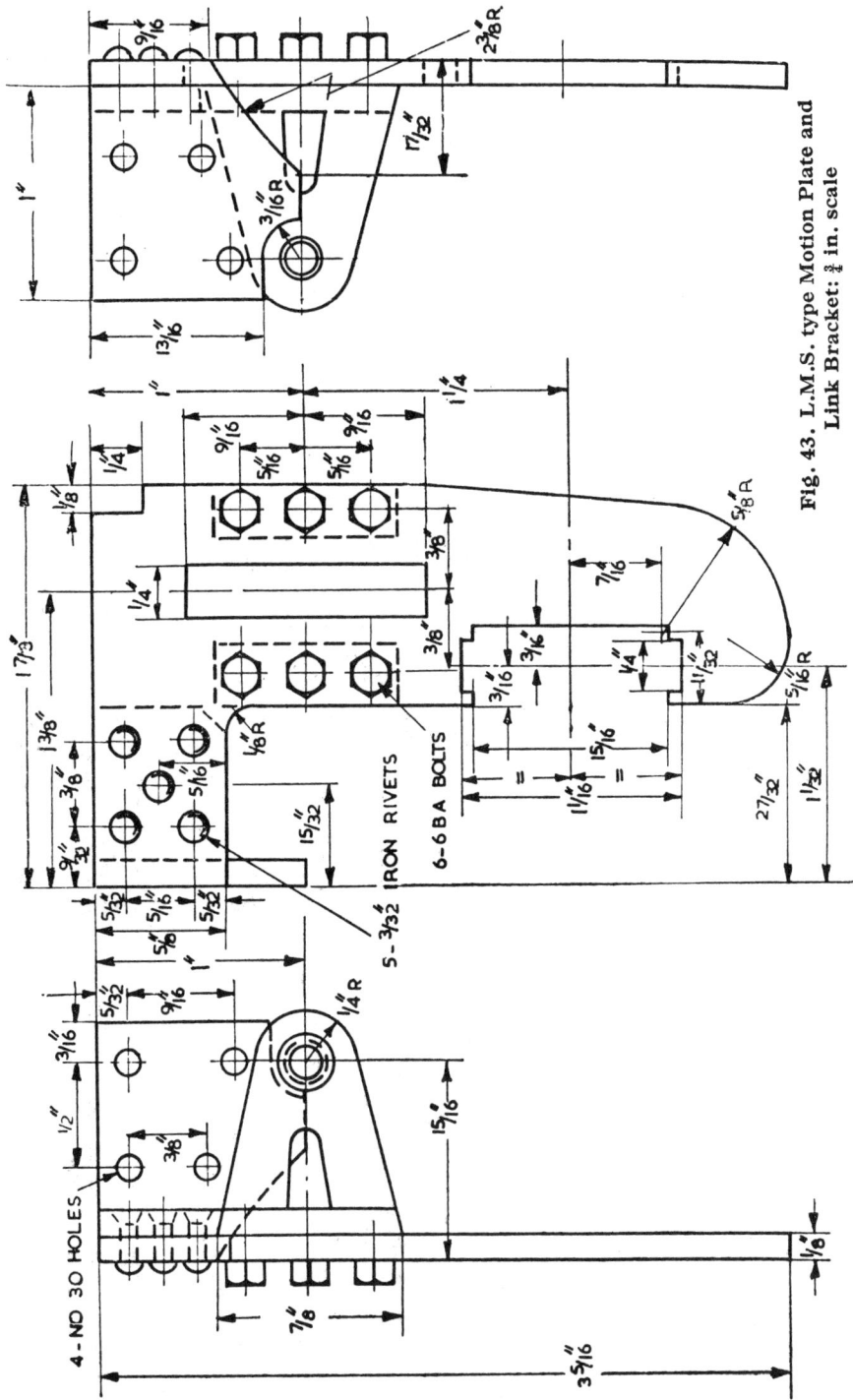

Fig. 43. L.M.S. type Motion Plate and Link Bracket: ¾ in. scale

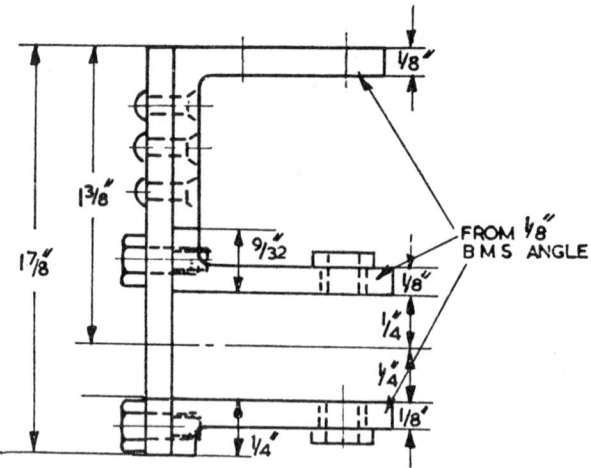

Fig. 43a. Plan of Motion Plate shown on previous page

Coupling Rods

On most modern locomotives, the coupling rods are fluted very deeply both front and back; to take an extreme case, the L.N.E.R. "A.4" class use rods of 5 in. × 2¼ in. section yet the fluting is so deep that the thickness of the web is only ⅜ in. This is made possible by the use of very high grade nickel-chrome steel. The rods are bushed with bronze lined with white metal at each crankpin, while the "knuckle" joint required on 6 or 8 coupled engines may be either bronze bushed or have a case-hardened steel bush.

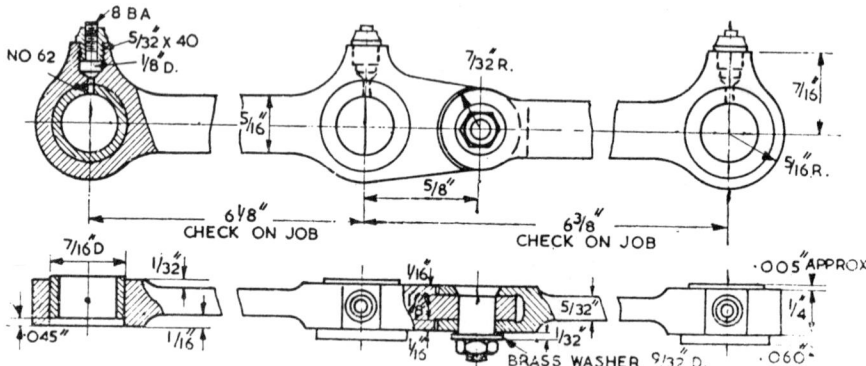

Fig. 44. Coupling Rods for a ¾ in. scale engine

On a few locomotives, the coupling rods are fitted with an additional joint the pivot of which is vertical. The purpose of this is to give lateral play, which allows the engine to take sharp curves more easily. This joint is very seldom used in models owing to the extra work involved, though there would appear to be no reason why it should not assist flexibility.

In model coupling rods, it is not usually considered worth while to adopt nickel-chrome steel, such material being very tough to machine especially with the type of equipment usually available to the amateur. Bright mild steel serves as a very good substitute and if made a little thicker than the scale equivalent is quite strong enough; in any case the fluting, if required for appearance's sake, need only be done on the outside of the rod.

The marking out of model coupling rods should be done with great care as it is of importance that the centres of the rods correspond exactly with the centres of the driving and coupled wheels of the locomotive. In the case of 6 or 8 coupled engines, it is not a bad plan to make and fit the knuckle joints in the coupling rod blanks before marking out the centres for the crankpins, the blanks can then be dismantled again for the remaining machining and finishing operations.

The rods should be held together in pairs for drilling and reaming for the bushes, after which they may be bolted together for shaping the outsides. This can be done in a horizontal milling machine or even in the lathe if a substantial vertical slide is available and the lathe cross-slide has sufficient travel. If no machine operation can be arranged, coupling rods may be shaped up by sawing and filing, the bosses being formed by the well-known method of swinging the rod on a suitable peg turned on the end of a piece of square bar which is clamped under the lathe toolholder. The rod is swung by hand against an end-mill of suitable diameter held in the chuck. It must be moved against the direction of rotation of the cutter as far as possible or the latter may "catch up" and spoil the rod.

A good method of ensuring that coupling rods are of the right length between centres is to first drill and ream them an exact fit for the crank-pins and try them on the locomotive. If they won't go on at all, it should be evident where they are incorrect; if they do go on, but produce a "tight spot" on rotating the wheels, a bright mark will quickly show up where the rod is tight, when the hole in the rod can be drawn over, and then opened out ready for fitting the bushes. The bushes for the driving crankpins should always be made a close working fit, but a little play may be allowed in leading and trailing bushes. For all sizes of models, a good quality phosphor-bronze is suitable for coupling rod bushes, either drawn or cast, and they are made a press fit into the rods; in models over $\tfrac{3}{4}$ in. scale, they are generally keyed or pinned in addition.

Fluting of coupling and similar rods can be done with a small diameter slotting or side and face cutter of requisite width, or with a Woodruffe cutter, the latter being suitable for the smaller gauges. If the job has to be done in the lathe, the cutter can be held in a collet or in the 3 jaw chuck, and the rod to be fluted bolted down to a length of heavy steel angle which is itself bolted to the vertical slide. This angle must of course be set quite square and level before cutting is commenced. The rod to be fluted is held firmly to the angle by Allen screws and washers through the bearing holes, this being done before the bushes are fitted.

When coupling rods are fluted on their outsides only, there is often a tendency to warp, and this should be corrected after machining and before fitting to the engine.

On some outside cylinder locomotives with leading coupled wheels, the leading coupling rod boss may require special treatment due to the proximity of the connecting rod or crosshead. The bush is generally made narrower, and the retaining collar of the crankpin (see Chapter 5) is partly recessed into the rod.

Connecting Rods for Outside Cylinders

The connecting rods are the mediums through which the reciprocating motion of the crossheads is converted into rotary motion at the cranks, and consequently the wheels; at one end, called the small end, they work upon the crosshead gudgeon pins, and at the other, the big end, they work upon the crankpins.

In full-size practice, connecting rods are usually made from special alloy steels owing to the great stresses and strains which have to be allowed for, though some small shunting and goods engines may use mild steel. Mild steel however is generally very suitable for model connecting rods, while for very small models German-silver or gunmetal are possible alternatives.

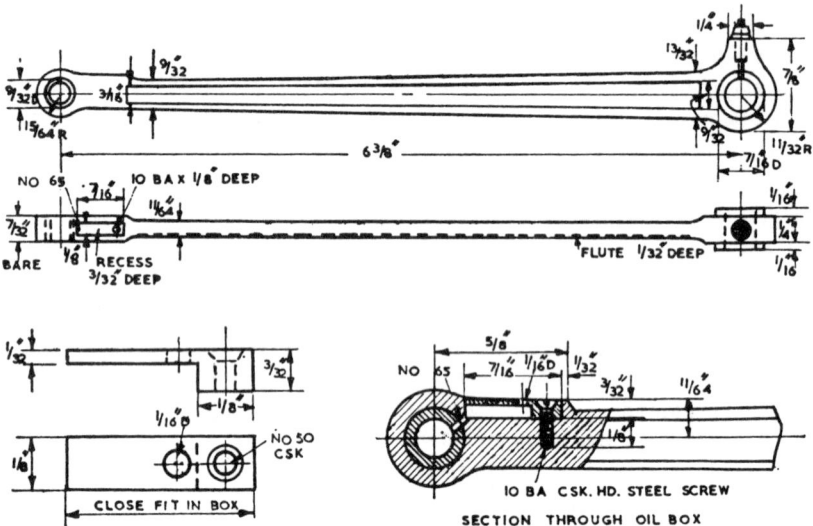

Fig. 45. L.M.S. type Outside Connecting Rod

The design of connecting rods for both outside and inside cylinders varies a great deal, though most modern locomotives have now adopted quite a simple type for the former, the boss being of large diameter cut from the solid with its oil box, a plain cylindrical bronze bush with white metal linings being used, while the rod itself is an H section, deeply fluted on both sides. This type of rod is most used in model locomotives except that it is not essential to flute on both sides, nor are white metal linings regarded as necessary except on the very largest models.

The small ends of steel connecting rods for ½ in. scale models are often case-hardened, but in larger models, the phos-bronze bush is preferable. The big end bushes of outside connecting rods should as a general rule be nearly twice the diameter of the small end bushes; while their length should be a little more than those of the coupling rods where these bear upon the driving crankpins.

On older locomotives, the rectangular big end having brasses adjustable by means of a taper cotter and glut are used. This type can be copied in large-scale models without very much difficulty, and two methods of construction are given later in this chapter.

In recent years, the use of roller bearings in connecting rod big ends has increased and some enterprising model engineers have followed this arrangement by using small needle roller bearings, in which the rollers bear directly on the locomotive crankpin, which must therefore be properly hardened. This type of bearing gives very long wear with the minimum of friction, its only objection may be its appearance, being somewhat large when applied to models below $1\frac{1}{2}$ in. scale.

Inside Connecting Rods

Inside connecting rods are somewhat more difficult to produce than the outside type, owing to the fact that their big ends must be made readily detachable from the crank axle. At one time the Marine type was used a good deal in full-size practice, the big end being comparatively simple in design and quite robust, while the rod is usually of round section, but with the greatly increased power of the modern locomotive, the H section rod has come into use.

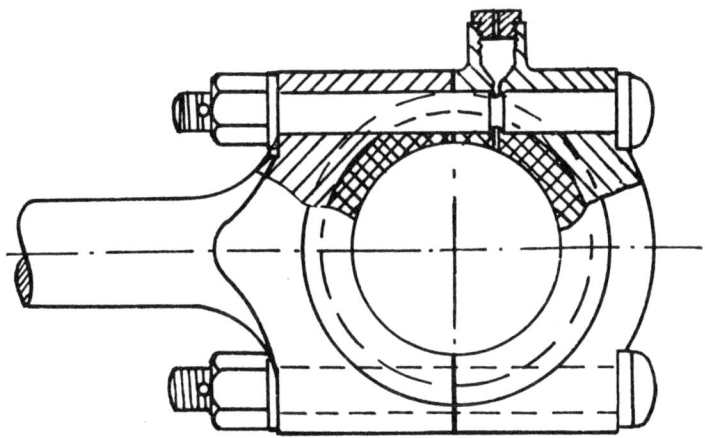

Fig. 46. Marine type Connecting Rod Big End

On the ex-L.M.S. Railway, a big end was adopted having the jaws machined out of the solid, the brasses being put in up against the leading end of the jaws, followed by a "clip" embracing the whole of the jaws, and a large taper cotter of 1 in 16 taper driven in against the lot. A small safety split cotter was then driven in through the bottom of the main cotter, while two bolts with square washers on each side were put through the main cotter with locking plates each side of the latter.

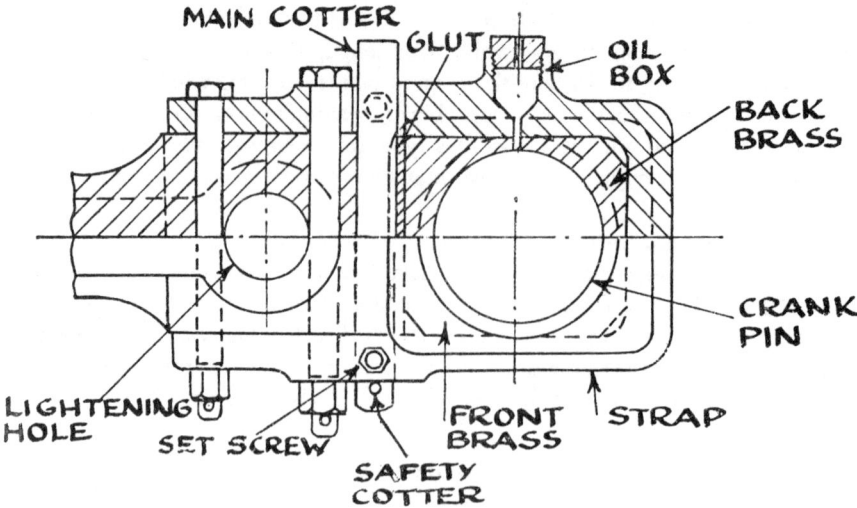

Fig. 47. Inside Connecting Rod Big End, L.M.S. type

The former L.N.E. Railway used a rather unusual type of big end on their inside connecting rods. The strap, which was of high carbon steel, was bent into a U shape and the two bolts machined integral with the strap thus preserving the grain. The circular split brasses were held between the rod and this strap and were

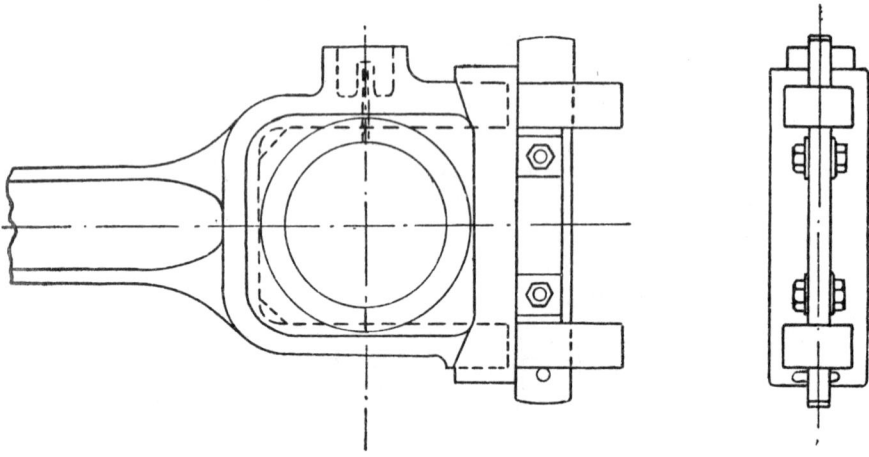

Fig. 48. Another type of Inside Connecting Rod Big End

prevented from turning by a steel key. The bolts were fitted with locknuts and cotters. Felt pads were provided, held in position by wires, to retain the lubricant, while the oil was fed through a pin trimming from an oil box integral with the strap.

The connecting rod itself was made from nickel chrome steel of fluted section, measuring (overall) $5\frac{1}{2}$ in. × $2\frac{1}{2}$ in. close to the big end, and 4 in. × $2\frac{1}{2}$ in. at the small end. This type of connecting rod would not be easy to model owing to the difficulty of bending the strap accurately enough after threading the main bolts One solution would be to bend up the strap without bolts and to tap the ends of the strap for studs after the bending had been satisfactorily completed.

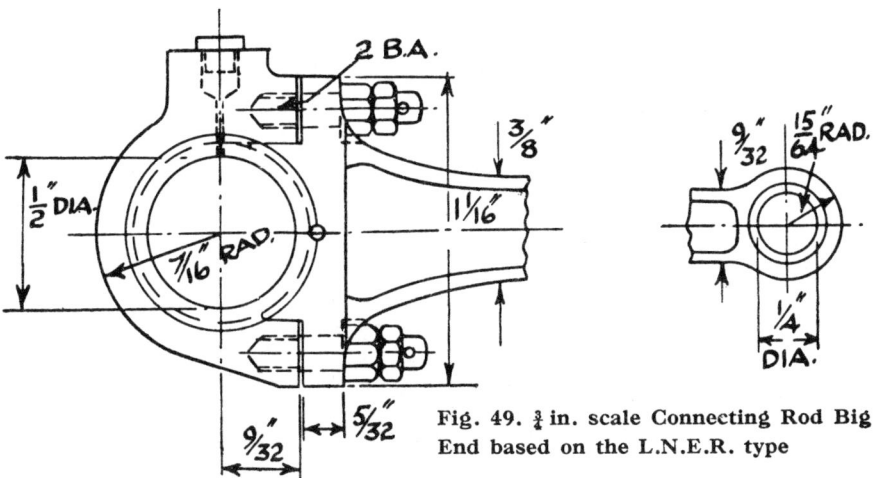

Fig. 49. ¾ in. scale Connecting Rod Big End based on the L.N.E.R. type

Construction of Model Connecting Rods

For small gauge models, the making of outside connecting rods is very simple, the rod being first marked out on a suitable length of flat bar, the holes drilled, the outside and the bosses marked out and the blank bolted to another length of bar so that the two rods can be cut out and filed to shape together.

In models of ½ in. scale and larger it is usual to flute connecting rods, at least on their outsides and as the flute is nearly always tapered to match the outside shape of the rod, it is well worth while to do this in the model.

The author's method of machining a tapered flute is as follows: the two connecting rod blanks are cut rather longer (¾ in. to 1½ in.) than finally required at one end. After marking out one blank and drilling the two together the blanks are held down on the milling machine, or in the case of a lathe operation, on a heavy angle attached to the vertical slide as described for fluting coupling rods, but in this case an Allen screw and washer is put through the small end hole only, the other end being held down by a clamp just clear of the big end hole. The flute is now machined as for a normal parallel rod to final depth, the cutter (a small side and face or a Woodruffe) is then brought back to the small end of the rod, the Allen screw partly slackened off, the clamp also slackened and the rod swung round, pivoting on the Allen screw, to give the desired width of flute at the big end, when the screw and clamp are again tightened and machining completed.

The older type outside connecting rod fitted with adjustable brasses to the big end may be modelled, in the smaller scales, by simply turning the bush from rectangular bronze bar and pressing into the rod, a dummy cotter and bolt being fitted to the rear of the bush. For large models, and for big ends of inside connecting rods, the "jaw" may be formed in the body of the rod itself, or it may be a separate item, machined to take the brasses and made to slide over the end of the connecting rod to which it is secured by two bolts. In either case the jaw may be milled out and the blank for the brasses milled to suit, the brasses being of course double flanged. When the brasses are a nice fit in the strap, they are sawn in half, the two halves cleaned up and soft soldered together again; they can then be drilled and reamed for the crankpin and finally melted apart.

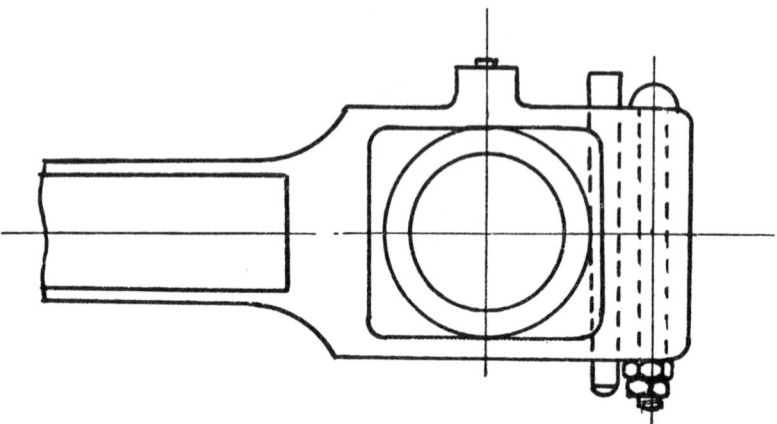

Fig. 50. A simple Outside Connecting Rod Big End for small locomotives

Except in the very largest models, it is not essential to use a taper glut, the cotter may bear directly against the brasses, the block or rod or whichever is next to the cotter being tapered to match the latter which should be of slow taper. The cotter should be locked by a screw or a small safety cotter.

The Marine type of big end for connecting rods is quite easily made, though the rod is often of rectangular section in model work, the rod having a head to which the brasses are clamped by a cap and two horizontal bolts which cut through the brasses. Should difficulty be experienced in obtaining an oil way from the oil box to the crankpin in this type of big end, the upper bolt may be slightly reduced in diameter immediately under the oil box to allow oil to pass. This is in any case quite legitimate practice as the threaded end of the bolt is the weakest part of it. The bolts should be fitted with locknuts and split pins though Simmonds or GKN anti-vibration nuts could also be used with success.

The shaping of the oil box on big ends should not present any difficulty, the oil reservoir itself taking the form of a large drilled hole with a very fine hole through the brasses, communicating with the crankpin, while small oil grooves may be formed in the brasses themselves. A top cap may be screwed in to the top of the oil reservoir to represent the cork and cane generally fitted to the full-size engine.

CROSSHEADS AND MOTION DETAILS

The oil box for the small end of connecting rods presents rather more difficulty owing to the lack of clearance in most model crossheads, but Figure 45 shows one solution, while another is simply to drill a vertical hole half-way through the rod close to the small end bush, and then to drill a fine connecting hole at 45° from this, breaking into the gudgeon pin bush.

Eccentrics and Straps

An eccentric is a crank in which the diameter of the crankpin is sufficiently large to enclose the shaft. It will not transform reciprocating into rotary motion, but only rotary into reciprocating.

Eccentrics are principally used in valve gears, generally inside the frames, but are also used in model locomotives for driving feed water pumps and mechanical lubricators.

Eccentric sheaves are usually made in mild steel, though cast iron is also suitable, while the straps are nearly always gunmetal castings. The sheaves are often grooved with a rib machined on the strap to match the groove, in order to retain the strap on the sheave. Another method is to machine the rib on the sheaves and to recess the strap to match, while a third and easiest method is to dispense with the rib altogether and machine the sheave with a small flange on each side of it.

Where two sheaves lie side by side, as for instance in Stephenson's valve gear, the sheaves may be flanged only on their outsides, though double flanged sheaves run with less friction.

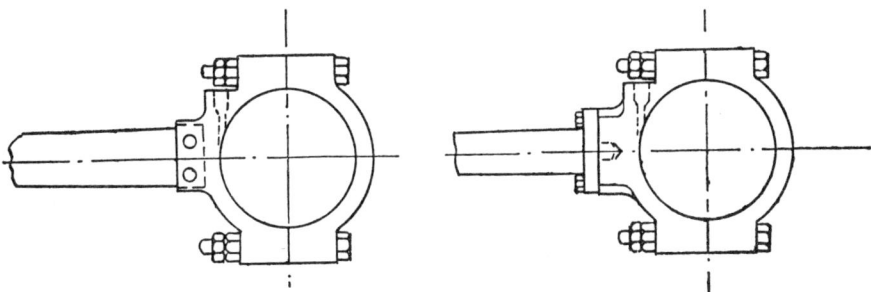

Fig. 51. Methods of fitting Eccentric Straps to rods

Valve gear eccentric sheaves may be held securely on their axles by means of Allen grub screws. These should be of as large a diameter as can conveniently be accommodated and put through the larger diameter of the sheave. The head of the grub screw may also be run over with soft solder after valve setting is completed, though this is not absolutely essential.

When machining eccentric sheaves, the flanges may be formed by using a stout parting tool ground off quite square on the cutting edge, the lathe run slowly and plenty of cutting oil used. They may be drilled and/or bored and reamed in the lathe by holding them in a four-jaw chuck; to avoid crushing the thin flanges, a brass split ring may be turned up and sprung over the working part of the eccentric.

Before machining the eccentric straps, they should be partly cleaned up with a file to remove sand and scale, the holes for the securing bolts drilled right through tapping size, opened out half way with the clearance size drill and then tapped. The two halves can then be sawn apart, and the jointing faces machined, or filed flat. They are then bolted together temporarily and set up to run as truly as possible in the four-jaw chuck for boring the inside.

It is not a bad plan to previously turn up a short piece of bar to exactly the same diameter as the sheave and use this as a plug gauge for the straps. This piece of bar can then be used again to hold the straps while the two sides are machined. The screws are slackened off and a strip of paper put between the straps and the bar; on re-tightening, the straps will be firm enough to enable a light cut to be taken over each side.

The eccentric rods themselves are generally made from mild steel and there are two commonly used methods of fitting them to their straps; one is by slotting the strap, inserting the end of the rod and riveting through the two, the other, used in the larger models, is to form a head on the eccentric rod and to fit studs to the strap for bolting the two together.

CHAPTER NINE

Valve Gears : Link Motions

THE FIRST ESSENTIAL IN A locomotive valve gear is to provide the driver with some means of reversing his engine; the second requirement is some method of varying the cut-off, in order to make the most economical use of the steam.

As mentioned in Chapter 7, slide valves must be provided with lap. The setting of a slide valve without lap is exactly 90° in advance or retard of the crankpin. When a valve is provided with lap or with lap and lead, the eccentric is advanced by that amount; the angle of advance of an eccentric is the angle it is moved ahead of the normal 90°.

The only really simple reversing valve gear is the slip-eccentric gear, this can be applied to a valve with as much lap and lead as is required and gives a good steam distribution. It cannot however, be reversed from the cab, nor can the point of cut-off be varied from the cab. This gear was employed on the Webb 3 cylinder compounds of the L.N.W.R. to operate the valve of the low pressure cylinder.

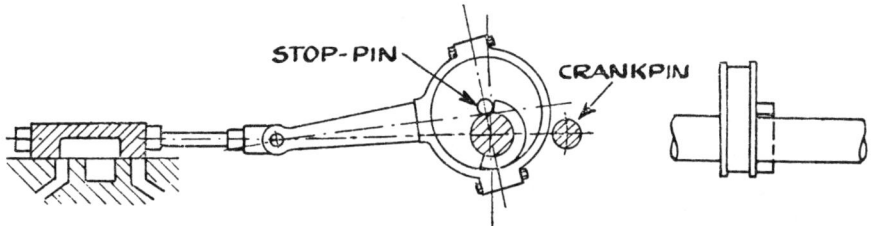

Fig. 52. Slip-eccentric Valve Gear

The single eccentric is made loose on the axle and is operated by a stud or pin mounted in a collar which is secured to the axle alongside the eccentric by means of a set screw.

Valve gears which are fully controllable from the cab are divided into two main classes: Link motions and Radial valve gears. The principal link motions are the Stephenson, the Gooch and the Allan straight-link; while the best known Radial gears are the Joy, the Walschaerts' and the Baker.

Stephenson Valve Gear

The Stephenson's link valve gear was at one time the most widely used in Great Britain, and though it has now been very largely superseded by the Walschaerts, Baker gear, and the various types of Poppet valve gear, it is still a very efficient gear when properly designed.

The Stephenson gear uses two eccentrics, one for each direction of working, the eccentric rods being connected to each end of a curved slotted link. In the "locomotive type" link, the eccentric rods are connected on the curved centre line of the link, above and below the link slot, thus the total travel of the eccentrics must be made more than the valve travel required in full gear. The locomotive

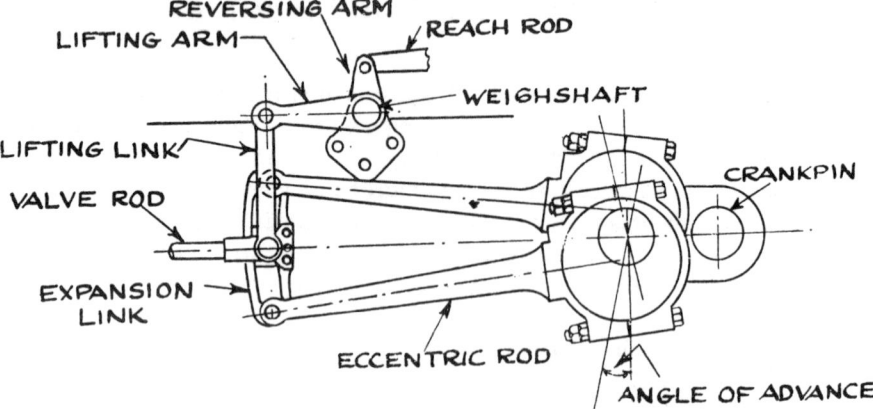

Fig. 53. Stephenson's Valve Gear with loco type link

type link is normally suspended at its centre point by means of a lifting link which is connected to the weighshaft. The valve rod, which is supported either by a guide fixed to the motion plate, or by a swinging lever, obtains its motion from a "die-block", upon which the curved slot of the link can slide up and down as controlled by the lifting link.

An interesting feature of the Stephenson gear is that with "open" eccentric rods, the lead increases towards mid-gear, while with "crossed" eccentric rods, the lead diminishes towards mid-gear. This is due to the angularity of the rods and the effect is greater with short eccentric rods.

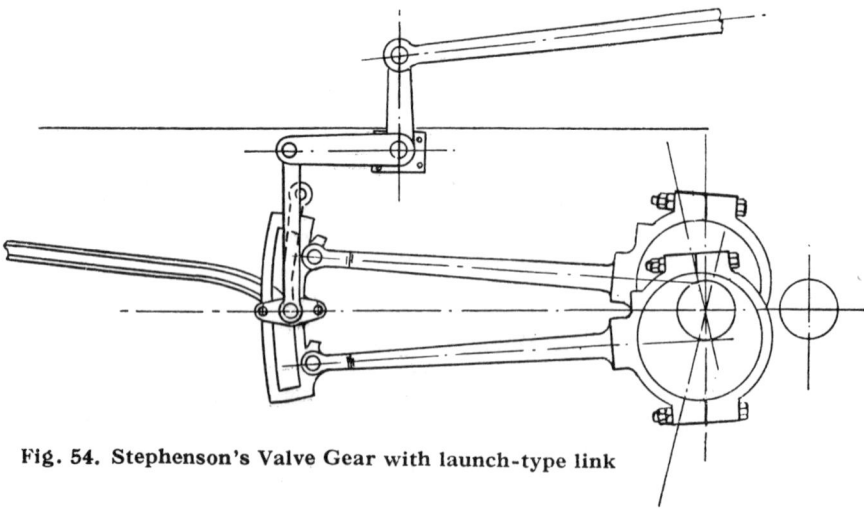

Fig. 54. Stephenson's Valve Gear with launch-type link

Another type of Stephenson gear is that where the expansion link used is the "Launch-type" link. The true Launch link has the point of suspension on the curved centre-line of the link slot but beyond the end of the slot, but in the Launch-type link, the suspension is arranged on the horizontal centre-line of the motion.

Alexander Allan of the L.N.W.R. was probably the first to realise the possibilities of the Launch-type link with Stephenson's valve gear, but it was G. J. Churchward of the old Great Western Railway who developed this type to its present high efficiency, by adapting it for the use of long valve travels.

About the year 1904, Churchward adopted long valve travels and large steam laps for his express locomotives; he soon realised however that if he was to use the usual locomotive type link, the length of link required and the large size of eccentric sheaves and straps needed, would make the arrangement quite impracticable. He therefore used the Launch-type link with comparatively short eccentric rods, and as the latter gave a large increase of lead towards mid-gear, he arranged for the valves to be set with "negative" lead in full gear.

Designing Stephenson's Link Valve Gear for models

Before dealing with the actual proportions of Stephenson's link valve gear, the full gear cut-off desired should be considered.

In full-size locomotive work, the point of cut-off in full gear is usually decided by the class of work the engine is required to perform. A two-cylinder contractor's shunting locomotive would probably be given a full gear cut-off of 85 per cent. of

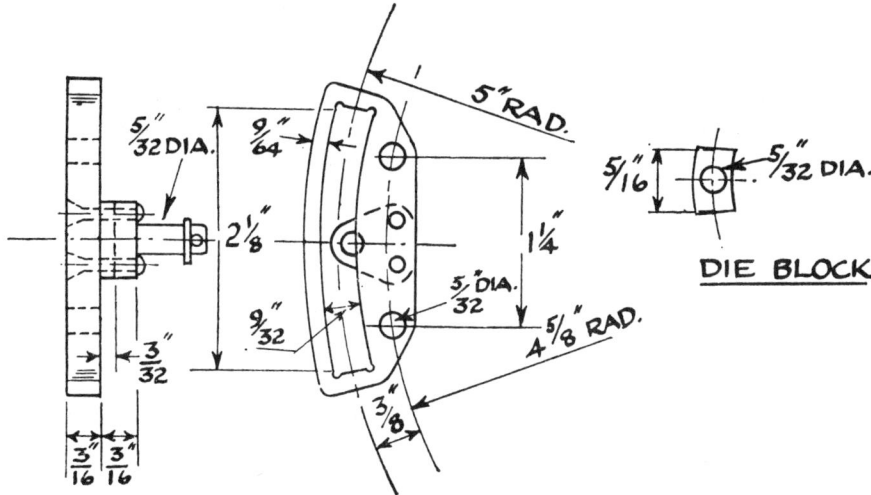

Fig. 55. Launch-type Link for 5 in. gauge model

the stroke, a shunting or goods engine around 80 per cent., while an express passenger locomotive would be given about 75 per cent., as it would not be required to start and stop nearly so frequently.

In the case of model locomotives, which may be used equally on a fast continuous track or on a short "up and down" track, it is advisable to make the full gear cut-off fairly late. It is of course true that at late cut-offs the angle of the connecting rod is very small, in relation to the position of the driving crankpin, even so however, it may be taken that anything up to 85 per cent. cut-off is useful in starting a two-cylinder locomotive. In any case, provided that the mechanical layout allows for it, there are no disadvantages attending the use of a late cut-off in full gear; there are however two distinct advantages. One is that a late cut-off gives full steam port opening early in the stroke; the other is that a locomotive so arranged has a more even turning movement at slow speeds, so that the tendency to slip at starting is reduced.

To obtain a full gear cut-off of 80 per cent. of the stroke, the full gear valve travel should be made $4\frac{1}{2}$ times the lap of the valve; for 85 per cent., the full gear travel should be 5 times the lap. This of course ignores any lead, but with launch-type links with comparatively short eccentric rods, the valves should have no lead at all in full gear, but should be set line-for-line with the outside edges of the steam ports, with the cranks on dead centre.

Proportions of Stephenson's Valve Gear

If success is to be achieved, the various parts of Stephenson's gear need to be carefully proportioned and the following dimensions, evolved from highly successful working models, may be relied upon:—

1. Throw of eccentrics (for launch-type links) = $\frac{1}{2}$ full gear valve travel.
2. Thickness of eccentric straps should be between $\frac{1}{5}$ and $\frac{1}{6}$ of piston diameter, to the nearest round figure.
3. Motion pins should be approximately $\frac{1}{8}$ of piston diameter.
4. Boss diameters on links, eccentric rods and valve rods = twice motion pin dia.
5. Width of curved slot of expansion link = pin diameter × $1\frac{3}{4}$ approx.
6. Thickness of expansion link should be between 1/5 and 1/7 of piston diameter, according to space available.
7. Length of curved slot of link should be eccentric rod pin centres × $1\frac{5}{8}$.
8. Distance between eccentric rod pins should be full gear valve travel multiplied by 2 for short eccentric rods or by $2\frac{1}{4}$ for long eccentric rods (by short rods in this context is meant rods of a scale equivalent of less than 4 ft. 6 in.).
9. Length of die-block = motion pin diameter × $2\frac{1}{8}$ to the nearest round figures.

The Point of Suspension of the Expansion Link

The point of suspension of the expansion link in Stephenson's gear makes a great deal of difference to the valve events obtained. On some models, the lifting link is attached to one of the eccentric rod pins, this however is not good practice, and is only done to avoid the extra work involved in arranging a proper central suspension.

In locomotives fitted with the Stephenson's link motion, it is important that the eccentric sheaves and eccentric rods should be so fitted up that the engine has "open" eccentric rods, enabling the lead to increase towards mid gear. To ensure that this is so the right-hand motion of the model should be drawn out, to as large a scale as possible with the right-hand crankpin on the back dead-centre. Then the outside eccentric rod nearest to the right-hand mainframe is the "forward" one, and is connected to the top boss of the expansion link. The inside eccentric rod is the "backward" one, and is connected to the bottom boss of the expansion link.

In this position, the forward eccentric will be up, and the backward eccentric down, and the expansion link will stand exactly vertical to the horizontal centre-line of the motion. The lifting link should now lie quite vertical and from this the correct position for the weighshaft may be decided.

If the valve gear actuates the valves through the medium of a rocking shaft, the eccentric rods are connected as described previously, but the eccentric sheaves are set exactly opposite to the previous position with the crankpin on back dead-centre. This means that the forward eccentric sheave is down and the backward sheave is up, and the eccentric rods are therefore crossed at this position of the crankpin.

In order to arrive at the best possible position for the suspension of the expansion link by the lifting links where long valve travels are required, it is necessary to consider what errors, caused by the obliquity of the link when fully inclined forward or backward, have to be neutralised. With the launch-type link, there are two main kinds of "link-slip", therefore the point of suspension of the link must be so chosen that each of these two kinds of "link-slip" is not decreased at the expense of an increase in the other.

By suspending the expansion link on its horizontal centre-line certain advantages are gained. Firstly the suspension point is never very far away from the die-block in any position of the gear, so that the lifting links always have a good leverage to hold the link with a minimum of link-slip. Secondly the steam distribution improves, and link-slip decreases, as the valve gear is "notched up" towards mid-gear, as this brings the suspension centre still closer to the die-block. Also as the suspension centre is midway along the link, the steam distribution will be equally good in forward or backward gear.

Another advantage of suspending the expansion link on its horizontal centre-line is that the swing of the lifting link is very small; this of course reduces wear, but more important it means that there is very little swinging effect transmitted from the lifting links to the expansion link itself, which would otherwise tend to move the link vertically up and down on the die-block.

It is now necessary to decide upon what point, on this horizontal centre-line, to locate the pins for the lifting links. If the expansion link is suspended at the point where this horizontal centre-line cuts the curved centre-line of the link slot, it will be found that this position allows of rather too much link-slip owing to the fact that this point of suspension is too far forward from the points from which the expansion link is driven, i.e. the eccentric rod pins. The eccentric rods have less control over the action of the link at the position where the die-block is located, and thus allow the link to rise and fall upon the die-block to some extent, making the cut off earlier at one end of the cylinder than at the other.

If the expansion link is suspended at the point where a line drawn between the two eccentric rod pins crosses the horizontal centre-line, it is found that the lifting links do not swing so much during the movement of the expansion link as they are now pivoted on a neutral centre. However it is also found that the rocking action of the eccentric rods is now transmitted to the expansion link in a more marked degree, thus introducing a more severe link-slip, the expansion link sliding up and down the die-block to some extent, giving a faulty steam distribution.

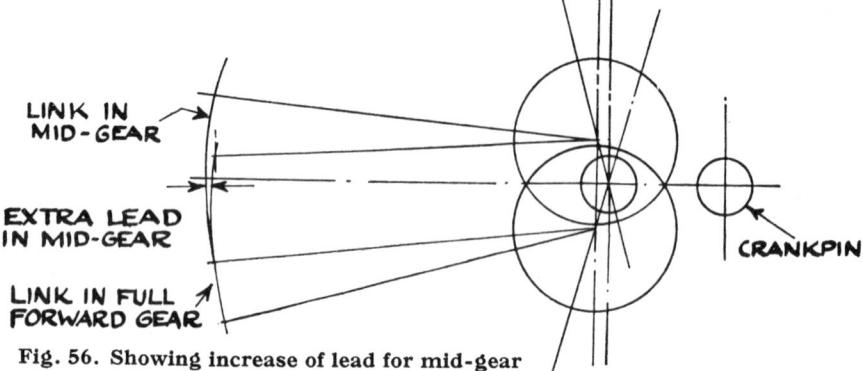

Fig. 56. Showing increase of lead for mid-gear

It will now be apparent that the position for the attachment of the lifting links should lie between these two positions and rather nearer to the former. The ideal position depends finally upon the proportionate length of the eccentric rods. With short eccentric rods, the second or more virulent error is more likely and therefore the point of suspension may be further forward, i.e. nearer to the curved centre-line of the link slot; if a line is drawn between the centres of the two die-block positions in full forward and backward gear respectively, this may be taken as the most *forward* position advisable, while for long eccentric rods (i.e. rods of a scale 5 feet length or over) the most *backward* position advisable may be taken as the point where the horizontal centre-line cuts the rear edge of the curved slot in the link.

When space permits, two lifting links should be used, one on each side of the expansion link and suitable brackets should be riveted to the link to carry them with the necessary clearance for the valve rod fork to embrace the die-block.

With Stephenson and other link valve gears, it is most important that all the eccentric rods are made exactly the same length, otherwise serious errors in the steam distribution may arise. To avoid the latter, it is advisable to make up a simple jig. This might consist of a length of steel bar of suitable dimensions on which is set out the overall length of the eccentric rods as accurately as possible; a silver-steel peg is then pressed in at one end, this peg being made a close fit in the eccentric rod forks; at the other end, a circular disc, turned to exactly the same diameter as the eccentric sheaves in use, is fitted, the disc being shouldered down and pressed into the rod. When each complete eccentric rod and strap will fit on such a jig, they will be relatively the same length to quite fine limits.

It is also important that the lifting links are made exactly the same length, and the lifting arms, which are attached to the weighshaft, arranged exactly parallel to one another. To ensure this, one method is to lightly clamp the boss of the lifting arm to the weighshaft with a grub screw and when the adjustment is correct, the grub screw is tightened and a taper pin fitted, through the boss and the shaft.

Full Gear Lead

When setting the valves of Stephenson's gear, the problem always arises of how much lead to allow the valves in full gear. As was mentioned earlier, with the normal arrangement of "open" eccentric rods, the lead increases towards mid gear. The amount of increase may be calculated as follows:—

$$\text{Increase} = \frac{c}{l} \times t \cos P.$$

Where $c = \frac{1}{2}$ the distance between eccentric rod pins.
$l = $ length of eccentric rod.
$t = $ throw of eccentric.
$P = $ angle of advance.

It will thus be seen that the length of the eccentric rods as well as the lap of the valves has an important bearing on the matter. With long lap valves and comparatively short eccentric rods (as described previously) the valves should be set with no lead at all in full gear. If long eccentric rods are used, some lead may be given though it is not possible to advise an exact figure owing to the many other factors which have a bearing on the matter. As a rough guide however it may be said that for the conventional type of Stephenson's gear with loco. type links and long eccentric rods, the lead in full gear should be about 1/10 of the lap.

Making Expansion Links

The expansion link is perhaps the most important individual component in the valve gear and care in its manufacture is always well rewarded. The ideal material to use is probably "gauge plate", which can be hardened before final assembly. Bright mild steel, case-hardened, makes a good substitute and is more easily worked. The curved slot can be cut by hand without very much difficulty, a row of holes being first drilled close together on the curved centre-line of the slot; needle files are then used to complete the slot, the die-block, which should be made previously, being used as a gauge.

There are several methods of machining the curved slot. If a vertical milling machine is available, the set up is quite a simple one, while the lathe may also be pressed into service, the link blank being bolted to a suitable bar in such a way that it can be swung on a pin at the required radius. It is then set up on an angle plate facing the lathe mandrel, with the pivot pin at centre height, an end-mill of suitable diameter being used in a collet or in the 3 jaw chuck.

Another method is to bolt the link blank to the lathe faceplate at the required distance from the centre, a horizontal milling spindle being used to end-mill the slot. In this method, the lowest speed of back gear may be engaged and the faceplate rotated the required amount by pulling the lathe belt by hand.

The Gooch Valve Gear

The Gooch or Stationary Link motion differs from the Stephenson in that the expansion link is hung from its centre point and is not moved up or down. It is arranged so as to be concave towards the cylinder end of the motion. Two eccentrics and straps and eccentric rods are used as in Stephenson's gear, while the valve or radius rod is lifted or lowered by the reversing arm attached to the weighshaft.

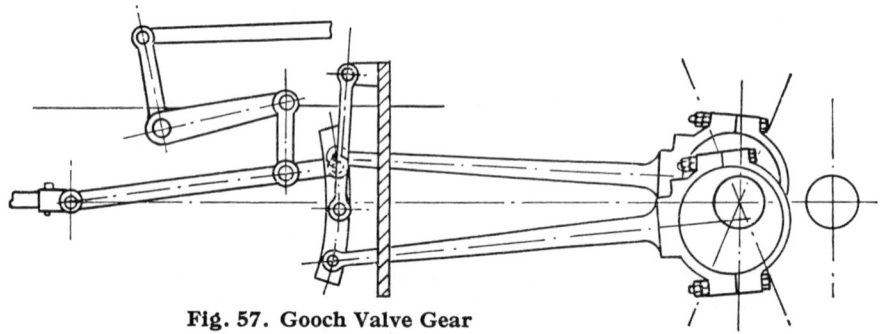

Fig. 57. Gooch Valve Gear

The expansion link itself is generally of the "box" type, consisting of two curved channels of radius equal to the length of the radius rod placed facing one another, distance pieces being inserted at each end. With this construction, the throw of the eccentrics can be made half the full gear valve travel required, or very slightly more.

The expansion link is hung from fairly long suspension links, so that the rise of the link at each end of its swing shall cause the least interference with its proper movement. As the radius of the expansion link is equal to the length of the radius rod, when the crank is at dead-centre and the port open to lead steam, reversing the motion simply lifts or lowers the radius rod and does not move the valve, thus the lead is constant for all positions of the reversing lever.

It is usual in Gooch gear to modify it so as to make the steam distribution more nearly correct in forward gear at the expense to some extent of backward gear. This is done by hanging the expansion link with its centre just below the centre-line of the motion, the back gear eccentric rod being lengthened and the angle of advance of the back gear eccentric reduced to suit. Die slip cannot be entirely eliminated as the radius rod has not the power to hold the die-block with the same vertical rigidity as the valve spindle guides usually employed with Stephenson's valve gear,

The Gooch valve gear is easier to reverse than the Stephenson, as only the radius rod requires to be moved, whereas in the Stephenson gear, the expansion link and eccentric rods have to be raised and lowered, and the friction of the eccentric straps overcome. This however need not concern the model engineer as even in a 3 inch scale locomotive, the force required to reverse a Stephenson gear is not excessive.

The Allan "Straight-Link" Valve Gear

In the Allan valve gear, both the expansion link and the radius rod are moved when reversing, but in opposite directions, and as the action is more direct, die-slip is reduced.

This valve motion uses two eccentrics on the axle, the eccentric rods being coupled direct to the top and bottom of the expansion link. The radius rod carries a die-block working in the link slot, the weighshaft having two arms, one on each

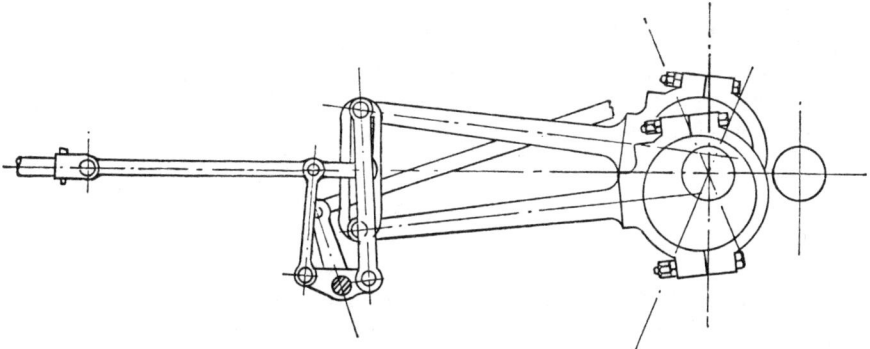

Fig. 58. Allan Valve Gear

side, coupled to the radius rod and the link respectively. The weighshaft is often placed below the motion, the arm coupled to the expansion link being attached to the top pin of the link.

The respective lengths of the radius and eccentric rods are proportioned so that the arcs described by the radius rod and link are always tangential to each other thus the die-block will move in a straight line when the engine is reversed.

While the steam distribution with this valve gear is good where long radius rods and short valve travels are employed, neither Allan nor Gooch gear compares with the Stephenson launch-type arrangement, when long valve travels are used and where space for the radius rods is limited.

CHAPTER TEN

Valve Gears : Radial Gears

THE RADIAL VALVE GEARS differ from the link motions in that they partly or wholly dispense with the use of eccentrics. The best-known are as follows: Walschaerts gear, invented by Egide Walschaerts, a Belgian locomotive engineer in 1844 and modified by Von Waldegg in 1851, Hackworth's, invented in 1859, Joy Valve gear, and Baker's which is extensively used in the U.S.A.

Joy Valve Gear

The motion in Joy gear is taken from the connecting rod through a system of levers, and no eccentrics at all are used. This valve gear was extensively used in this country at one time, especially by the L.N.W.R. It was mainly adopted for inside cylinder locomotives, but was used with outside cylinders in one or two cases.

The connecting rod has an enlarged boss formed in it at a suitable point about one-third of the length of the rod from the small end. This boss is bored out and fitted with a bush through which a pin passes, projecting on either side to carry the

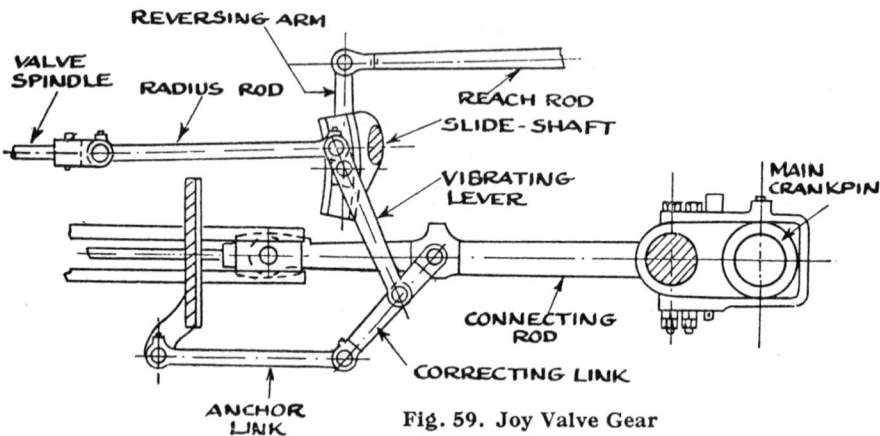

Fig. 59. Joy Valve Gear

forked end of a lever called the "correcting" link. The latter is coupled at its outer end to an "anchor" link which in turn is allowed to vibrate about a fixed point below the motion. This fixed point is generally a bracket attached to the motion plate, it may however be a frame stay or a shaft fixed across the frames, as is found most suitable for the particular engine.

The correcting link has a bearing in its central portion to which is connected the valve lever, usually named the vibrating lever. This is further provided with two other bearings, one at the top end for the attachment of the valve rod, and the other close to it for the pin upon which work die-blocks, which are able to slide up and down curved guides attached to the weighshaft, these guides and weighshaft being collectively termed the slide-shaft.

It will be seen that the vibration of the connecting rod when the locomotive is in motion moves the die-blocks up and down in the slide-shaft, causing the valve rod to take a course depending upon the position of the guides. Thus when the slide-shaft is in a vertical position, the valve will have the least movement horizontally and the gear will be in mid-gear. On movement of the weighshaft, the guides are tilted, the top end towards the cylinders for forward gear, and away from the cylinders for backward gear.

The Joy valve gear, in full-size practice, gave a fairly good steam distribution, though it was better suited to the earlier locomotives with slide valves and short valve travels than more modern engines. One drawback of the gear is the fact that it is affected by the up and down movement of the axleboxes in the horns. This drawback applies even more to a model locomotive, as miniature tracks are relatively rougher, and axlebox rise and fall relatively more.

As no eccentrics are required with Joy's gear, it appeals to the model engineer, even though the slide-shaft, with its curved guides, is not an easy component to make.

Designing Joy Valve Gear

When designing a Joy valve gear for a model locomotive, the first thing to decide is of course the full-gear valve travel, the proportions of the ports and the dimensions of the valve itself. The next point to be decided is the exact position on the connecting rod to locate the bush and pin for the correcting link. It was mentioned

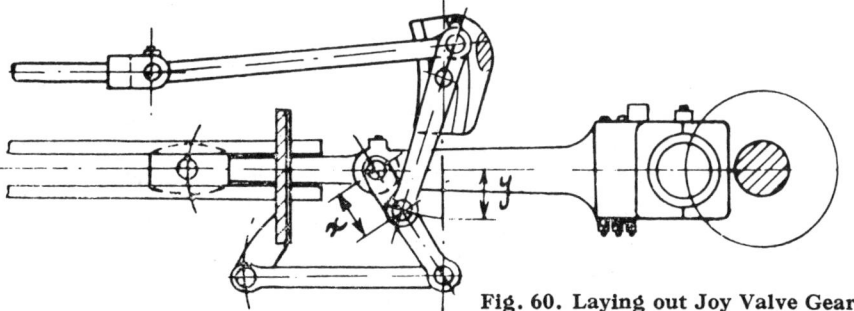

Fig. 60. Laying out Joy Valve Gear

previously that this position is generally about ⅓ the length of the connecting rod measured from the small end.

A simple method of deciding the exact position is as follows: The motion is drawn at least twice full size, the horizontal centre-line of the motion and the centre of the driving axle being drawn in; the connecting rod and crankpin are now drawn in four positions, the front and back dead-centre positions, and the positions where the connecting rod is at its highest and lowest positions relative to the horizontal centre-line of the motion. It is now only necessary to locate the pin hole in the connecting rod such that its maximum movement in a vertical direction (vertical amplitude) is twice the full gear valve travel required, or very slightly more.

A vertical line should now be drawn at this position, and this locates the correct "fore and aft" position (to borrow a nautical phrase) for the weighshaft.

The length of the correcting link can now be decided. Its lower end, which is attached to the anchor link, must be sufficiently far away to allow of the angle between its two extreme positions being less than a right angle.

The anchor link should be made as long as conveniently possible, so as to allow the end of the correcting link to rise and fall as nearly as possible in a vertical line. It is generally more convenient to fix the anchor link to a point forward of the correcting link.

To locate the correct position for the weighshaft in the vertical plane, the following procedure may be recommended. On the centre-line of the valve spindle, mark out vertical lines on either side of the vertical line previously drawn (when deciding the position for the pin in the connecting rod) at a distance from it equal to the required lap plus lead.

To take an example—if the required lap is $\frac{1}{8}$ in. and the lead 0·025 in., then these lines will be 0·150 in. on either side of the original line, or 0·30 in. from each other.

Now assuming the crank to be upon its front dead-centre, and the correcting link coupled to the anchor link, choose a point in the correcting link, which has for the moment to be assumed, rather nearer its upper pin than its lower pin. Draw a line representing the vibrating lever from this assumed point to the intersection of the rear vertical "lap and lead" line with the horizontal centre-line of the valve spindle; where this line crosses the central vertical line is the position for the weighshaft.

In practice the weighshaft is often placed a little higher than this, in order to give more clearance between the valve rod and the motion plate and between the weighshaft and the central boss of the connecting rod. It should, where possible, be a little below the horizontal centre-line of the valve spindle.

The distance between the two upper pins in the vibrating lever are now also determined, as the upper pin is of course the point where the line representing the vibrating lever intersected the horizontal centre-line of the valve spindle.

The exact length of the vibrating lever is determined by the position of the central pin in the correcting link. This position must be such that when an arc the length of the vibrating lever is swung to the vertical centre-line (see Figure 60) then $x = y$. In other words the length of the vibrating lever is best determined by a simple process of trial and error on the drawing board.

It will be seen that the centre of oscillation of the die-blocks and the centre of the weighshaft trunnions exactly coincide with one another when the piston is at either end of its stroke. Thus it is possible to reverse the motion from full forward to full backward gear without giving any movement to the valve rod, and the lead is therefore constant in all gears.

The radius rod in Joy gear should not be made too short, while the radius of the curved guides in the slide-shaft must be made equal to the length of the radius rod.

In full size practice, some locomotives fitted with Joy valve gear experienced failure through the connecting rods bending or breaking. This is not likely to cause trouble in models, provided that plenty of metal is allowed around the boss in the middle of the connecting rod.

Construction of Joy Slide-shafts

The only item of Joy's valve gear which might cause trouble in manufacture to the average model engineer is probably the Slide-shaft.

One method of making the curved guides themselves is to clamp a suitable bar of steel to the lathe faceplate, its centre being arranged at a distance from the lathe centre equal to the radius required. A parting tool, ground with top rake and plenty of side clearance on both sides, is then set up crosswise in the lathe tool-holder, at a distance out equal to the radius of the curved guides. Cutting should be carried out at the lowest speed with plenty of cutting oil.

Another method, which generally produces a better finish, is to use an end-mill or slot-drill held in a milling spindle attached to the lathe top-slide or cross-slide, the back gear being engaged and the faceplate slowly rotated against the cutter. Alternatively the end-mill could be held in the 3-jaw chuck or a collet, and the blank for the curved guides held on a stout plate attached to the vertical slide, arranged facing the headstock. The blank is then rotated on a pin at the required radius.

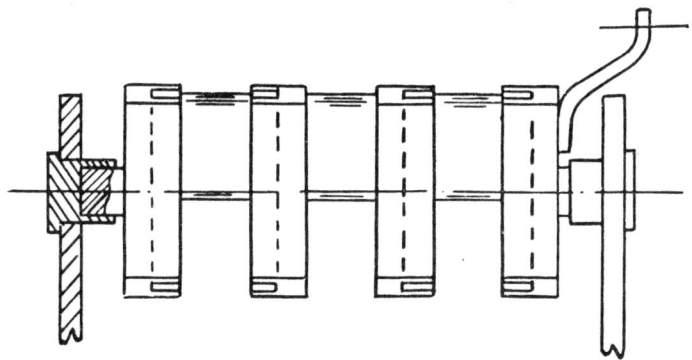

Fig. 61. End elevation of Joy Slide Shaft

When sufficient "channel" has been produced in this way to make the four sections of curved guides, these are cut-off and cleaned up to size externally. The weighshaft is then cut from rectangular steel bar and the four sections held to it by one small screw each. After carefully lining up the sections, they are brazed to the weighshaft.

The reversing arm, which is attached to the driver's reach rod, is then fitted to one end, this being usually cranked outwards to bring the reach rod outside the mainframes, and the two trunnion pins, which work in bushes in the frames, are pressed home at either end. It is a very good plan to make the overall length of the complete slide-shaft, measured over the trunnion pins, exactly the same as the width between the mainframes, the trunnion bushes being put in from the outside and screwed to the frames. In this way, it is always possible to slip the slide-shaft out from the frames, without having to disturb the frames themselves or any other components apart from the vibrating links and radius rods.

Hackworth Valve Gear

The Hackworth valve gear is one in which the valve motion is taken from one eccentric, which is fixed on the driving axle exactly opposite the crank-pin, and has its rod working vertically, with the end attached to a die-block which slides in a pair of straight guides.

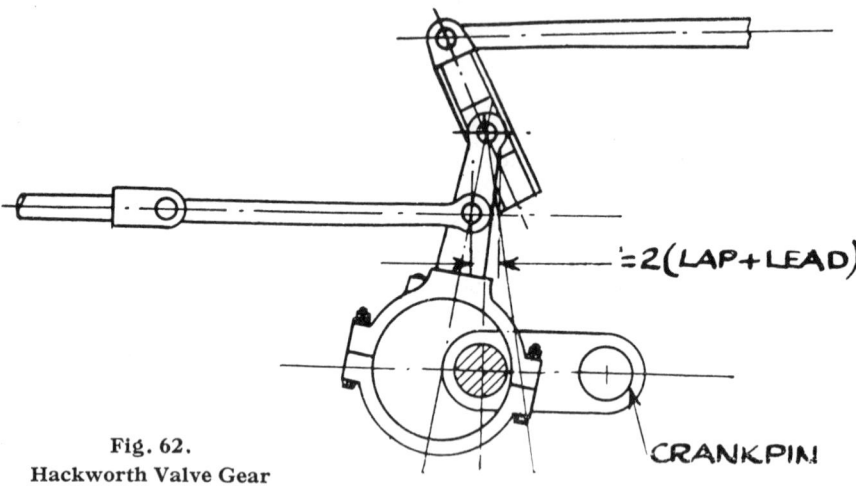

Fig. 62.
Hackworth Valve Gear

These guides are pivoted, so that they can be turned to an angle to the vertical by means of the reversing rod. At a suitable point in the eccentric rod, a pin is provided for connecting the valve rod, the extreme end of which is attached to the valve spindle in the usual way.

When the guides are exactly vertical, i.e. the mid-gear position, the valve rod connection is moved through an oval path, the horizontal amplitude of which is made equal to twice the lap plus lead. In full forward and backward gear, the guides are rotated sufficiently to increase this horizontal amplitude to the required full gear valve travel. With this gear, the lead is of course constant for all positions of the reversing lever.

The Hackworth valve gear is an easy one to make, and has few parts, but it cannot be recommended for model locomotives as unless the eccentric rod is made very short, trouble may be experienced in obtaining sufficient clearance for the guides underneath the boiler. Also the vertical movement of the axleboxes in the horns upsets the valve events to some extent.

Walschaerts' Valve Gear

The Walschaerts' valve gear is the most widely used locomotive valve gear at the present time, and is popular all over the world. If properly designed, it is also one of the most efficient, while it can be used with equal effect outside or inside the locomotive frames.

Walschaerts' gear is not, strictly speaking, a radial gear, as no ellipses are described by it. The travel of the valve is controlled by two quite separate movements, one being that of the crosshead, and the other that of an eccentric fixed upon the crank axle, or in the case of an outside cylinder engine, a "return crank" fixed on the end of the driving crankpin.

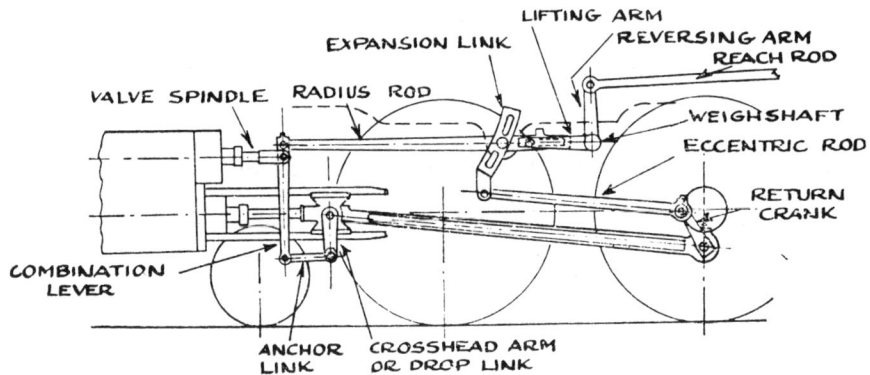

Fig. 63. Walschaerts' Valve Gear for Piston Valve Cylinders

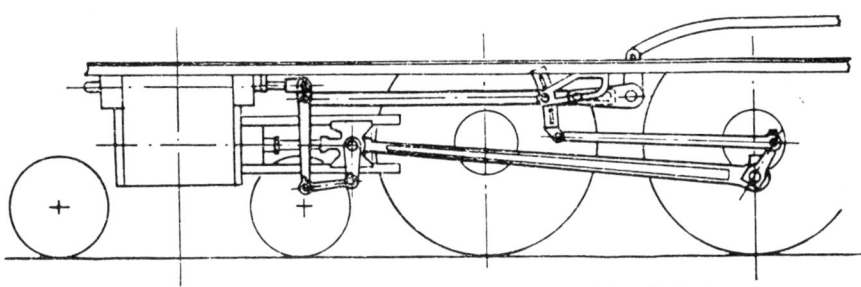

Fig. 64. Walschaerts' Valve Gear for Slide Valve Cylinders

Walschaerts' valve gear may differ a great deal in mechanical details, notably in the design of the expansion link, its suspension and the weighshaft arrangements. It may be required to operate valves with outside steam admission, or piston valves with inside admission; this necessitates a 180° reversal of both the advance functions and the eccentric or return crank drive.

Where slide valves with outside admission are used, the vibrating or combination lever is arranged so that the valve spindle is attached to it above the radius rod connection, while with the normal position for the die-block—in the bottom of the expansion link for forward gear—the return crank is arranged 90° in advance of the main crankpin.

When inside admission piston valves are in use, the connections at the top end of the combination lever are reversed, the radius rod connection being above the valve spindle, while the normal arrangement of expansion link necessitates the return crank being 90° in retard of the main crankpin.

Walschaerts' valve gear is most convenient when the valves are arranged above the cylinders, and the valve spindles offset to the outside of the engine. In the case of inside cylinders, the offset of the valve spindles is usually towards the centre of the locomotive.

Average valve spindle offsets are as follows:

Gauge I	$\frac{5}{32}$ in.
$2\frac{1}{2}$ in. gauge	$\frac{1}{4}$ in.
$3\frac{1}{2}$ in. gauge	$\frac{5}{16}$ in.
5 in. gauge	$\frac{7}{16}$ in.
$7\frac{1}{4}$ in. gauge	$\frac{5}{8}$ in.

Designing Walschaerts' Gear for Models

As with other valve gears, the first things to be decided are the proportions of the valves and ports.

It was mentioned in the last chapter that large steam laps with long valve travels are recommended, though care must be taken to ensure that the valve travel required will not produce a valve gear that is mechanically impossible in the available space. The lead, being controlled by the combination lever, is constant at all positions of the reversing lever in Walschaerts' gear, and the amount of lead to allow was fully discussed in Chapter 7.

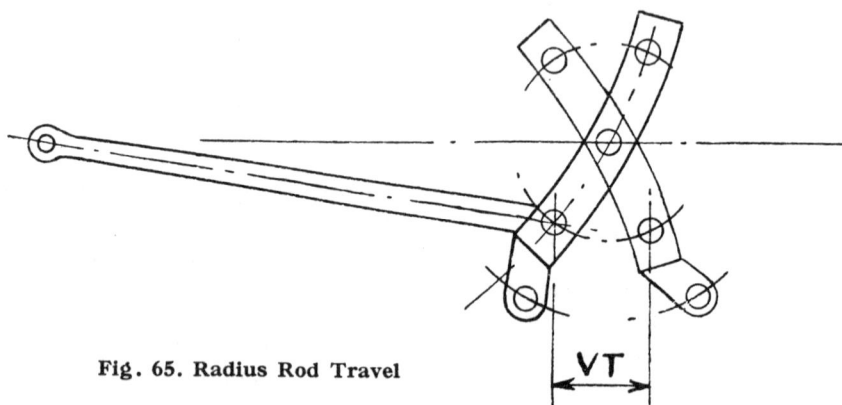

Fig. 65. Radius Rod Travel

The total travel of the valve in full gear and for a normal full port opening is equal to the amount of the lap plus the port width multiplied by 2.

In Walschaerts' gear, the swing of the expansion link must not be made too great, or difficulty will be experienced in reversing the engine. Generally speaking it should not be made more than 25° to the vertical, i.e. a total swing of 50°.

VALVE GEARS: RADIAL GEARS

Expansion Link Movement

Having decided the angle of swing of the expansion link, the effective length of this must be determined, in order to give the full gear valve travel desired. In the diagram Figure 65, the distance VT must be made equal to the full gear valve travel, or very slightly more, to allow for the inevitable slight lost motion in the pins and die-block.

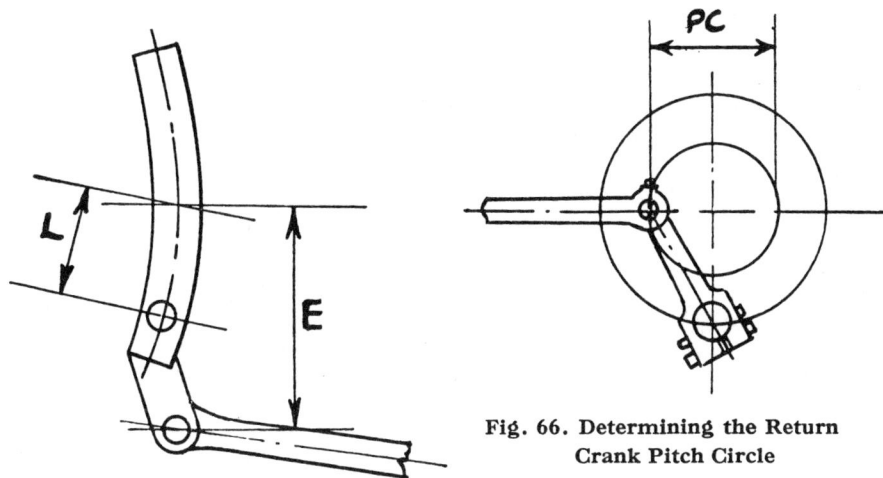

Fig. 66. Determining the Return Crank Pitch Circle

The position for the eccentric rod connection is next settled, and the pitch circle diameter of the return crank necessary to give the desired movement (Figure 66). For an inside cylinder locomotive, where an eccentric is used in place of the return crank, the dimensions L and E are almost equal. The return crank pitch circle may then be calculated as follows:—

$$PC = \frac{VT \times E}{L}$$

The Combination Lever

The Combination lever is operated by the main crank, its attachment usually being made to the crosshead by means of an "anchor" link, though a "drop" link is frequently used to lower the position of the bottom pin of the combination lever.

The movement of the combination lever is thus 90° out of phase with the movement obtained from the expansion link. Independently of the position of the reversing lever, the valve is moved by the combination lever to an amount equal to the lap + lead.

The top joint proportions of the combination lever are now decided upon as shown in Fig. 67.

For slide valves $\dfrac{A}{B} = \dfrac{2 \,(\text{Lap} + \text{Lead})}{\text{Stroke}}$

For piston valves (int. adm.) $\dfrac{C}{D} = \dfrac{2\,(\text{Lap} + \text{Lead})}{\text{Stroke}}$

The actual length of the combination lever is entirely a matter of convenience, for if it is made too short, trouble will be experienced in arranging the top pins clear of one another—hence the drop link often employed on the crosshead.

When modelling prototype locomotives having inside-admission piston valves, if it is desired to use slide valves trouble may be experienced owing to the reversed connections at the top of the combination lever. As a rule this involves lowering the whole arrangement of the radius rod, expansion link and lifting links, which may cause trouble in obtaining the necessary clearances.

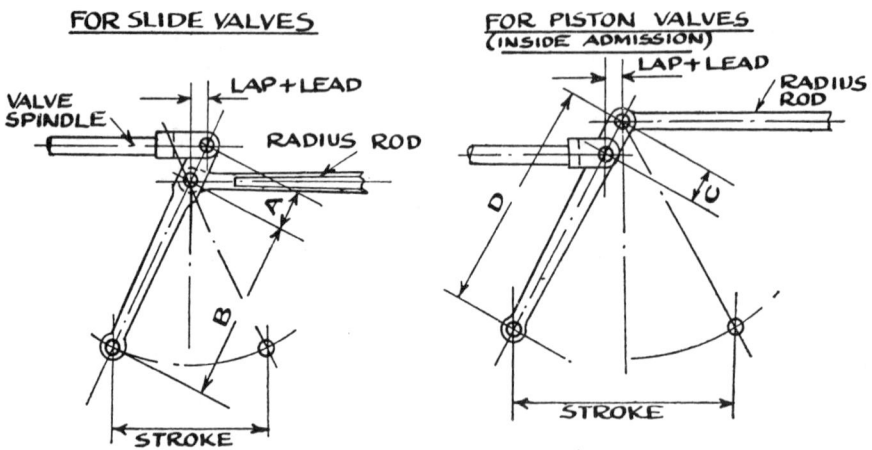

Fig. 67. Setting out the Combination Lever

There are three solutions to this problem; the valve crosshead may be offset vertically, to raise the combination lever; a separate guide may be employed, as suggested by Henry Greenly, the guide being attached to the gear frame; or the radius rod may be inclined downwards towards the valve spindle, the expansion link centre remaining in its original position. The latter method cannot be recommended unless the radius rod is fairly long as slight errors in valve movement may be introduced, the valve events in back gear being different from fore gear for a given radial setting of the lifting arms.

Suspension of the Expansion Link

Wherever possible, Walschaerts' valve gear should be laid out so that all parts operate on centre lines which are either parallel to the horizontal centre-line of the motion or exactly at right angles to same.

The cylinders may be inclined, for various reasons, and this may have a slightly adverse effect on the valve movements due to excessive up and down movement of the driving axle, but it makes no difference to the setting out of the valve gear, the whole drawing may in fact be tilted to the required angle of the cylinders to simplify matters.

The horizontal position for the expansion link may now be decided upon, and this should if possible be arranged half-way between the driving axle and the valve spindle crosshead. The design of the casting or framework which supports the link varies in almost every class of locomotive. The L.N.E.R. used a steel casting which projected from the mainframes between the driving wheels and then forward again to a convenient point for the link bearings. The design of such a bracket should be gone into carefully as with many types of links it is necessary to be able to assemble the link in situ, the outer support being placed into position after the expansion link itself.

Separate girder frames were often employed on the L.M.S. the frames spanning the space occupied by the driving wheels.

Walschaerts' valve gear should always be drawn out in plan and in end elevation as well as in side elevation to ensure that the necessary clearances are provided, particularly between the lower half of the expansion link and the connecting rod. The combination lever should be drawn at front and rear dead centres, to ensure that it clears the slide bars and boss of the crosshead and does not foul the rear cylinder cover or packing gland when right forward.

"Back-set" of the Expansion Link

We come now to the design of the Expansion link itself, and the determination of the correct amount of "back-set" for the eccentric rod pin in relation to the curved centre-line of the link. It is important that the expansion link should swing an equal amount on each side of its central position. Referring to Figure 68 the

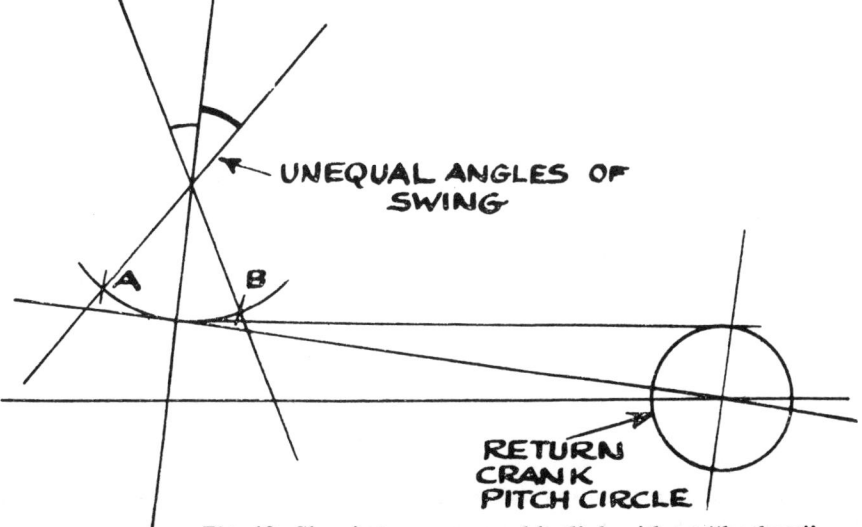

Fig. 68. Showing error caused by link without "backset"

theoretically correct arrangement is shown, but due to the angularity of the eccentric rod, this is not possible, and the pin in the "tail" of the expansion link must be set back sufficiently to counteract this angularity.

The effect of too much back-set is shown in Figure 69, an unequal angle of swing being given to the expansion link. The correct solution is shown in Figure 70.

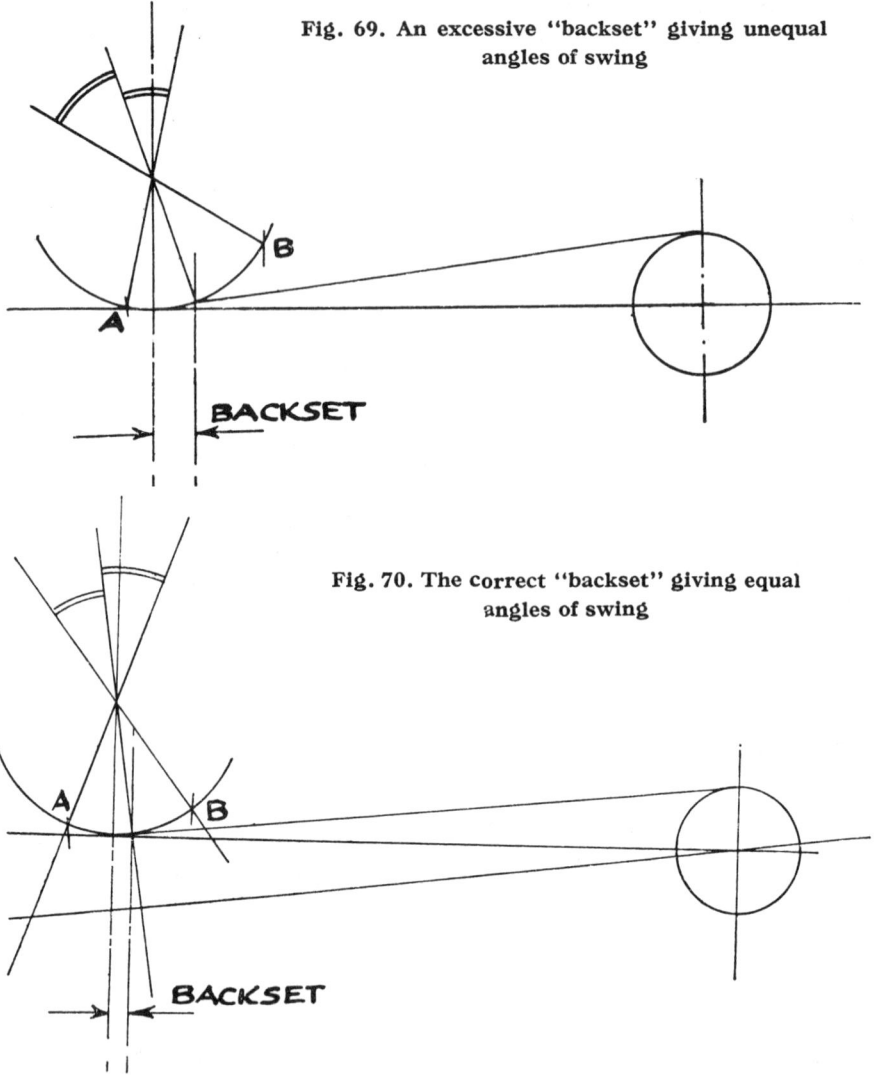

Fig. 69. An excessive "backset" giving unequal angles of swing

Fig. 70. The correct "backset" giving equal angles of swing

The amount of back-set is normally regarded as the distance of the eccentric rod pin in the link from the normal vertical centre-line of the link in the middle of its angular swing.

The correct amount is best determined on the drawing board by a process of trial and error, dividers being used to determine the positions A, B in the diagrams.

In some arrangements of Walschaerts' gear, notably in American locomotives, the "tail" of the expansion link is made longer, so that the eccentric rod pin falls on the horizontal centre-line of the motion, giving an "all-square" layout. With this arrangement, the back-set appears greater than with the inclined connection more common to British locomotives.

The Design of the Expansion Link

In some models, the expansion link is cut from plain mild steel plate of suitable thickness, and rivetted or brazed to its trunnion pin, this pin being on one side of the link only, the radius rod with a single die-block lying on the other side. This scheme is quite satisfactory in small models provided the trunnion pin is of sufficient length; an improvement is to use "gauge plate" rather than mild steel.

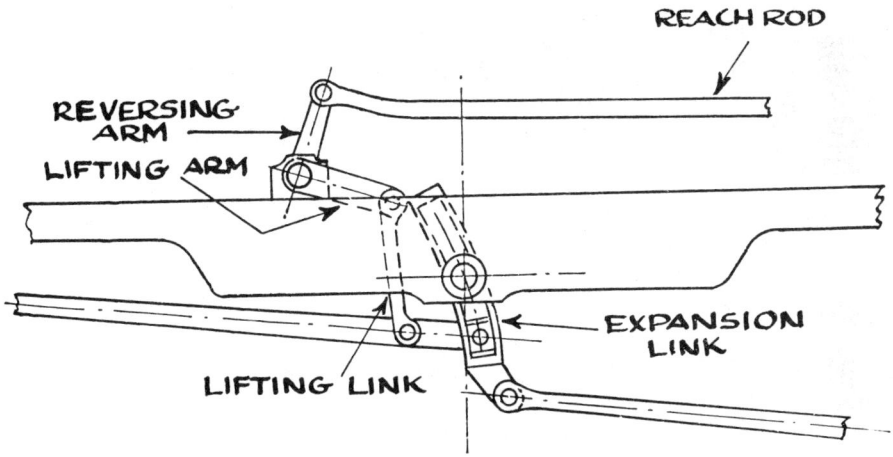

Fig. 71. S.R. type Expansion and Lifting Links

A better method for models over ½ inch scale is to arrange for a double bracket to be fitted to the link, each arm of the bracket carrying a trunnion pin; the radius rod is then forked to embrace the link itself. This method is used on many S.R. locomotives and is shown in Figure 71. If this design is adopted, the lifting link should be made as long as possible to minimise die-slip.

Many railways had a preference for an arrangement whereby the radius rod is raised and lowered by means of a lifting link behind the expansion link and for this scheme, the expansion link must be so designed that the radius rod can pass right through it. With this arrangement there is very little die-slip in forward gear.

The usual L.M.S. arrangement provided for a sliding type of lifting link, the end of the radius rod beyond the expansion link being slotted and this has the advantage that the weighshaft is in line with the radius rod, when the latter is in the mid gear position, and therefore well clear of the boiler. Figure 72 shows the

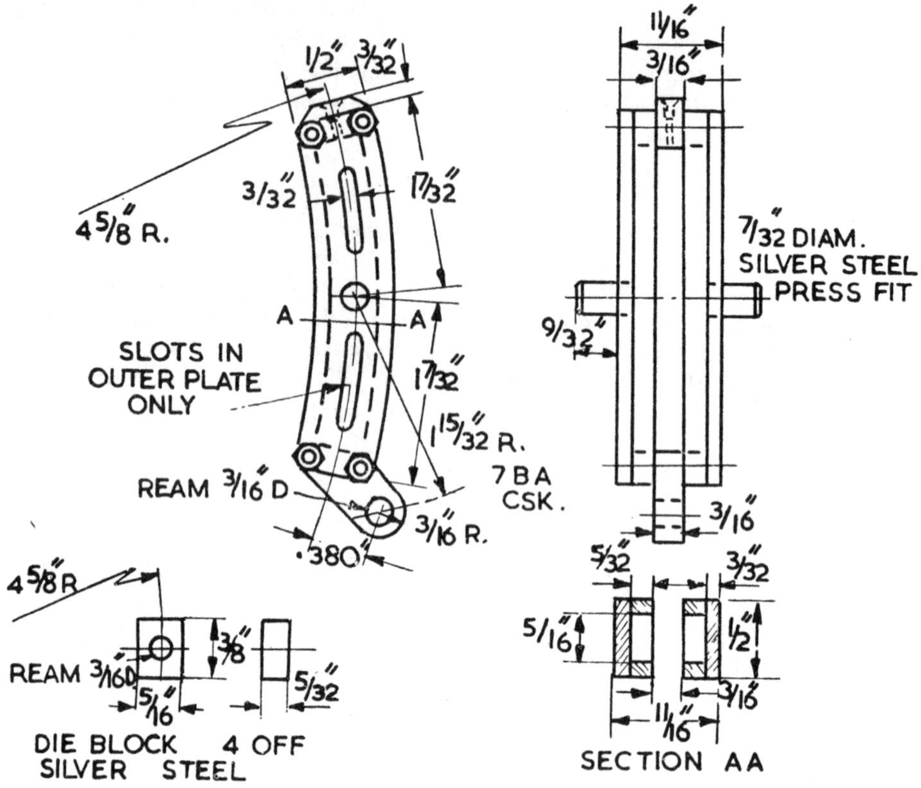

100   MODEL STEAM LOCOMOTIVE CONSTRUCTION

Fig. 72. 5 in. gauge L.M.S.-type Expansion Link

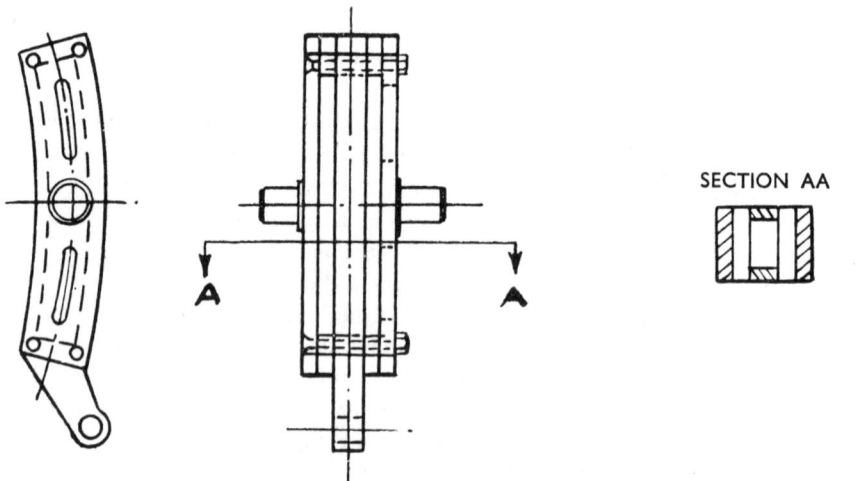

Fig. 73. The 3-piece Expansion Link

VALVE GEARS: RADIAL GEARS

author's design for an expansion link of the L.M.S. type arranged for a 5 inch gauge engine. The "tail", or extension for the eccentric rod connection, and the top spacing piece are made of $\frac{3}{16}$ in. thick bright mild steel; the outer plates, which carry the trunnion pins are of $\frac{3}{32}$ in. material, while the slotted plates are of $\frac{5}{32}$ in. steel either mild steel case-hardened, or "gauge-plate"; the parts are held together by four 7 B.A. countersunk steel screws so that the link can be assembled in position between the link brackets. In this type of expansion link, the slotted plates can be hand filed quite easily, the die-blocks being used as a gauge.

On some ex-L.N.E.R. locomotives, the expansion link was made in three pieces, the radius rod being doubled where it passes through the link. Provided that the trunnion pins are arranged exactly in line, this type of link is not a difficult one to make; the central slotted member of the link may be end-milled or hand-filed.

The Return Crank

The return crank is fixed to the outer end of the main crankpin, and with the die-block in the lower end of the expansion link for forward gear, is in advance of the crankpin for slide-valve cylinders, or in retard for piston valve (inside admission) cylinders. The angle of advance or retard must be exactly 90°, though the actual

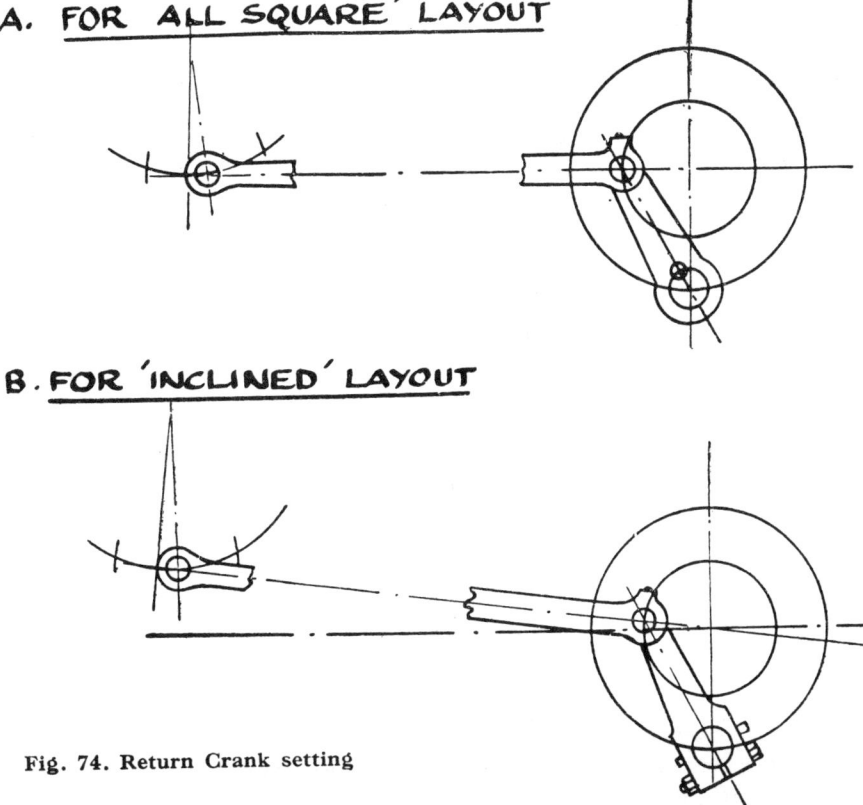

Fig. 74. Return Crank setting

position of the eccentric rod connection will depend on whether the setting is an "all-square" one or an inclined one in relation to the horizontal centre-line of the motion; this will also affect the exact length of the return crank.

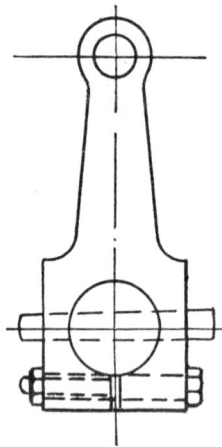

Fig. 75. Return Crank Fixing

The fixing of the return crank is an important point in model locomotives, as there must be no possibility whatever of the crank shifting in service. A very good scheme for models of $\frac{1}{2}$ inch. scale and above is to split the lower end of the return crank, a clamping bolt being put through this just clear of the crankpin. After the return crank has been correctly set, a standard taper pin of suitable size is put through the middle of both crankpin and crank. This method ensures that, should the return crank have to be dismantled at any time, it can be replaced in its correct position without any difficulty.

In full-size practice, the end of the main crankpin is sometimes squared, the return crank being clamped to this by a bolt immediately below the square; another method is to mill a slot across the face of the crankpin, the crank having a tongue to fit this for driving purposes, the securing being done by four set screws or studs. Neither of these methods can be recommended for model work, owing to the difficulty of obtaining the correct setting before machining either the end of the crankpin or the crank.

The setting of the return crank in its correct position can be done as follows: the axleboxes are first jacked up to the designed running position. The expansion link is then temporarily clamped in its mid position, that is such a position that the die blocks can be run from top to bottom of the link without imparting any movement to the combination lever. The main crank is now set exactly on front dead centre, while the return crank is set as near as possible by eye in order that its pin describes a circle of the diameter required by the design of the valve gear (P.C. in Figure 66). With a pair of dividers, measure the distance from the centre of the hole in the "tail" of the expansion link to the centre of the return crank pin.

Now shift the main crank around to the back dead centre position and apply the dividers, without shifting them, as before. If they tally, the return crank is correctly set and can be bolted up and pinned, if they don't tally, the return crank should be shifted by half the amount of the difference. The same process should then be repeated, and it should be noted that when the dividers do tally in the two positions, they give THE EXACT LENGTH REQUIRED FOR THE ECCENTRIC ROD.

In recent years, miniature ball bearings and needle roller bearings have been used with success for the eccentric rod bearings of larger models. For the latter, both the pin and the rod itself must be hardened. In either case a proper dust-excluding cap should be provided.

VALVE GEARS: RADIAL GEARS 103

The Baker Valve Gear

This valve gear, invented by Abner D. Baker of Ohio, U.S.A. in 1903, is a modified form of the Walschaerts' motion wherein the expansion link is replaced by a system of cranks and levers. The return crank is set to give considerably more throw than in Walschaerts' gear, and this drives an eccentric rod which is connected to a lever known as the gear-connecting lever. This lever is connected at its top end to a bell crank which in turn drives the valve rod. The gear-connecting lever is pivoted to another lever known as the radius bar which is itself pivoted to the reversing yoke.

The fulcrum point of the gear-connecting lever can thus be moved from its neutral position—in line with the radius bar—to a position either side of it, giving an angular movement to the bell crank and thus a longitudinal movement to the valve rod.

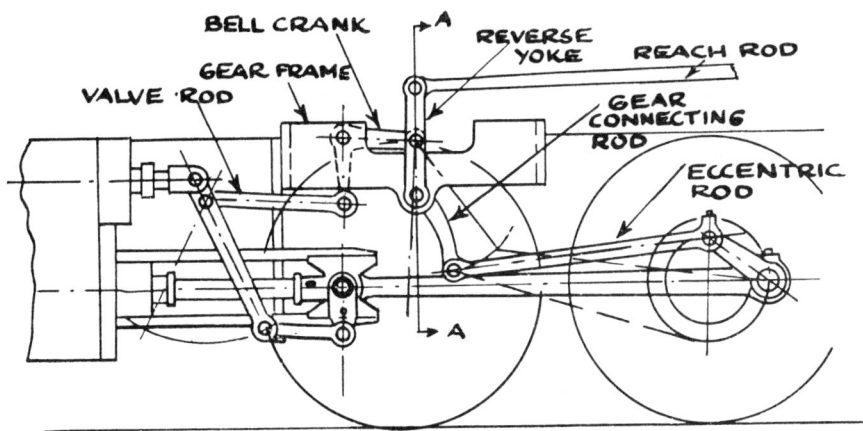

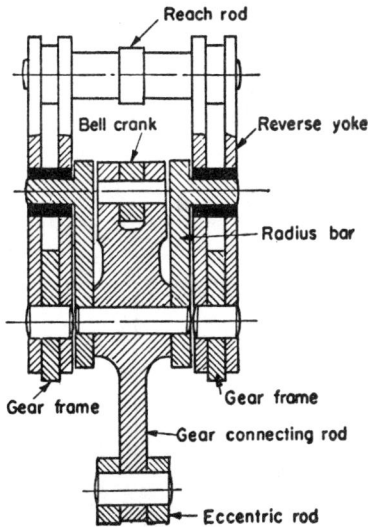

Fig. 76. Baker Valve Gear

104   MODEL STEAM LOCOMOTIVE CONSTRUCTION

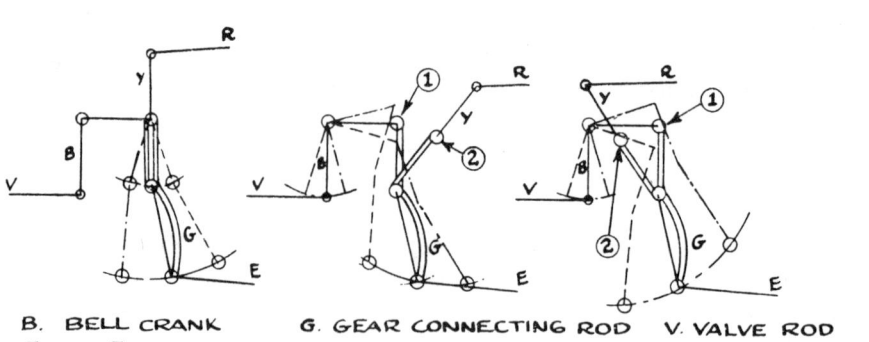

B. BELL CRANK
E. ECCENTRIC ROD
G. GEAR CONNECTING ROD
R. REACH ROD
V. VALVE ROD
Y. REVERSING YOKE

Fig. 77. The Baker Gear

In the diagram Figure 77, the valve travel is increased the more points 1 and 2 are moved apart.

Although the Baker gear is not used on British locomotives, it is a useful gear for the model engineer, owing to the ease with which it can be fitted up, the necessary levers being attached to a "gear frame" which can be angled to the mainframes.

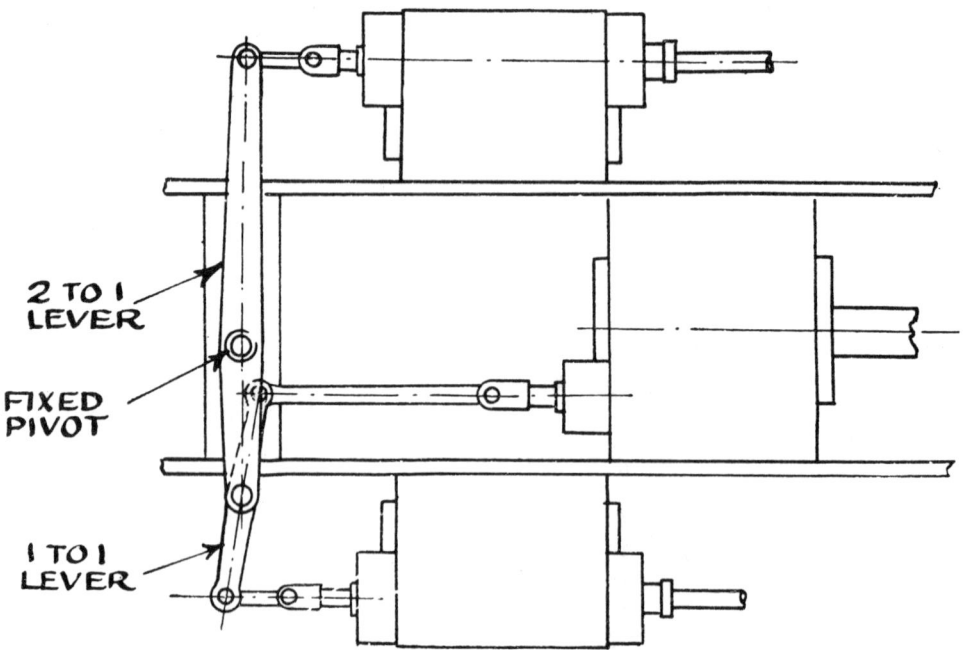

Fig. 78. The Gresley Gear

Gresley Valve Gear

The Gresley conjugated valve gear, used on the ex-L.N.E.R. 3 cylinder locomotives is a useful gear for 3 cylinder engines as the usual inside valve gear with its eccentric is dispensed with. By a simple linkage of levers, the inside valve is operated by the two outside valve spindles. The cranks must be set at 120°, although if the inside cylinder is inclined at a different angle to the outside cylinders, allowance for this difference must be made when adjusting the driving wheels on the crank axle.

The valve spindles of the outside cylinders are usually extended beyond the front of the cylinders. One of them is connected to one end of a lever pivoted at its centre, the other end of this (1 to 1) lever being connected to the inside cylinder valve spindle. The other outside valve spindle is connected to a long (2 to 1) lever, pivoted at a point two-thirds along its length, the opposite end of this lever forming the fulcrum for the shorter lever.

While this valve gear is quite satisfactory in model work, it is important that there be no appreciable lost motion in the various pins, and that the outside valve gears be accurately set up, as any irregularities in the latter will adversely affect the inside valve events.

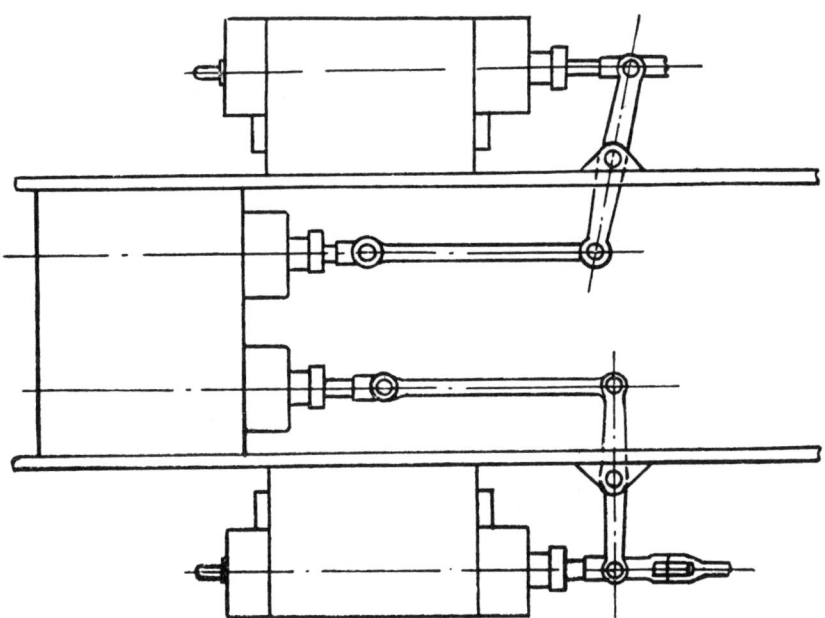

Fig. 79. Outside to Inside Gear

Valve Gears for 4 Cylinder Locomotives

It is quite common practice in 4 cylinder locomotives to use only two sets of valve gear to operate all four valve spindles. The valve gears may be outside the mainframes, or inside the frames as in G.W.R. engines. The valve events of the outside cylinder occur at 180° to its associated inside cylinder, therefore the cranks of these two cylinders must be set at 180° to one another.

The G.W.R. "Stars", "Castles", and "Kings" used inside Walschaerts' valve gear, the radius rods being forked to clear the inside valve spindle and its guides, while a bent-lever connected the inside spindle to the outside via a differential screw.

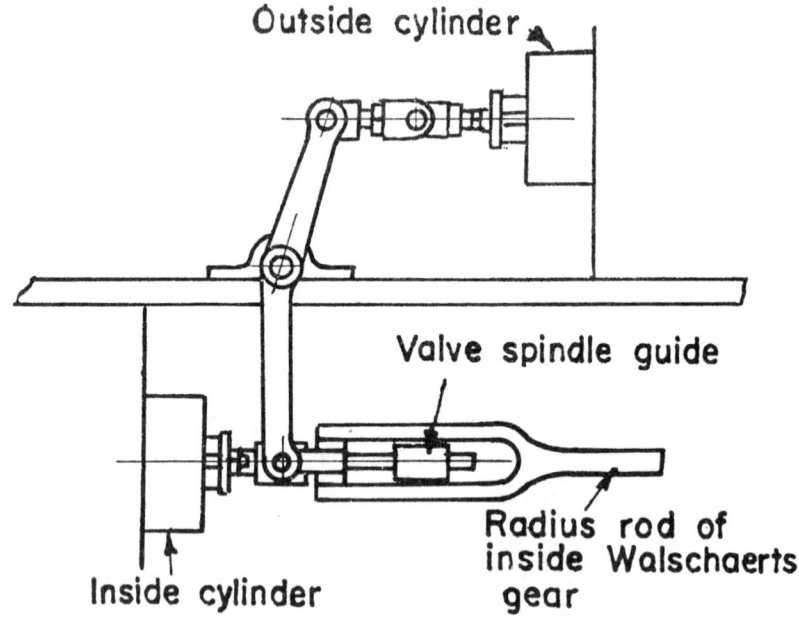

Fig. 80. Inside to Outside Gear

Poppet Valve Gears

The Poppet valve differs from the slide and piston types in its method of opening, the valve being moved away from its seating during the time steam is passing through the latter. It also remains stationary during the time it is closed. Separate valves are used for both admission and exhaust at each end of the cylinder.

The cam gear for operating poppet valves may be described as either oscillating or rotary; the former have cams which oscillate through about a quarter of a revolution, and may be operated by a link or radial type gear, the latter have cams which receive a rotary movement from the driving axle, usually through gears.

Poppet valves were first tried in the early part of the nineteenth century but it was not until 1906 that they were successfully adopted in locomotives. Although more complicated than the link or radial gears, there is no reason why poppet valve gears should not be applied to models with success.

VALVE GEARS: RADIAL GEARS 107

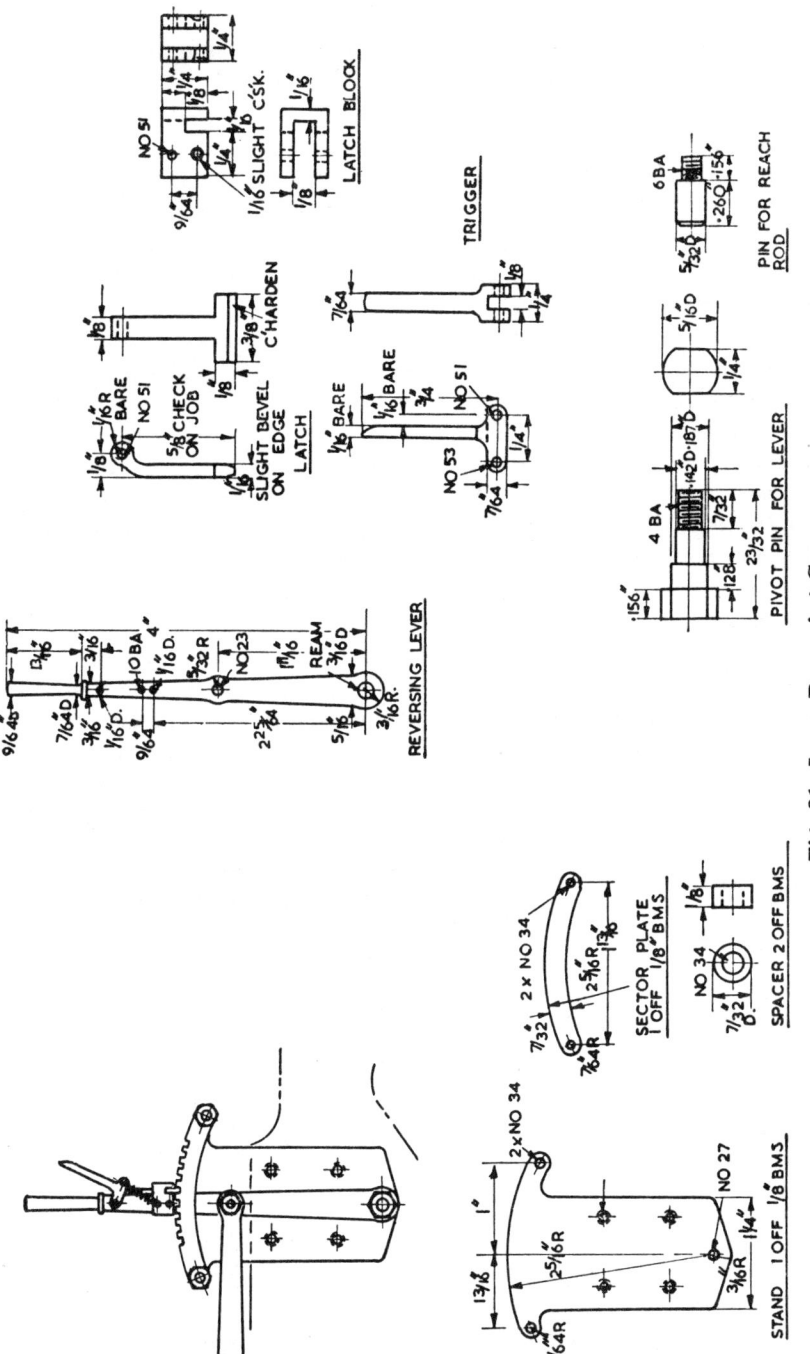

Fig. 81. Lever Reversing Gear

Cab Reversing Gear

The bridle or reach rod of nearly all types of valve gear is connected inside the cab to either a long reversing lever or to a screw.

Most full-size locomotives, except for shunting engines, now use the screw reversing gear, but in model practice where the engine may be required to work upon an "up and down" line, the hand lever may be found more convenient. Whichever type is chosen, the whole gear should be made quite rigid. The stand of the reversing gear should be of stout material and secured rigidly direct either to the mainframes or to the drag beam by means of a heavy section angle and sufficient screws for the purpose.

With screw reverse the nut itself must be made a good fit on the thread, which may with advantage be made left-hand, the nut sliding in guides to prevent any rocking motion being imparted to it.

Coming now to the reach rod, if this made to "scale" dimensions, it will probably whip quite considerably, it should therefore either be provided with a support or guide half-way along its length, or be made of fairly heavy section.

The locating of the "notches" in the lever type reversing gear may be done by moving the reversing lever forward very slowly, while turning the wheels in a forward direction. When the position of the lever is such that the valve is receiving its designed full gear travel, the lever is clamped, and the position for the forward full gear notch marked out. The operation is then repeated for backward gear. For the mid gear position, the lever is moved to such a position that no longitudinal movement is given to the radius rod by the expansion link. The location of the intermediate notches can then be marked out in between the full and mid gear notches as convenient.

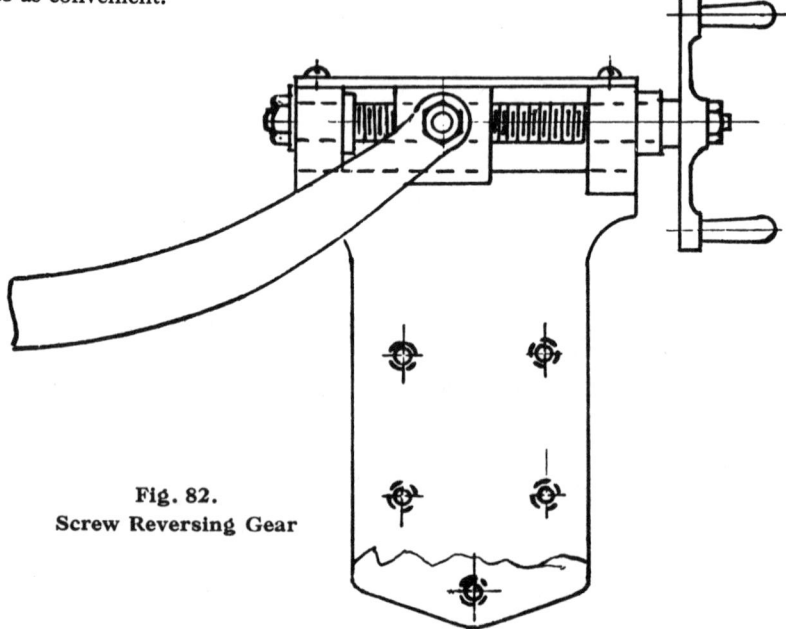

Fig. 82.
Screw Reversing Gear

CHAPTER ELEVEN

Boilers

THE DESIGN OF THE model locomotive boiler, although it may be based on that fitted to the full-size engine, needs very considerable modification and great care in design if it is to be efficient, safe and reliable in service. It is perhaps not surprising that many highly skilled model engineers, who would think little of designing and building a four-cylinder locomotive chassis, fight shy of designing, or even of making the coal-fired boiler required for it. The truth is that there are few if any suitable formulae to assist the designer of a model locomotive boiler, hence the great majority of model engineers have tended to rely on the published designs of two or three experts with long practical experience in this field.

However a careful study of both successful full-size and model boilers helps one greatly to grasp the essentials of good design, and points out the pitfalls to be avoided.

Simple Boilers for "O" and "1" Gauges

The majority of model locomotives built for 1¼ in. and 1¾ in. gauges are fitted with water-tube boilers. The simple "pot" boiler without water-tubes is generally used only in the "semi-toy" type of model and need not concern us here. As far as water-tube boilers are concerned, the chief points to note for success are as follows:—

1. The barrel should be of seamless copper tube, as thin as possible consistent with safety.
2. The water tubes should be of thin-gauge seamless copper.
3. The water tubes should be of reasonable diameter and not spaced too closely.
4. The water tubes should be fitted so that they slant downwards from the front of the barrel (see Fig. 83) and hard-soldered direct to the barrel, no turned or screwed fittings being required.
5. All joints should be hard-soldered, no soft solder being used at all.
6. The ends of the barrel, except for sizes under 2 in. dia., must be stayed, and should be of thicker material than the barrel itself.
7. The barrel should not be too small in relation to the outer wrapper.
8. The outer wrapper should preferably be made of steel and lined with asbestos to minimise heat losses.
9. Bushes of copper or gunmetal should be silver-soldered in to the barrel for the fittings.
10. No castings should be used.
11. Where possible a dome should be fitted, near to the middle of the boiler, to ensure dry steam.

For the guidance of the beginner, the following may be taken as suitable dimensions, for small water-tube boilers working at 60 to 80 lb. per sq. inch pressure:

Outer casing	...	$1\frac{3}{4}$ in. dia.	2 in. dia.	$2\frac{1}{4}$ in. dia.	3 in. dia.
Barrel	...	$1\frac{1}{4} \times 20$ s.w.g.	$1\frac{1}{2} \times 20$ s.w.g.	$1\frac{3}{4} \times 20$ s.w.g.	$2\frac{1}{4} \times 18$ s.w.g.
End Plates	...	18 s.w.g.	18 s.w.g.	16 s.w.g.	16 s.w.g.
Centre stay	...	—	$1 \times \frac{1}{8}$ in. dia.	$1 \times \frac{5}{32}$ in.	$1 \times \frac{3}{16}$ in.
Water tubes	...	$2 \times \frac{5}{32}$ in.	$3 \times \frac{5}{32}$ in.	$3 \times \frac{3}{16}$ in.	$4 \times \frac{1}{4}$ in.

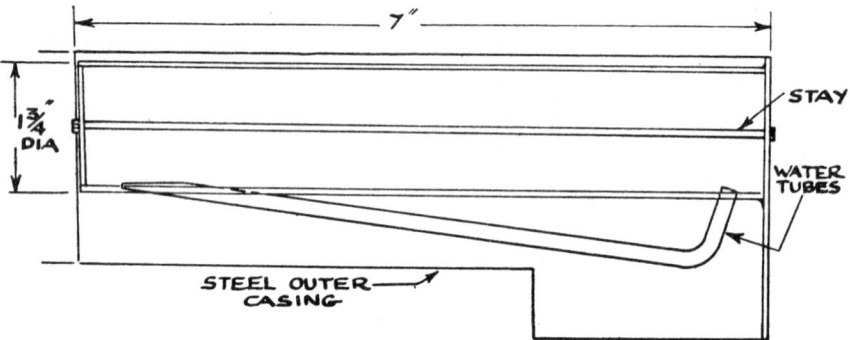

Fig. 83. Water Tube Boiler for Gauge 1 locomotive

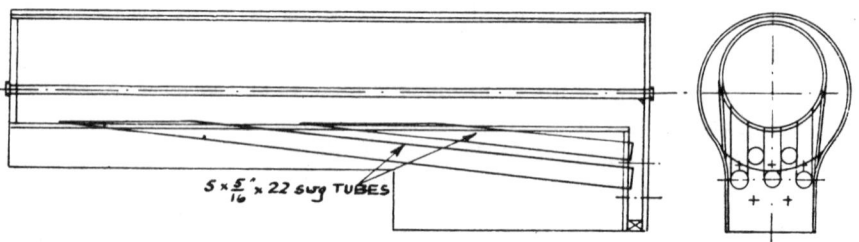

Fig. 84. $\frac{1}{4}$ in. scale Water Tube Boiler

The ends of the barrel should, for preference, be flanged inwards, this will be found convenient for silver-soldering. In order to fit the tubes at the front end of the barrel a hole should be drilled, and then elongated by inserting a piece of steel rod of the same diameter as the tube and forcing it over to the angle required. This operation will be found much easier if the barrel is annealed first by heating to a dull red and plunging into cold water.

In order to give more space for the attachment of fittings, the water space at the rear end of the boiler may be continued below the barrel by means of a throatplate and a deeper backhead, the lower end of the water tubes being silver-soldered into the throatplate; see Fig. 84.

Locomotive Type Boilers

Although the simple water-tube boiler gives good results for Gauge "O" and "1" models, there is no doubt that for models of ½ in. scale and above, the extra work and expense involved in building the proper locomotive type boiler is fully justified. The normal loco. type boiler consists of a barrel fitted to an internal firebox located at the rear of the engine, the furnace being fitted with firegrate and ashpan below. The products of combustion pass through the barrel to the smokebox by means of a number of small diameter tubes.

The so-called "dry-back" type of loco. boiler has been used for models, but it cannot be recommended as too much valuable heating surface is lost.

There are two main types of locomotive boilers. Those having a long and deep firebox narrow enough to go between the mainframes and those with a shorter but very wide firebox coming behind the driving and coupled wheels and supported by extensions from the mainframes and by bogies or pony trucks. The barrel of the locomotive type boiler may be parallel or tapered. Several advantages are claimed for the taper barrel; the greatest cross-sectional area is obtained next to the firebox where the heat value is at its greatest. As the products of combustion are drawn through the tubes and flues, their temperature is dropping, and it is therefore only natural that one should arrange for the volume of the water to be heated to fall in unison. Another advantage of the taper barrel is that the end-to-end surge of the water in the boiler due to acceleration or braking is less than in the parallel barrel, while the opportunity can be taken to increase the height of the chimney which helps to clear the exhaust from the locomotive so preserving a clear lookout for the driver.

Another variation in boiler design should be noted, the top of the firebox may be round, or it may be flat or nearly so, the sides also being flattened. The latter type, known as the Belpaire, gives greater water and steam volume over the top of the furnace, thus it is basically more efficient as a steam raiser, though more difficult to build.

The diameter of the tubes in the boiler and the relation between this and their length was discussed in Chapter 3, although if the boiler is an exceptionally long one it is not advisable to follow the formula given as otherwise the tubes would be too large and too few. A better solution is to adopt the combustion chamber; as far as British prototypes are concerned, the boilers fitted to the 4-6-2 "Pacific" locomotives are usually of such a size that the addition of a combustion chamber is called for.

Materials for Model Boilers

There is no doubt that the best material for the model boiler up to 2 in. scale is copper. It is often asked whether steel can be used for at least the larger model boilers, chiefly on the grounds of cheaper cost. While steel is considerably stronger than copper for a given thickness, owing to the problem of corrosion steel plates must be made a good deal thicker than would be warranted on the score of strength alone. Then again steel does not conduct the heat through to the water quite so quickly as copper, and it is less ductile and thus more difficult to work.

Stainless steel has been suggested for model boilers and there seems no reason why it should not be used for barrels and certain of the plates, but the difficulty of flanging this material will probably deter most model engineers from using it.

Brazing Equipment

Before attempting to build a model locomotive boiler, the model engineer should first make certain that he has suitable equipment to cope with this type of work. Few amateurs are likely to possess Oxy-Acetylene equipment, and those who do would be well advised to consult the British Oxygen Company who will be glad to assist in any way required. There are however several other types of equipment which are equally satisfactory.

The technique required for Oxy-Acetylene work is very different from ordinary silver-soldering and brazing. The heat applied is local and the temperature reached is such that welding is resorted to rather than brazing; the welding bronze is not nearly so fluid as silver-solder and it is therefore built up into a "fillet" on the surface of the joint. Flanged joints for welding must therefore allow for this difference, joints for silver-soldering must be close fitting.

Apart from Oxy-Acetylene equipment, probably the most efficient method of brazing model boilers is the use of the modern self-contained bottle-gas (Propane) outfits. These Propane brazing torches now obtainable are available with a great variety of burners, the largest of which will provide sufficient heat to braze a 1 in. scale locomotive boiler, while the smaller sizes are ideal for the silver-soldering of small boiler fittings, etc.

Another type of brazing equipment in general use is the Air/Town Gas outfit. An Air/Gas torch having a burner 1 in. diameter and a suitable supply of air will supply enough heat to braze $\frac{3}{4}$ in. scale boilers. The air may be supplied by a rotary type blower driven by an electric motor of about $\frac{1}{4}$ h.p.

The paraffin blowlamp will be known to most readers, and while the largest ones (5 to 6 pint) are somewhat frightening machines to use, they will do the job. As a guide to their capacity, it may be said that a 1-pint blowlamp will silver-solder a water-tube boiler up to $\frac{1}{2}$ in. scale, but for a $\frac{3}{4}$ in. scale loco.-type boiler, the largest size will be necessary.

After the model engineer has equipped himself with a suitable brazing torch, a brazing pan or forge will be required. For $\frac{3}{4}$ in. scale boilers, a convenient size would be about 30 in. long by 15 in. wide by 10 in. deep, the side nearest the operator being left open. Such a brazing pan can quickly be made up from black steel sheet bolted to steel angle, the height of the bottom of the pan being made about 30 in. from ground level. The back of the pan can be lined with a few bricks, while coke should be heaped up around the job as required.

Other items which are essential are a large pair of tongs to lift the boiler when hot, and a length of steel rod sharpened to a point at one end, useful for scratching the joint while brazing, and finally a large tank for "pickling" after each brazing

BOILERS 113

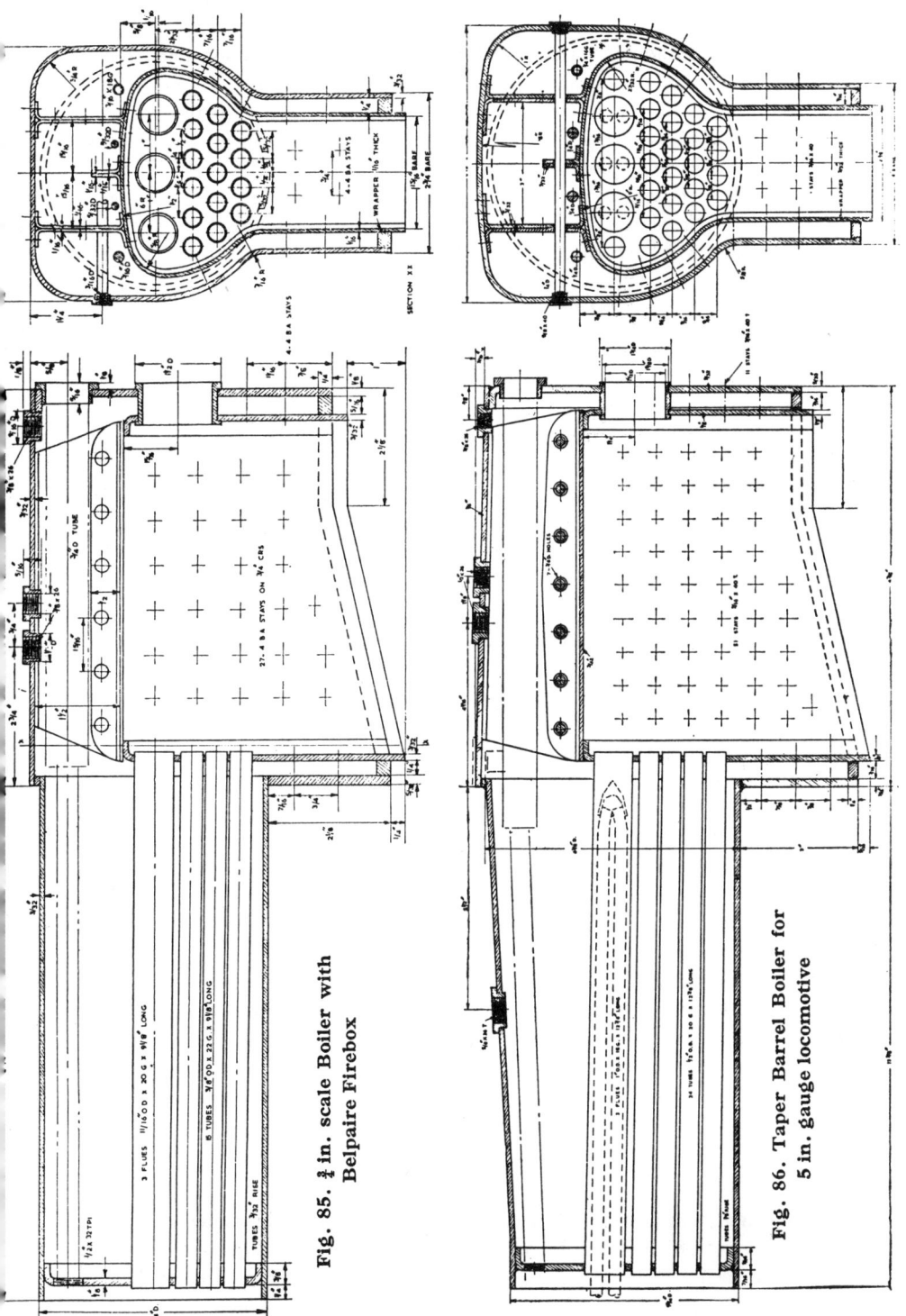

Fig. 85. ¾ in. scale Boiler with Belpaire Firebox

Fig. 86. Taper Barrel Boiler for 5 in. gauge locomotive

operation. The ideal would be a wooden box lined with lead and filled with dilute sulphuric acid, although a large rubber bucket would suffice for small boilers. When purchasing the acid, the "commercial" concentrated acid should be asked for, and this is added to the water in a strength of about 1 in 50 parts. It must be noted that water should never be put into concentrated acid, always the other way around, otherwise an explosion may take place.

As regards silver solders and brazing spelters for use with blowlamps, the makers' advice should be taken. The author generally uses "B.6" alloy, "Easyflo No. 1" and "Easyflo No. 2" according to the particular operation in hand.

Building Locomotive-type Boilers

Work should be commenced on the barrel. If possible, seamless copper tube should be used, and for working pressures of 80–90 lb. per sq. in. the thickness chosen may be as follows: up to $2\frac{1}{2}$ in. outside diameter—18 s.w.g. or $\frac{3}{64}$ in. $2\frac{3}{4}$ in. to $3\frac{3}{4}$ in. o.d.—16 s.w.g. or $\frac{1}{16}$ in. 4 in. to 5 in. o.d.—13 s.w.g. or $\frac{3}{32}$ in. $5\frac{1}{4}$ in. to $6\frac{1}{4}$ in. o.d.—$\frac{1}{8}$ in. and $6\frac{1}{2}$ in. to 8 in.—$\frac{5}{32}$ in.

When suitable seamless tube is unobtainable, the barrel may be rolled up from sheet copper, well annealed, a coppersmith's joint being used; alternately the edges may be brought together and an overlapping strip laid the full length of the barrel on the inside (apart from the depth allowed for the flange of the smokebox tubeplate) this strip being riveted to the two edges and the whole joint afterwards brazed.

Before any brazing or silver-soldering is attempted, the metal must be absolutely clean and all joints coated with the appropriate flux. The job should be brought up to such a temperature that the brazing strip will flow freely even if the flame from the blowlamp is withdrawn for a moment. The joint should be scratched with the scratch rod mentioned previously before it is accepted as sound and the flame withdrawn. This will break up any flux blisters and ensure that the brazing metal will reach every nook and cranny.

The job may then be allowed to cool to black and placed very carefully in the pickle tank—splashes from the acid must be avoided with care. After ten minutes in the acid, the barrel should be washed thoroughly under the tap with Vim or similar cleanser. It will then be possible to see exactly where the silver-solder has run and thus whether the joint is sound.

Taper barrels may also be rolled up from sheet, although these are sometimes made by cutting a vee piece out of a seamless tube, annealing and bringing the two edges together as before.

The ends of taper barrels are normally squared by filing, a square being used for checking, but parallel barrels can be turned in the lathe by plugging the ends with wooden discs, the outer end being supported by the tailstock.

The Firebox Wrapper

In the case of some types of "round-top" boilers, the firebox outer wrapper can be formed out of the boiler barrel tube itself by cutting and opening out; if the sides so formed are not long enough to reach to the bottom of the firebox, they may

Weighshaft and expansion link, "Britannia" class locomotive

Plate 21

Box type expansion link: ¾ in. scale chassis

Walschaerts' gear fitted to "Schools" class locomotive

Plate 22

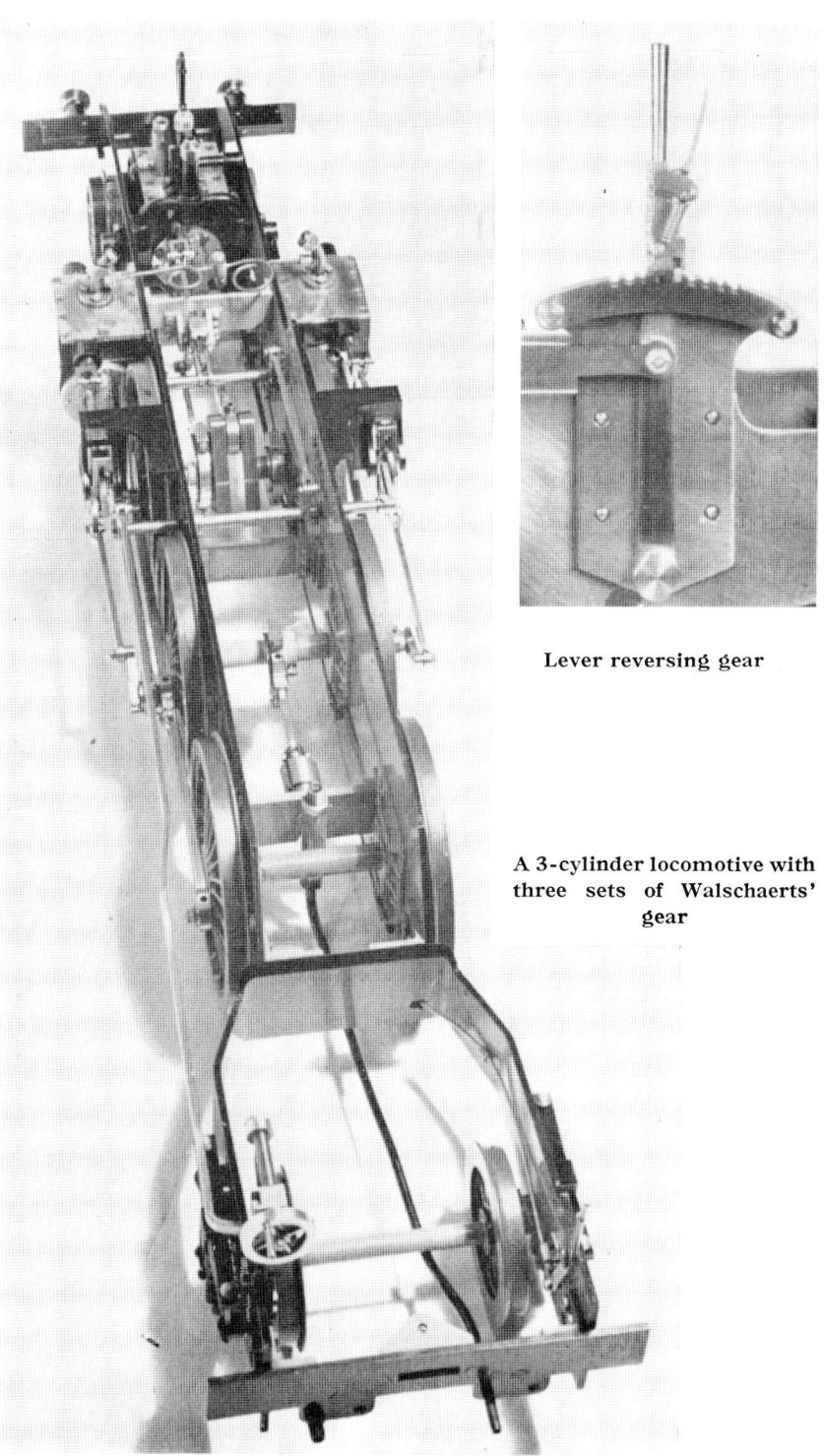

Lever reversing gear

A 3-cylinder locomotive with three sets of Walschaerts' gear

Plate 23

A magnificent ¾ in. scale boiler: Mr. B. Palmer of Durban

Plate 24

STAGES IN BOILER CONSTRUCTION

Bending up a firebox wrapper

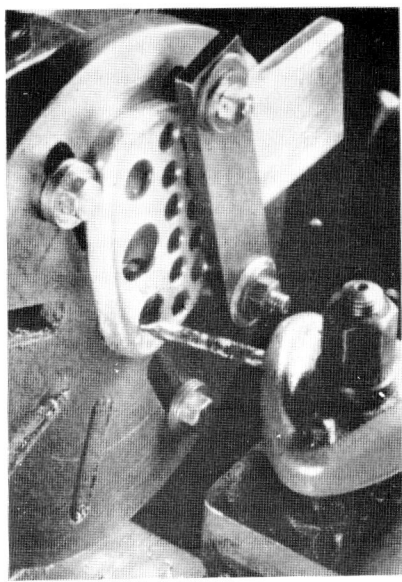

Boring flue-holes in firebox tube plate

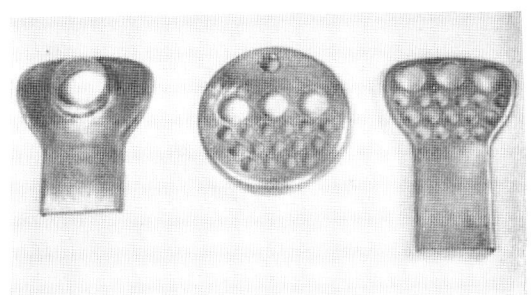

Hand-flanged boiler plates

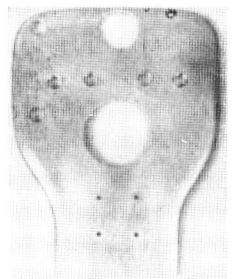

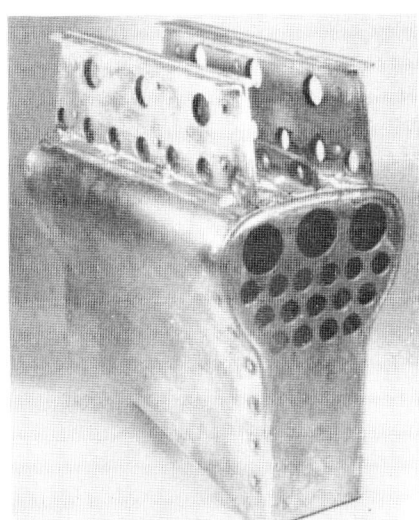

Firebox, showing tubeplate ready for insertion of tubes

Inner firebox, showing firehole ring

FURTHER STAGES IN BOILER CONSTRUCTION

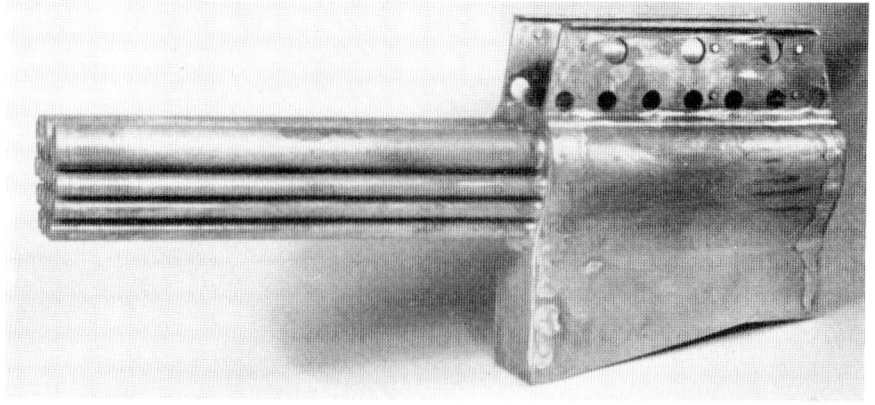

Firebox and tubes—after brazing

Firebox and tubes assembled in shell

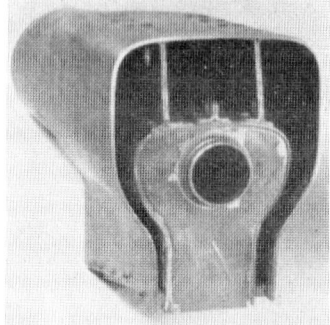

Boiler before fitting backhead

View of boiler after brazing smokebox tubeplate

Plate 26

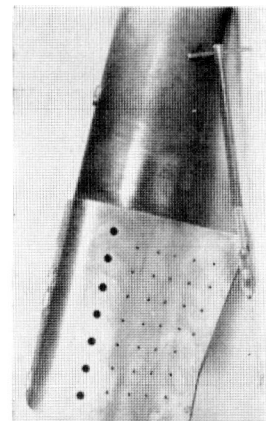

View showing stay holes before tapping, and special tap holder

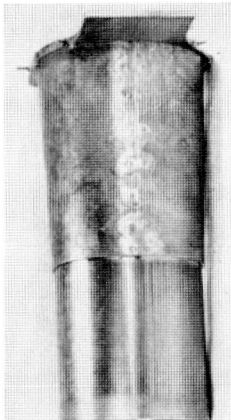

Boiler barrel for a 5 in. gauge G.W.R. locomotive. Throatplate partly fitted

An experimental stay-less boiler built by Mr. Hughes of Massachusetts

Plate 27

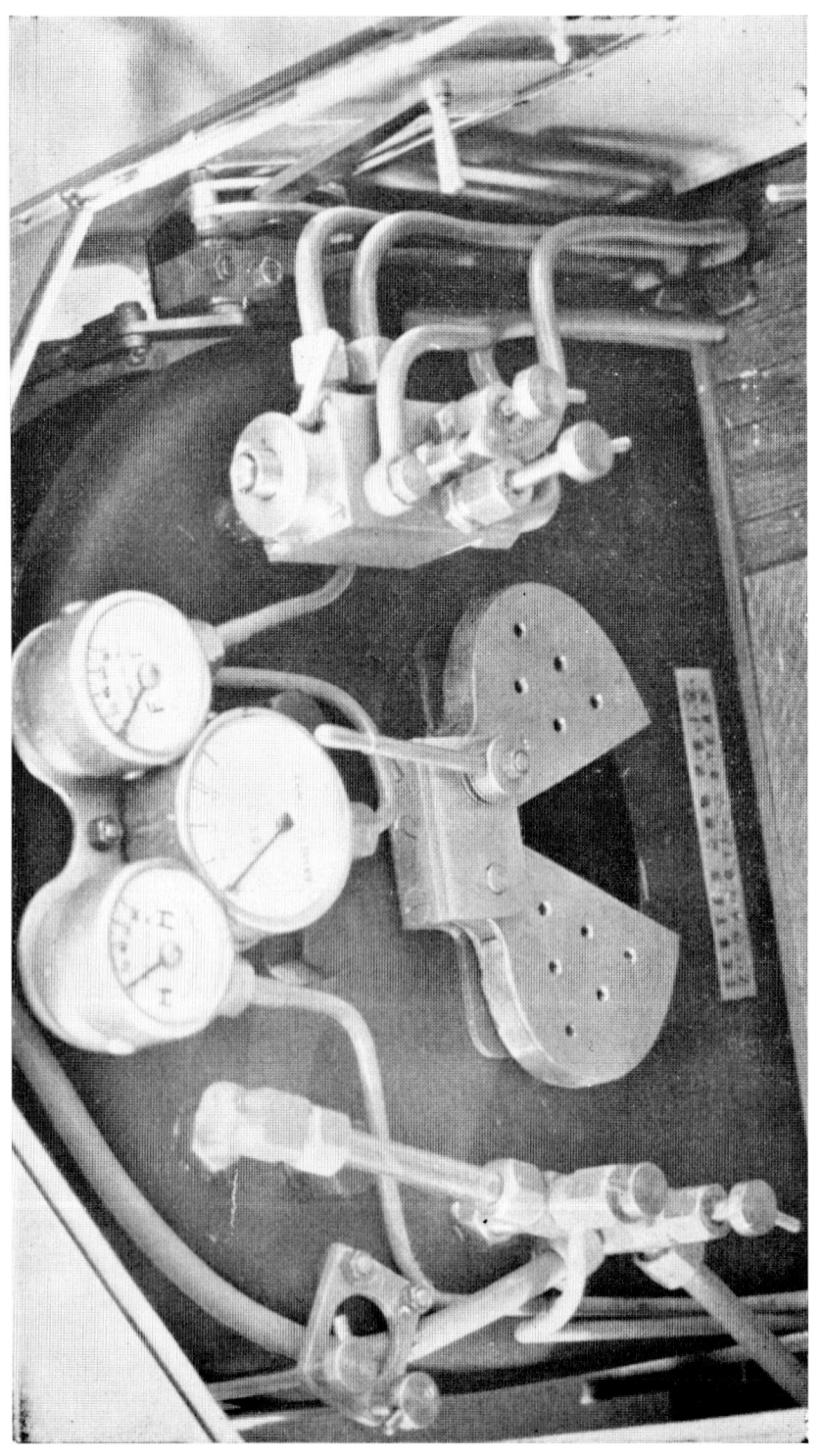

Cab fittings of a model Beyer-Garratt locomotive, showing butterfly-type firedoor

Plate 28

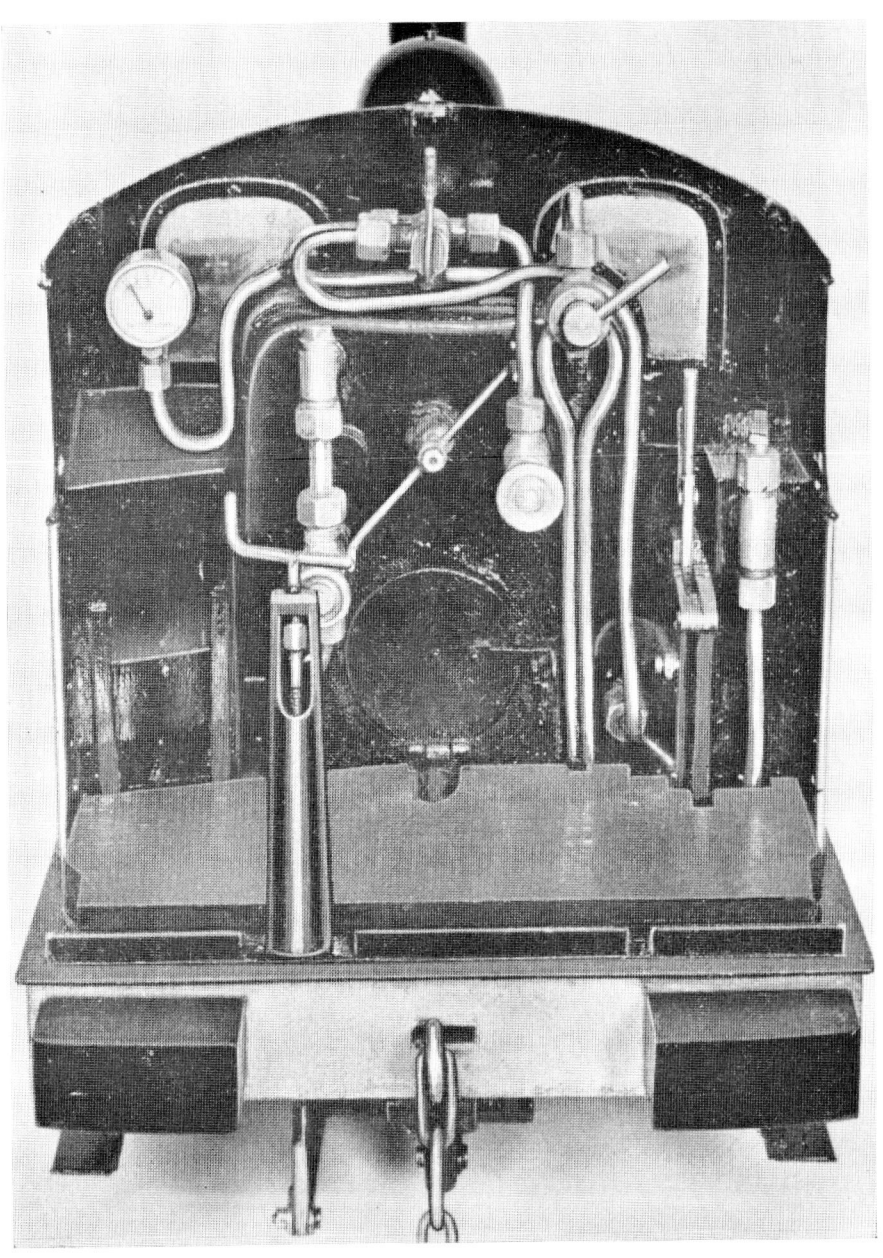

Cab fittings of a model dock shunter

Underside view of grate and ashpan

Turning a smokebox in the lathe

A safety valve, blower and whistle valve

The parts of a disc-type regulator before assembly

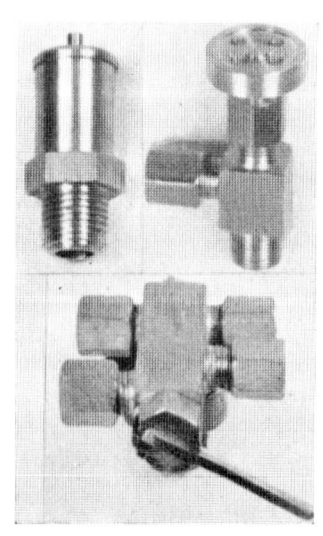

Plate 30

Locomotive backhead, showing pressure and water gauges, etc. ¾ in. scale "Britannia" loco

Plate 31

Underside of mechanical lubricator, showing drive

A mechanical lubricator

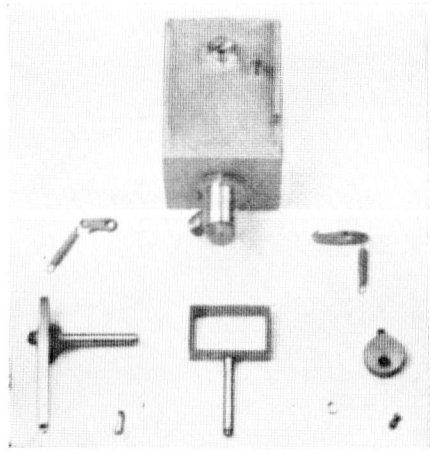

The above lubricator shown dismantled

Blast pipe and steam connections to cylinders on a ¾ in. scale locomotive

Plate 32

Twin water feed pumps between frames

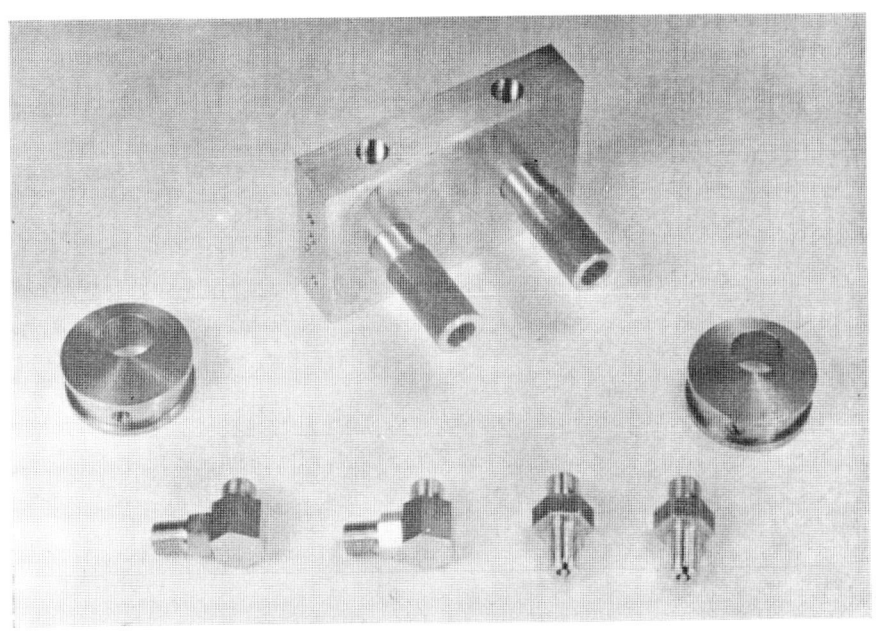

Components of the twin pump

Plate 33

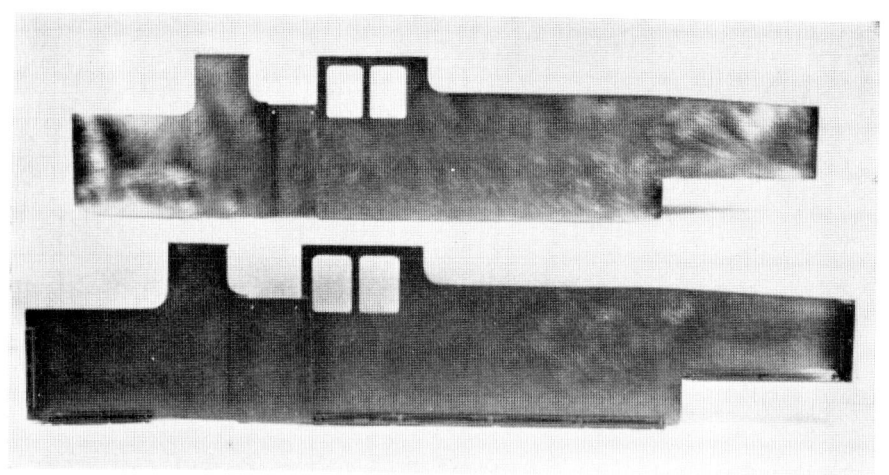

Side tanks and cab during construction

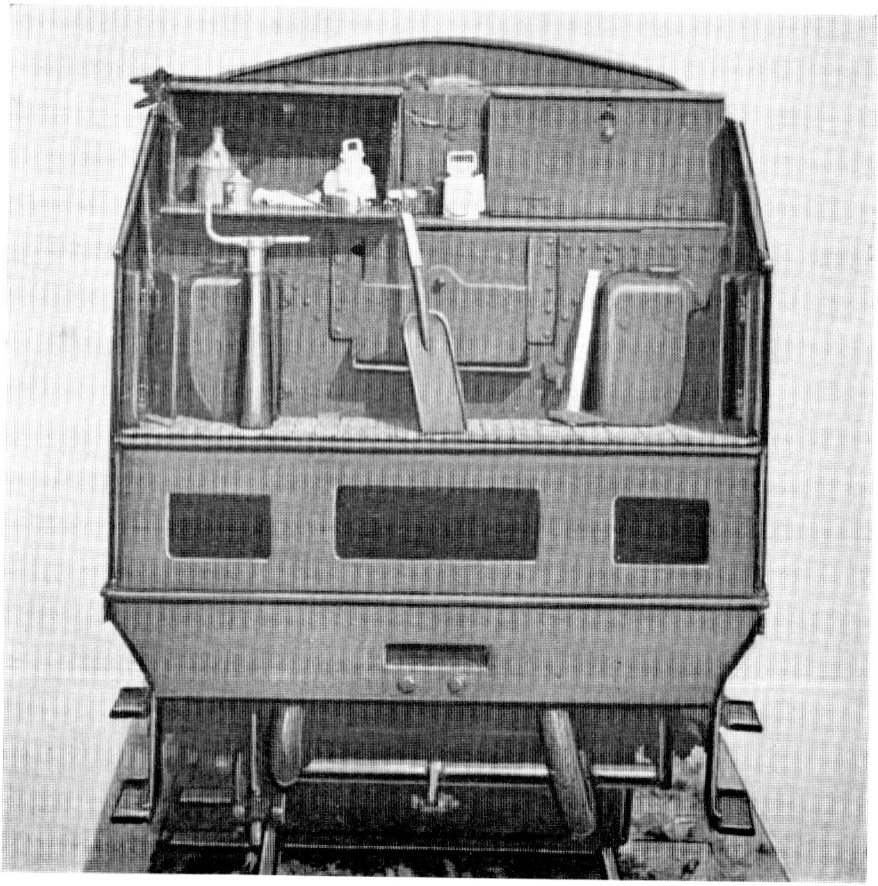

Front end of a ¾ in. scale tender

Plate 34

A Gauge "1" tender chassis

A tender fitted up for spirit firing

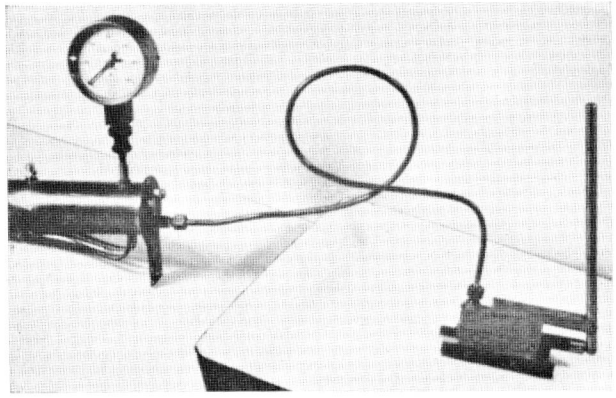

A hydraulic test on a small water-tube boiler

Plate 35

Cab view of a ¾ in. scale tank engine

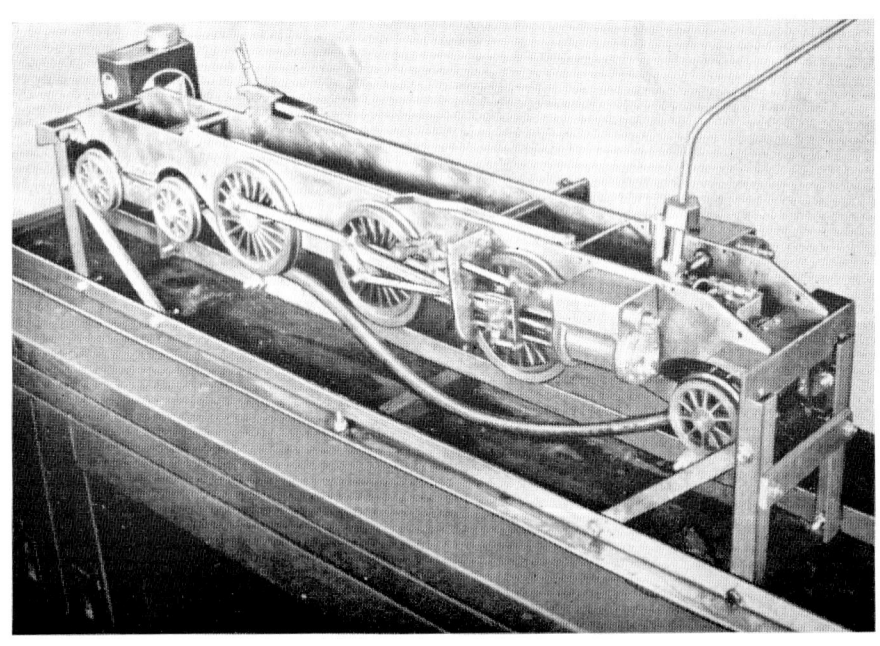

The author's 2-6-4 tank locomotive chassis under test on the bench

Plate 36

be extended by separate pieces of sheet brazed on. Another method is to use one separate piece of sheet for the wrapper, and attach it to the barrel by means of a turned ring. A "throatplate" is then required to close the front, underneath the barrel, and this should be made by flanging over a former of steel.

Flanged plates for model boilers should not be made from castings; they should be made from annealed copper sheet by beating over steel formers of suitable thickness which are cut to the shape required, with allowance for the thickness of the sheet itself. A soft hammer is advisable and the plate must be re-annealed immediately it shows signs of going hard—a thick plate may require annealing three or four times before flanging is complete.

The Firebox

When the barrel and outer firebox wrapper are ready, the next item to tackle is the inner firebox. The formers for the firebox tubeplate and firebox backplate are cut out, the first mentioned being drilled for the tubes and flues so that it can later be used as a jig for drilling the smoke-box tubeplate. In many boilers, one former suffices for both the firebox plates. After the firebox tubeplate has been flanged, the tube and flue holes should be drilled and reamed a tight push fit for the tubes and also countersunk on the outside (that is the side nearest to the smokebox).

Fireholes

Before proceeding further with the firebox, the size and position of the firehole should be considered. This should always be made a good deal larger than the scale equivalent for convenience in firing, and placed somewhat higher up, especially in tank locomotives. Either a round or oval firehole is recommended rather than a rectangular shape. A good method of constructing the firehole is to turn up a ring from thick-walled copper tube, both ends being turned so as to form a step in the middle. This can then be put through a hole of suitable size cut in the firebox backplate and flanged over on the inside.

The firebox wrapper can now be bent around the two flanged plates and riveted to them, using snaphead copper rivets. In the case of narrow-type fireboxes, it may be found that it is difficult to get a riveting "dolly" inside in certain places. The solution here is to make up gunmetal or copper screws, and drill and tap the wrapper and flange, which must be kept in close contact while the screws are put in.

If plate crown-stays are adopted these should now be made up and riveted to the crown of the firebox, when the whole unit may be brazed, care being taken to ensure that the brazing material flows throughout all the joints especially all along the base of the crown-stays, over all screws and rivet heads, and around the firehole ring. The hottest part of the flame should be kept away from the tube holes, or this part of the firebox may become overheated. As with all brazing operations, the job must then be "pickled" in the acid bath, washed thoroughly and carefully examined before the next part of the boiler is attempted.

M.M.S.L.—E

Fitting Tubes to Fireboxes

The author strongly recommends that tubes and flues be silver-soldered into the firebox tubeplate. At one time it was customary to thread the ends of tubes and screw them into the tubeplate, afterwards covering with soft solder. This method is a poor one; for one thing the tubes, which must be of fairly thin material if they are to be efficient, are dangerously weakened by threading, while the tubeplate is not thick enough to take more than a few threads unless specially thickened locally by flanging inwards, a difficult process if the tubes are close to one another.

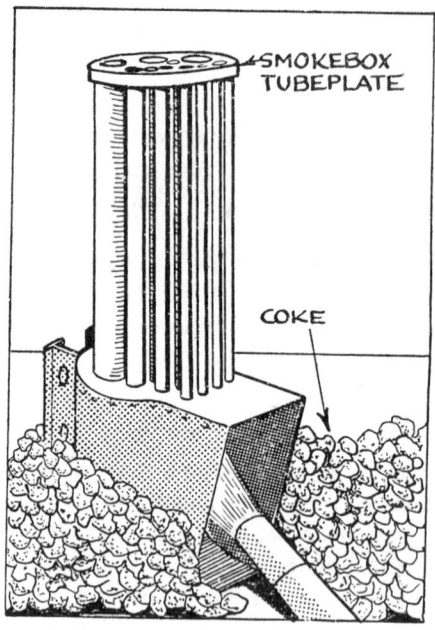

Fig. 87. Fixing Tubes to Firebox

Some builders screw their tubes into the tubeplate and then silver-solder them. This is better, but still does not entirely overcome the objections mentioned, as it is difficult to build up a "fillet" with silver-solder. In any case this method involves a great deal more work than the first-mentioned.

The smokebox tubeplate should be made up and used as a support to hold the outer ends of the tubes while the latter are being silver-soldered into the firebox tubeplate. As mentioned previously, the holes in the firebox tubeplate should be reamed so that they are a tight fit for the tubes and flues. The tubes should be annealed and thoroughly cleaned at both ends before being pressed home (see fig. 87). Plenty of flux must be used and the silver-solder, which should be of the best grade and in wire form, wrapped around every tube beforehand. On bringing the whole to a dull red heat, more solder may be fed in from all around before the flame is removed. Care must be taken in this operation not to overheat the thin-walled tubes. After pickling and washing, the inner firebox and tubes should now be ready for assembly in the barrel and outer firebox (see photographs, Plate 23).

The crownstays (if of the plate type) should be temporarily clamped to the firebox wrapper before the front and side sections of the foundation ring are fitted. The latter are generally made from square or rectangular copper bar, annealed and the lower edges bevelled before riveting in place. Plate crownstays should be riveted as well as brazed or silver-soldered to the wrapper. It is generally possible to insert a stout steel bar between the top of the firebox and the wrapper to support these rivets, though copper or gunmetal screws may also be used, but in this case care must be taken to silver-solder the heads outside the firebox.

BOILERS

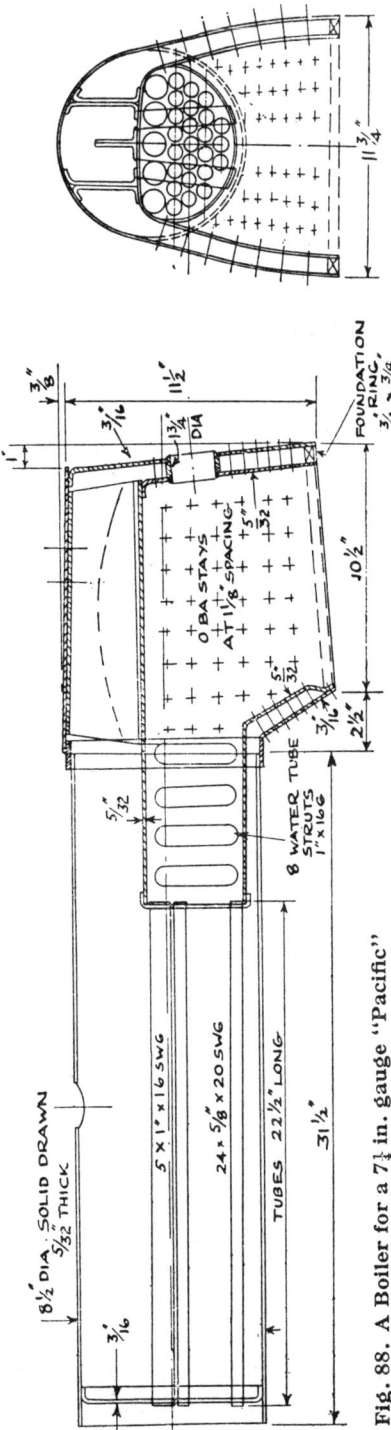

Fig. 88. A Boiler for a 7¼ in. gauge "Pacific"

Before the smokebox tubeplate is fitted, the holes for the tubes and flues should be countersunk. The flange of the tubeplate is generally put on the inside of the boiler, this method leaves a deep groove or recess all around which will be found convenient for running in the silver-solder. A few copper screws will hold the tubeplate in place while the ends of the tubes are expanded, this being done by means of a polished and greased taper drift.

The smokebox tubeplate can now be silver-soldered, best grade being used on the tubes themselves.

In the case of Belpaire fireboxes, before fitting the backhead, it is a good plan to check up on the location of the cross stays which pass right across the wrapper above the inner firebox. This will ensure that these stays do not foul the crownstays or longitudinal stays.

Before the backhead is fitted the bushes required for the various fittings may be pressed in and brazed on the inside, while the hole cut for the firehole ring can be checked off from the position of the ring itself. The remaining section of the foundation ring is then fitted, and the firehole ring expanded or flanged over the backhead, the latter being held for the moment by a number of copper screws put through the wrapper into its flange.

The final brazing operation—that of the foundation ring and backhead—requires the most heat, and if there is any doubt about there being enough heat available, the packing of the coke should be done very carefully. In any case, some asbestos sheet must be put inside the firebox to protect the tubes and crown, after which it may be filled with coke almost up to the level of the foundation ring. Coke can also be piled up all around the outside. Should difficulty still be experienced in reaching a sufficiently high temperature, there is no objection to the use of the best grade silver-solder here, apart from expense, as some quantity may be used.

Any other bushes required can now be fitted, being pressed in and silver-soldered. At this stage the boiler may be given a preliminary water test, all bushes being blanked off, and the pressure brought up to about 25 lb. A reliable gauge will be required, while a hand pump will suffice for supplying the pressure, the boiler being completely filled with water before pressure is applied.

Should the boiler be found to have leaks, these should be carefully examined, their cure being dependent on their position. A slight leak in the foundation ring could be cured by drilling and tapping it 10 or 8 b.a. and screwing in a short stub of copper suitably threaded, the threads being smeared with jointing. A leak at the smokebox tubeplate or backhead would probably require further attention from the blowlamp. If a leak is found in an inaccessible internal position, one way out is to use some soft solder as a caulking medium, the solder being put inside the boiler as near as possible to the leak, a few spoonfuls of a liquid flux added and the whole boiler heated to the melting point of the solder.

Stays

Longitudinal boiler stays can be made from a good quality drawn gunmetal or phos-bronze, threaded and nippled at each end. These nipples may either be run over with solder or plumbers jointing used on the threads. One of the longitudinal stays in model boilers is usually made hollow—a thick-walled copper tube being employed—to carry the blower steam to the smokebox. It is of course most important that all flat surfaces in the boiler are well supported with stays, and those required at the sides of the firebox, between the throatplate and firebox tubeplate, and between the firebox backplate and the backhead are generally of the threaded type, nutted on the inside.

The holes are tapped with a fine thread straight through the outer and inner plates in one operation, a special long taper tap being employed. The stays themselves can be turned from copper or gunmetal. The former are much easier to rivet, especially if annealed, as they should be, while the latter thread more easily. If gunmetal is used, it is not essential to rivet the head of the stay. The head can be partly turned in the lathe, the thread machined and the stock removed from the lathe. The stay is then screwed right home in the boiler and the remainder of the rod twisted off, the unfinished head being cleaned up with files. With copper, the same procedure can be followed, but the head is finished by rivetting.

On the inside of the stays, brass locknuts are satisfactory, though care should be taken not to over-tighten them or the threads may strip.

When all the stays in the boiler are fitted and lock-nutted, they may be sweated over with soft solder, the higher melting point solder being preferable. A liquid flux should be used, the whole boiler being gradually raised to the melting point of the solder and a fillet formed over every stay head and locknut, inside and out.

It is also possible to silver-solder over the stay heads; some boiler builders prefer this as the whole boiler can then be completed without any soft solder being used at all. This is considered an advantage should repairs be required at any time in the life of the boiler. It will be appreciated that once soft solder has been used on a boiler, it is almost impossible to use silver-solder again.

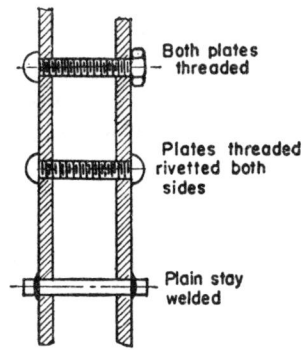

Fig. 89. Types of Stays

Another method of staying is to use plain stays of copper or gunmetal rod. The holes are simply drilled a tight push fit for the stays, which are then pressed into place, allowing a short projection inside and out, and the ends bronze-welded, using the Oxy-acetylene flame. While this method is quite satisfactory, it is not one that can be recommended to the beginner.

Crownstays

The crownstays of a "round-top" firebox should preferably be of the plate type, and if the crown of the firebox is made convex to the pressure (as it should be) a very strong job is produced. A central "tee" stay also helps to stiffen the crown if of stout metal.

Vertical rod type crownstays are satisfactory in Belpaire fireboxes, but they must be closely spaced, tapped right through both plates and nutted inside and out, the whole being run over with silver solder for additional security.

The plate type of crownstay should always be rivetted to the firebox crown and top, as well as silver-soldered, care being taken to ensure that the solder runs right through the joints.

Brick arches

Although brick arches are always used in full-size boilers, experience has shown that they have very little effect in model boilers smaller than $1\frac{1}{2}$ in. scale, and they also tend to be a hindrance when the tubes and flues are being swept. If used in boilers for large-scale models, they could be made from rustless steel sheet not less than $\frac{1}{8}$ in. thick, and held in place between the stay locknuts.

Stay-less boilers

In view of the labour involved in fitting stays to the conventional loco-type boiler, it is hardly surprising that attempts have been made to adopt a coal-fired boiler without stays, the barrel usually being of the normal type, but the water space of the usual firebox being replaced by a series of small diameter tubes which surround the furnace. Alternately the firebox may be heavily corrugated or completely circular. An example of the latter in full-size work was the special boilers fitted to certain of the 0-8-0's of the old Lancashire and Yorkshire Railway. An experimental stay-less boiler for a model locomotive is shown in plate 24.

Water and steam tests

Before a model locomotive boiler is passed ready for service, it must be given both a hydraulic and a steam test. For the former, which must be done first, the boiler is completely filled with cold water, all air being excluded, and all except two of the bushes being carefully blanked off. A large pressure gauge is now fitted to one of these bushes, a reliable gauge having a range about four times the desired working pressure of the boiler being essential. To the other free bush is fitted a suitable hand pump immersed in a tray of cold water. For this purpose the usual type of hand pump fitted to models for emergency purposes is quite suitable.

The pressure is now brought gradually up to twice the working pressure (or a little less) and the boiler is examined thoroughly for faults or leaks. The test pressure should be held for about twenty minutes if the boiler is a new one, though ten minutes should suffice for a boiler which has been tested before. If the hydraulic test proves satisfactory, a steam test should then be held. The steam test pressure may be about 50 per cent lower than the hydraulic test pressure. Steam may be raised by using a bunsen burner or a small blowlamp, and the test pressure need not be held for more than a few minutes. After all tests have been satisfactorily completed, the boiler fittings are put in place and steam raised once again to ensure that all fittings work correctly before the boiler is mounted on the chassis for good.

Hydraulic tests must be carried out on boilers in regular service at intervals of not more than twelve months, in the interests of safety. This is even more important where steel boilers are concerned, owing to the possibility of rusting. The safety valves should also be examined, cleaned and tested at frequent intervals.

CHAPTER TWELVE

Boiler Fittings

Firedoors

AFTER THE LOCOMOTIVE BOILER has been completed and tested, the firedoor is generally fitted. The type and shape of the door used is usually a question of personal preference. A door which is hinged at the top is most undesirable on models below 3 in. scale, as it prevents the driver from seeing the fire properly, A firedoor which is hinged at the bottom is not too satisfactory, owing to the tendency for the hinge to become jammed with coal dust etc. The simple swing door with hinges at the side is a very effective one and easy to make. The handle should be made long enough to enable the driver to reach it comfortably while on the move, while the latch should be sufficiently large to make the door an easy one to close properly.

The sliding type firedoor, as used on many G.W.R. and L.M.S. locomotives, is quite satisfactory in model form and looks better than the side-hinged type. Two panels are used, sliding in runners; the panels are connected by levers so that they move together in opposite directions under the control of the driver's lever. It is important, with the sliding type of door, to prevent the lower runner from becoming choked by coal dust. This can usually be achieved by leaving one side of the lower runner channel open immediately below the firehole itself.

The firedoor is generally provided with a few small air holes to allow a little extra air over the top of the fire. This helps to ensure the complete combustion of the fuel in the firebox and reduces smoke. Where possible a baffle should be arranged just inside the door itself to deflect this "top air" and to prevent its being drawn straight across to the tubes. Fig. 90 shows a typical round type firedoor fitted with a baffle, while Fig. 91 shows a sliding type firedoor based on the G.W.R. design.

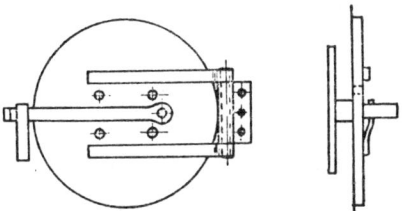

Fig. 90. Round type Firedoor

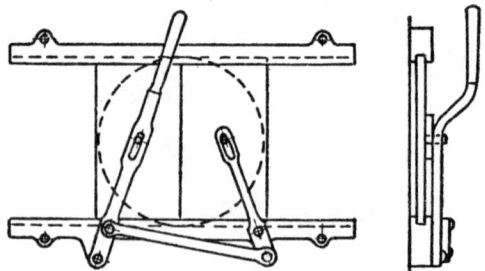

Fig. 91. Sliding type Firedoor

Firegrates

Firegrates are sometimes built up from mild steel strip, the space between the bars being made at least as great as the thickness of the bars themselves, preferably a little more. For locomotives up to $\frac{1}{2}$ in. scale the bars may be about $\frac{3}{32}$ in. × $\frac{5}{16}$ in. section; for $\frac{3}{4}$ in. scale about $\frac{1}{8}$ in. × $\frac{3}{8}$ or $\frac{1}{2}$ in. section with $\frac{5}{32}$ in. air spaces; for 1 in. scale about $\frac{3}{16}$ in. × $\frac{1}{2}$ or $\frac{5}{8}$ in., and for $1\frac{1}{2}$ in. scale boilers the bars may be $\frac{1}{4}$ in. × $\frac{3}{4}$ in.

When a locomotive is in regular use, mild steel firebars do not last very long, and the use of stainless steel for both firebars and bearers can be recommended. However a better plan is to make a pattern and have the whole grate cast in one piece in iron. Apart from the obvious advantage of easy replacement, the cast grate can be made with its firebars the correct shape, i.e. tapered towards the bottom, so that the spaces between the bars do not become jammed with the ashes.

The firegrate should not be attached permanently to the firebox, as it is useful to be able to drop the grate quickly in the event of emergency.

Ashpans

All locomotive-type boilers should be fitted with ashpans. Apart from preventing the ashes from falling all over the track, the ashpan helps to maintain an even flow of air through the furnace.

The ashpan should be arranged with the front end completely closed, the air being drawn in at the back. Where the grate has a bend in it, the bottom of the ashpan should if possible follow the contour of the grate. Where the rear end of the ashpan is of necessity too small to allow sufficient air to pass through it, there is no

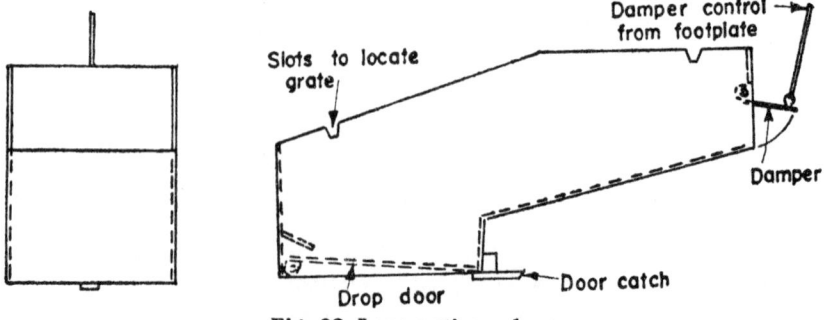

Fig. 92. Locomotive ashpan

BOILER FITTINGS

objection to the provision of a further small air gap in the middle of the ashpan. On large models, the flow of air through the fire can be controlled by means of a damper—that is an adjustable door at the rear end of the ashpan operated from the cab.

Ashpans are generally built up from black steel sheet, about 18 s.w.g. for a ¾ in. scale engine, other scales in proportion. Joints may be brazed, or angled and riveted. A flap to allow ash to drop through between the rails without disturbing the ashpan itself is a useful refinement and quite easy to make. The pivot pin of such a flap should be protected from the ashes by means of a ledge as shown in Fig. 92.

Smokeboxes

The smokebox of model locomotives up to about 1 in. scale is generally made from brass or copper tube; steel can also be used, though rusting sets in rather quickly in steel smokeboxes. The smokebox can either be screwed direct to the boiler barrel, or it may be fitted by means of a turned ring in order to allow for the thickness of lagging and cleading around the barrel. It should be made removeable in order to gain access to the various fittings, superheaters, etc.

The front of the smokebox is usually fitted with a turned ring to which is attached a hinged door giving access to the tubes, etc. This turned ring may, in small smokeboxes, be made a tight push fit into the smokebox tube, so that the full internal diameter of the latter may be used for sweeping tubes, etc. Although castings are often used for the smokebox door, a brass blank is sometimes preferred, the hinges and other details being attached after the door has been machined. It is most important that the smokebox should be quite airtight, otherwise the boiler will not steam. The gaps inevitably left around the blast pipe, and the steam pipes to the cylinders, where these pass through the bottom of the smokebox, should be carefully plugged with a putty made by kneading asbestos sheet with water. The joints between the smokebox and the barrel, and between the front ring and the smokebox,

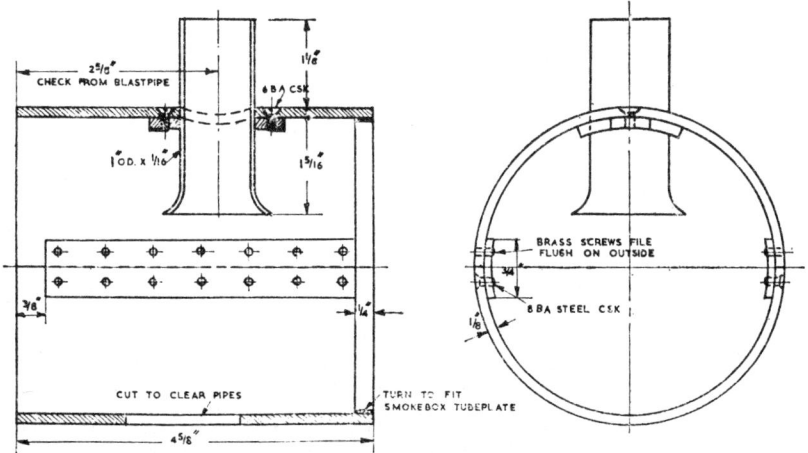

Fig. 93. Divided Smokebox

should be smeared with plumbers' jointing compound before finally bolting up. A removable crossbar is generally fitted across the inside of the door ring, a rectangular slot in which is engaged by the dart, thus enabling the door to be tightened up by the usual handles on the outside. The inner of these two handles is squared, to match the dart, while the outer handle is tapped.

In locomotives smaller than 1 in. scale, difficulty is often experienced in coupling up the various pipes inside the smokebox due to the small internal diameter. One way of overcoming this is to make the smokebox in two halves, split horizontally exactly on the centre-line. This enables all the pipes, etc. inside the smokebox to be put permanently in place without having to grope through the front at all. The smokebox tube can be split by means of a very thin slitting saw or by hacksawing, but in the latter case, a strip of metal would have to be silver-soldered to the edge of one half in order to make up for the metal lost in cutting. Another method is to use a fine metal fretsaw; this requires patience but the cut edges can be left without any cleaning up. The two halves of a smokebox of this type can be held together by means of a horizontal lap strip on each side, closely spaced countersunk screws being used, and the adjoining surfaces treated with jointing compound before final assembly.

Smokeboxes of the larger-boilered locomotives are generally fitted with a "petticoat pipe", this being an extension of the chimney inside the smokebox. (See Fig. 1.) In smaller models this may take the form of a length of tube belled out at the bottom, the chimney being made a tight push fit over the upper part of it. On some engines, the arrangement of blast pipe and petticoat makes access to the tubes for sweeping difficult. A petticoat which can be quickly removed through the smokebox door overcomes this, the lower portion being held in place by a screw set at an angle to the horizontal.

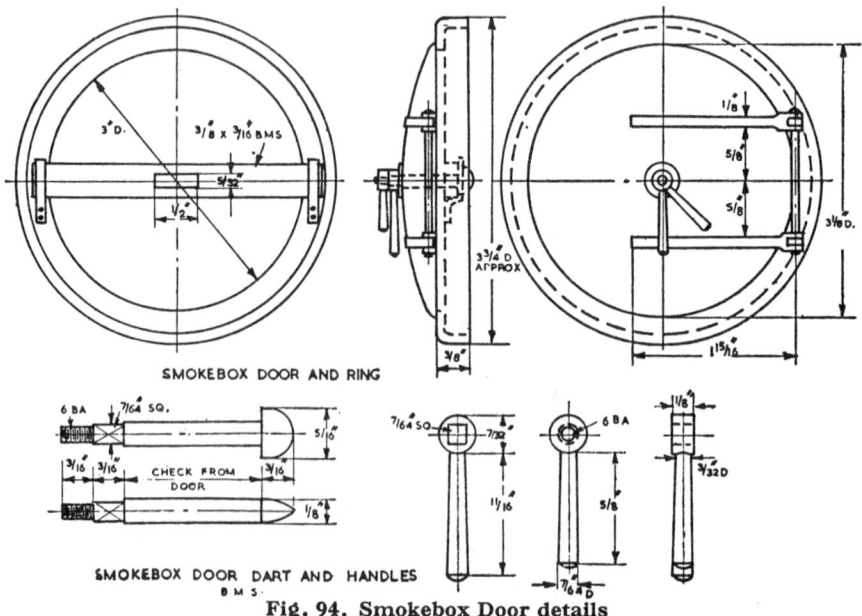

Fig. 94. Smokebox Door details

Superheater elements

With the usual arrangement of flue-tube superheater, the elements can be made of seamless copper tube of thickness not less than 20 s.w.g., and to give sufficient protection to the return bend, the latter may either be built up by welding, or better still a "block" return bend used. This consists of a block of solid copper or gunmetal, drilled to receive the two elements, and shaped as seen in Fig. 95. The bend should be brazed, using an alloy of fairly high melting point. Silver solder melts at rather too low a temperature to be advisable in this position.

Rustless steel tube can also be used for superheater elements, giving a longer life than copper.

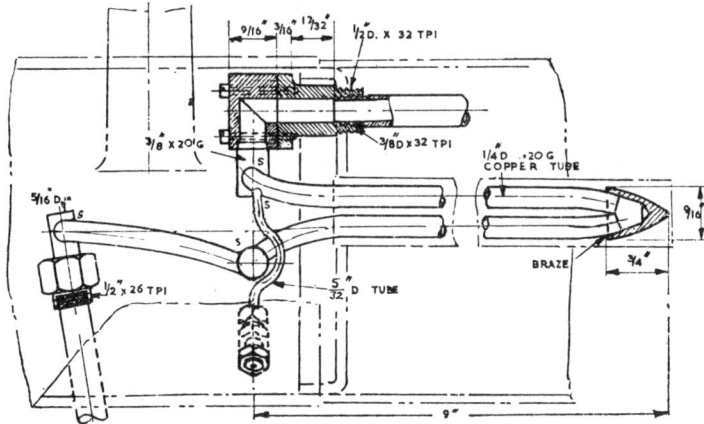

Fig. 95. Flue type Superheater: ¾ in. scale

In some model boilers, in order to obtain a higher superheat, the elements, of rustless steel, are led through one flue, right across the firebox, and back through another flue. This arrangement generally gives a high degree of superheat, but can only be recommended where cast-iron cylinders with proper rings are employed. Ordinary mild steel tube has also been used for superheater elements, giving quite a reasonable working life before severe rusting sets in.

Water gauges

All coal-fired boilers should be provided with at least one water gauge. Small water-tube boilers as fitted to Gauge O and Gauge 1 models can be fitted with two try cocks in lieu of a water gauge, one cock being placed a little above normal water level, and the other a little below.

Two water gauges are sometimes fitted to locomotives larger than $1\frac{1}{2}$ in. scale, but if the gauge is properly made and fitted, this is not by any means essential.

Where possible, the water gauge should be arranged with a vertical glass, and the glass should be of such a length that when the water level is flush with the top edge of the lower gland nut, there is still a little water over the top of the crown of the firebox. In allowing for this, it must be remembered that a small gauge, due to capillary attraction, always shows the water level as slightly higher than it actually is.

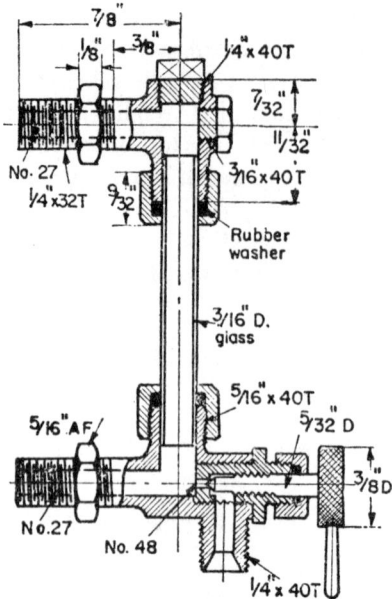

Fig. 96. A water gauge, ¾ in. scale

A glass of reasonable bore is advisable, i.e. $\frac{3}{16}$ in. diameter outside for ¾ in. scale boilers, ¼ in. dia. for 1 in. scale, or $\frac{5}{16}$ in. dia. for 1½ in. scale. The bore of the water and steam ways should be made slightly greater than the bore of the glass, and the connections into the boiler kept on the short side as long connections only collect scale. Cleaning plugs are generally fitted for both the steam and water ways, and a blow-down valve of not too small a bore so that a good rush of water can be passed when it is desired to clean the glass.

The shut-off cocks fitted to full-size water gauges are not essential in small gauges as glass breakages seldom take place if the glass is properly fitted. The large plug cocks sometimes seen on model water gauges spoil the appearance of the backhead and often stick in service. If some protection is desired, the use of mica may be considered. The gland nuts are made longer than would normally be required, and the outer ends of them turned circular. Mica sheet is then bent around the circular part of the nuts and secured by spring clips. The back of the glass is left open.

Water gauge fittings must be carefully lined up, using a length of silver steel rod of the same diameter as the glass, before the latter is tried in place. The fittings and gland nuts should always be made appreciably larger in the bore than the glass itself. Rubber washers are normally used, these can be made from thick rubber tube, being parted off with a razor blade while mounted on a length of metal rod. Synthetic rubber rings suitable for the purpose can also be obtained. When the glass is inserted, it should be noted whether there is plenty of room for the glass to expand; when the gland nuts are tightened, finger pressure will be found sufficient to prevent leakage. Spanners should never be used.

Regulators

The regulator is of course the main steam stop valve of the locomotive. It must control the passage of the steam to the cylinders so that the driver has full control over his engine, it must have a gradual opening yet at the same time be capable of passing all the steam required by the cylinders when fully open.

In small models, the screw-down type of valve may be considered; this type of valve will not stick, if made of the right materials and handled properly, and it will not leak steam. It is also easy to make and fit, whether the engine is provided with a dome or not. The only real drawback of this type of regulator is the large amount of handle movement required to give a reasonable opening, though the use of a coarse

BOILER FITTINGS

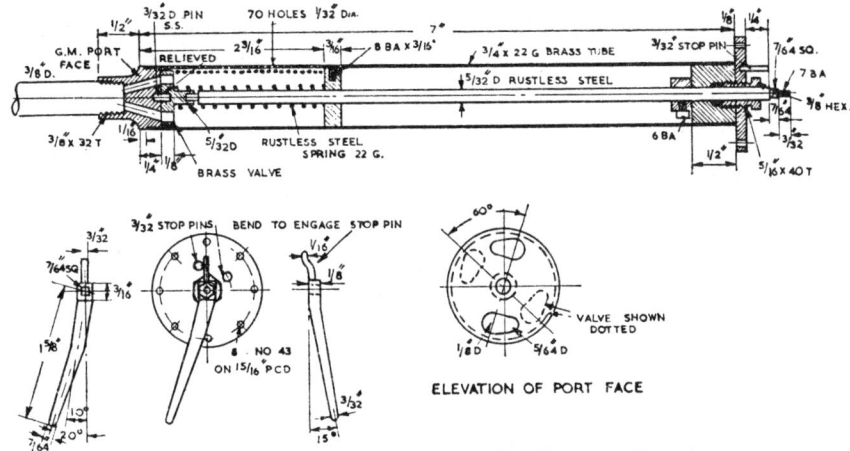

Fig. 97. Disc type Regulator

thread or even a two-start thread will generally overcome this. To ensure that the handle moves in the conventional direction of rotation, the thread could be a left-hand one.

For most $2\frac{1}{2}$ in. gauge engines, the main steam pipe can be about $\frac{3}{16}$ in. diameter internally; while for $\frac{3}{4}$ in. scale, $\frac{9}{32}$ in. to $\frac{5}{16}$ in. is advisable.

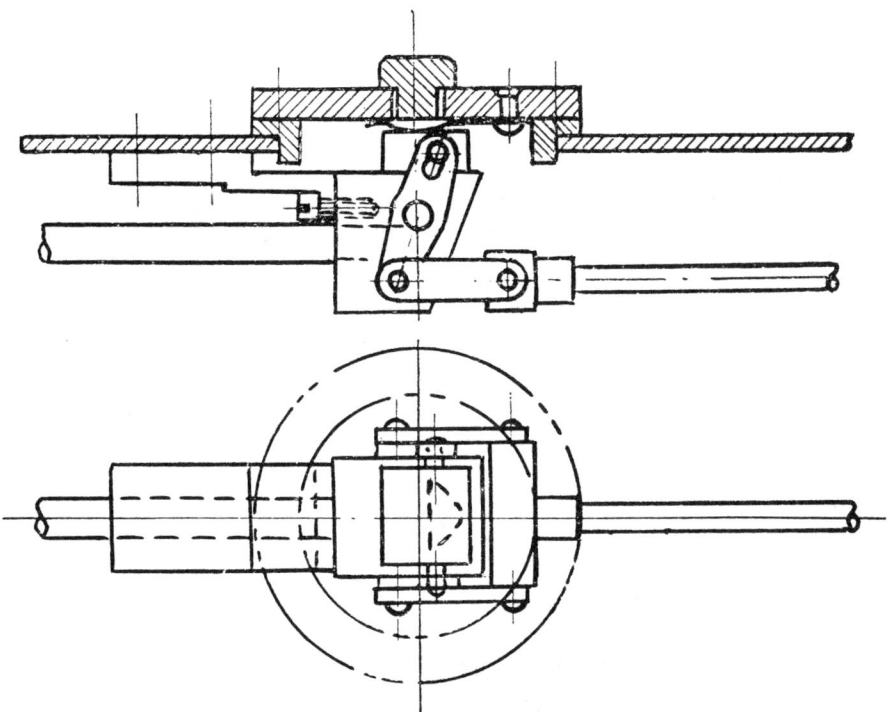

Fig. 98. Slide Valve Regulator

Fig. 97 shows a rotary type regulator. This type can be arranged with a large number of fine holes for the collection of the steam, or a single large stand-pipe can be fitted in the dome, the former arrangement being suitable for dome-less boilers. Another useful type of regulator is the slide-valve type, an example of which is shown in Fig. 98, while the poppet-valve regulator is a good one provided that care is taken in fitting it to a true surface on the backhead; if fitted direct to the backhead, leakage will occur sooner or later.

Although regulators of model boilers are sometimes fitted in the smokebox, this position is not an ideal one, owing to the much higher temperature reached. Also, it is usually found that assembly of the regulator from the smokebox end of the boiler is more difficult than from the backhead end.

The shape of the regulator handle is a matter for personal choice, the older type, working vertically in a quadrant, being very easy to operate unless the cab roof is low, while the more modern type suits a long, low-built cab. It is important to ensure that the handle is a secure fit on the control rod, either a squared fitting being used, or a small cotter and nut.

When considering suitable materials for regulators, a combination of rustless steel and drawn bronze, or cast bronze and drawn bronze should be considered. No mild steel can of course be used, while brass is only satisfactory for parts not subject to wear. The screws used to hold the flange of the regulator to the backhead may with advantage be made from rustless steel or phosphor bronze. These screws are subject to some stress, and may have to be removed on more than one occasion, so should be of ample strength for the job.

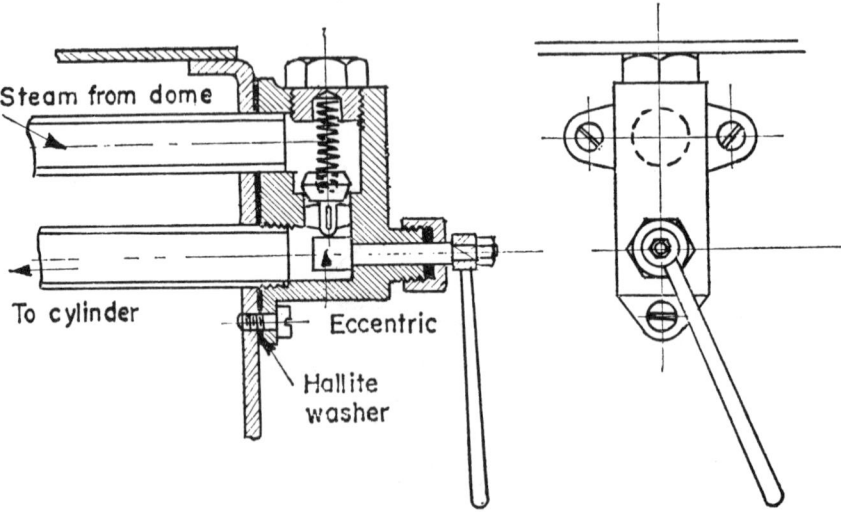

Fig. 99. Poppet Valve Regulator

BOILER FITTINGS 129

Safety valves

Most modern locomotives are fitted with the Ross "pop" type of safety valve. This is also quite a good valve to use in models and not at all difficult to make. The main advantage of the pop valve is the fact that the valve shuts down quickly with only a small drop in pressure, whereas the plain valve, particularly in small models, may allow an appreciable drop in boiler pressure before it closes properly.

In model boilers, pop valves are inclined to lift the water owing to the short distance between the valve seating and the water level. This defect can be overcome by plugging the bottom of the steam way and drilling a number of small inter-communicating holes at right angles. The use of the ball type of valve also reduces the violence of the pop action.

Where possible, two safety valves should be fitted to models larger than Gauge 1, one valve being set to blow off at a slightly higher pressure than the other. In the case of the valve fitted to Great Western locomotives, it is often difficult to arrange two valves inside the characteristic tapered brass casing, especially in the smaller scales. However one valve of large bore can be considered quite safe, provided that the valve is removed for cleaning at frequent intervals.

On some exceptionally large diameter boilers, difficulty is sometimes experienced in obtaining the necessary "headroom" for safety valves of the usual type, with the

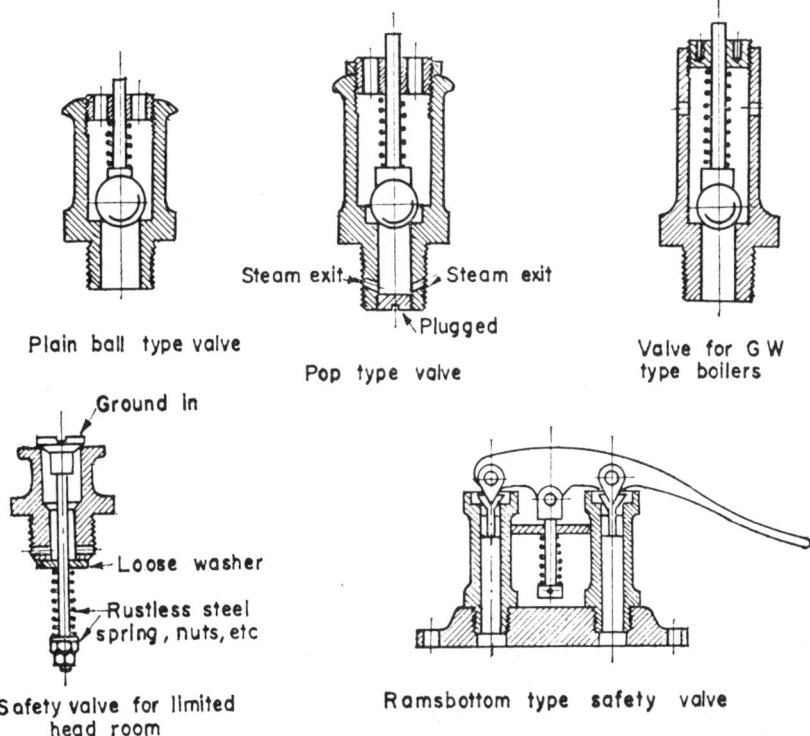

Fig. 100. Types of Safety Valves

springs above the valve seating. In such cases, the spring can be arranged below the valve which may have a coned face ground in against its seating. The spring must then be of rustless steel, otherwise rusting would set in very quickly.

Safety valves should be capable of ready adjustment without the necessity of removing them from the boiler. They are also generally provided with a comparatively coarse thread for screwing into the boiler bush. All safety valves should be removed frequently for examination, cleaning and adjustment.

As a guide to the size of orifice required in safety valves, the following dimensions may be found helpful:

Gauge O ...	...	One valve—$\frac{3}{32}$ in. dia. orifice.
Gauge 1 ...	...	One valve—$\frac{1}{8}$ in. dia., or two $\frac{3}{32}$ in. dia.
$2\frac{1}{2}$ in. gauge	...	One valve—$\frac{3}{16}$ in. dia. or two $\frac{5}{32}$ in. dia.
$3\frac{1}{2}$ in. gauge	...	One valve—$\frac{1}{4}$ in. dia. or two $\frac{3}{16}$ in. dia.
5 in. gauge	...	Two valves—$\frac{1}{4}$ in.–$\frac{9}{32}$ in. dia.
$7\frac{1}{4}$ in. gauge	..	Two valves—$\frac{5}{16}$ in.–$\frac{7}{16}$ in. dia.
$9\frac{1}{2}$ in. gauge	...	Two valves—$\frac{7}{16}$ in.–$\frac{9}{16}$ in. dia.

Check Valves

Check valves, also known as clack valves, are non-return valves which are fitted on all water pipes feeding water into the boiler of the locomotive, and also on oil delivery pipes. In the majority of model locomotives they are simple valves fitted with a single rustless steel or bronze ball. The lift of the ball is generally restricted according to the duty involved. For instance where mechanically driven pumps are involved, the lift of the ball may be restricted to about one-eighth of the ball diameter; for slow-speed pumps or hand operated pumps. the lift may be about one-sixth of the ball diameter, while for use with injectors, the lift would be set at about one-third of the ball diameter.

The usual method of constructing the actual seating for the ball is to first use a drill of suitable size, follow this with a reamer, put through slowly and carefully; the upper chamber is then opened out with a drill and a "D" bit of diameter some-

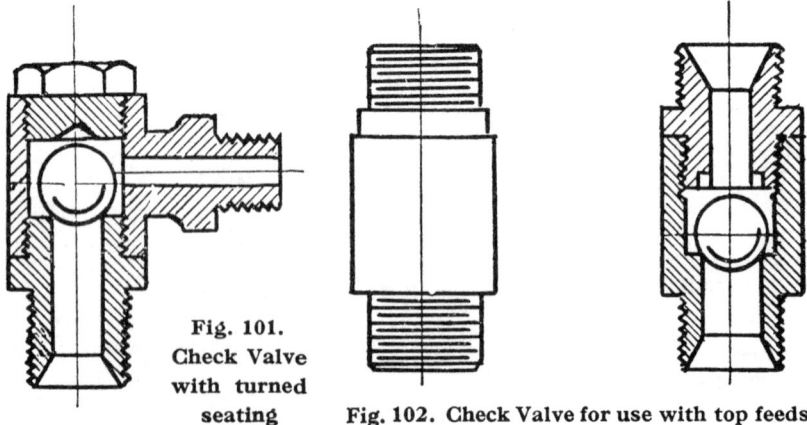

Fig. 101. Check Valve with turned seating

Fig. 102. Check Valve for use with top feeds

BOILER FITTINGS

what larger than the ball to be used. A steel ball of the same diameter as the ball to be used in the valve is then placed on the seating and given a sharp tap by means of a hammer and a length of brass rod. It is of course most important that the rod is held quite square, otherwise the seating will be spoiled.

A better method than the above is to make the seating for the ball as a separate fitting, so that it may be left with a turned finish, the fitting being afterwards pressed or screwed into the body of the check valve.

The best position for the admission of the feed water into the boiler is on top of the barrel, and not too close to the firebox. (i.e. "top-feed"). On Great Western locomotives, this top-feed takes the form of quite an elaborate series of trays through which the water is delivered in a number of very fine streams. In this way the feed water is heated thoroughly before it can come into contact with the metallic surfaces of the boiler.

In model boilers, it is not necessary to go to such lengths as the above arrangement, but the water can with advantage be directed towards the front of the barrel through a series of small holes as shown in Fig. 103. It is not essential to fit the check valves actually inside the top feed fitting; they may be arranged at some convenient position in between the pump (or injector) and the top-feed.

The check valves may also be fitted to the side of the barrel, as in Southern Railway and many other locomotives, or they may be put on the backhead, though this is not an ideal position unless the valves are receiving water only from injectors. The water delivery from injectors being hot, does no damage to the plates of the boiler.

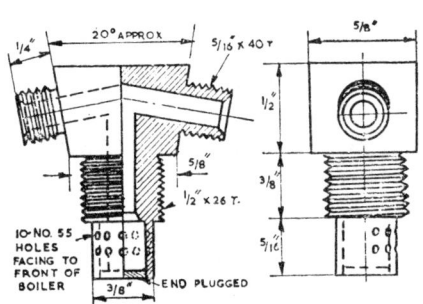

Fig. 103. Top Feed Fitting

Pressure Gauges

The making of the steam pressure gauge is not usually attempted by the model engineer as this is a fitting which, though simple in principle, lends itself more easily to quantity production than to hand work. The basic component of a small pressure gauge is the "C" tube. This is made from very thin brass sheet, closed and soft-soldered at the ends to render it steam-tight. One end of this tube is soldered to the union fitting, and a connection between the two made by carefully drilling through one wall of the C tube. The other end of the C tube is connected by a very light linkage to the pointer. When pressure is applied, the

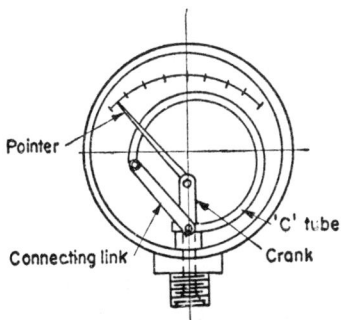

Fig. 104. Showing the principle of the model pressure gauge

C tube tends to straighten itself out, thus moving the pointer across the scale. Calibration is carried out against a large gauge of known reliability.

The pressure gauge should have a range at least 50 per cent higher than the normal working pressure of the boiler, and must be fitted to a U or syphon pipe to protect the internal mechanism from unnecessary heat. Although steam gauges can generally be obtained in sizes as small as ¾ in. dia. it should be remembered that the larger the gauge, the more likely it is to be reliable.

Steam Blowers

A steam blower is of course an essential fitting on any coal-fired locomotive. Without it, when the engine is standing, the furnace would quickly die out as its combustion depends entirely on an induced draught up the chimney.

Locomotives fired by methylated spirit lamps and paraffin blowlamps or high-pressure burners also require blowers, to avoid the possibility of a blow-back; the draught does not require to be nearly so strong as when solid-fuel is used.

In small models the blower usually consists of an auxiliary blast-pipe fitted with a fine jet laid alongside the main blast pipe, the jet being directed to the middle of the petticoat pipe or chimney. On larger models, the blower may be more elaborate, and have three or more jets, equidistant around the blast pipe.

The steam for the blower is generally conducted through a hollow longitudinal stay in the boiler, the blower control valve being mounted on the backhead end of this and taking its steam from some high point on the boiler.

Many model engineers prefer the single jet blower in engines up to ¾ in. scale, as where three jets are employed, these have of necessity to be of very small bore and

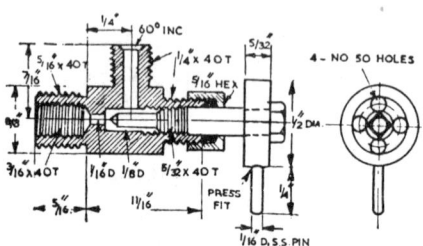

Fig. 105. Steam Blower Valve

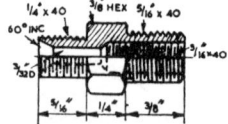

Fig. 106. Smokebox Connection for Blower

it is possible for one or even two of the jets to become blocked before the driver realises it, whereas if the single jet becomes blocked—a less likely happening because of its larger diameter—the driver is immediately aware of it.

Whatever design of blower is adopted, it is important to ensure that the jets are not easily knocked out of alignment, when sweeping tubes, etc.

BOILER FITTINGS 133

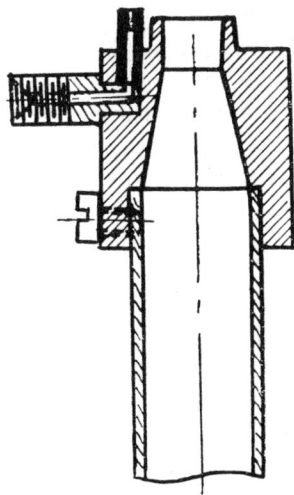

Suitable blower jet diameters are as follows:

Gauge O ...	One orifice ·030 in. dia.
Gauge 1 ...	One orifice ·033 in. dia.
½ in. scale...	One orifice ·036 in. dia.
¾ in. scale ...	One of ·050 in. or three of ·032 in.
1 in. scale ...	Three of ·036 in. dia.
1½ in. scale	Three of ·050 in. dia.
2 in. scale ...	Three of ·065 in. dia.

Snifting Valves

All locomotives fitted with piston valves or with slide valve cylinders with the valves on top should be provided with a snifting or anti-vacuum valve. It should be arranged so that the air is drawn into the "wet" header, thus when the regulator is closed and the engine is coasting, cool air is drawn through the superheater elements, preventing them from becoming overheated. If no snifter is fitted, the action of the pistons, when the regulator is shut, would create a partial vacuum in the superheater and steam pipes and there is always the danger of ashes and grit being sucked down the blast pipe.

Fig. 107. Blast pipe with single-jet blower

On L.N.E.R. models, the snifting valve is usually placed on top of the smokebox just behind the chimney. This is in fact quite a good position, as the valve can then

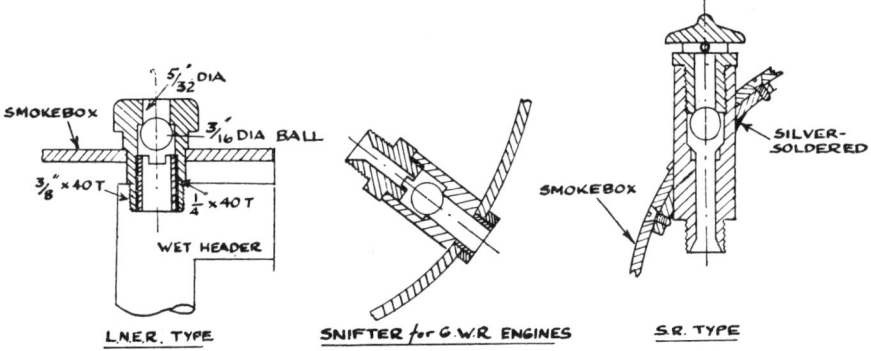

Fig. 108. Snifting Valves

be screwed straight into the header. On some Southern Railway locomotives, two snifting valves were provided, one on each side of the smokebox, while on many G.W.R. and L.M.S. engines, the snifter was situated in the lower part of the smokebox, just above or to the rear of the saddle. In G.W.R. and similar models, the snifting valve may be connected to the wet header by means of a pipe, laid inside the smokebox and close against the inside wall of the latter so as to avoid the blast pipe, main steam pipe, etc.

When fitting snifting valves, great care should be taken to ensure that there is no leak of steam, where the valve is attached to the header, and also that there is no possibility of air getting into the smokebox, otherwise the steaming of the locomotive will be impaired.

Steam Whistles

The difficulty in the model steam whistle is to obtain a realistic note, at the same time keeping the overall dimensions within reasonable limits. If the whistle is made to scale proportions, the note emitted would be a very poor one, of small volume and too high in pitch. On some railways, the pitch of the whistles used was very high, e.g. the old Great Northern and the L.N.E.R., and in such a case the problem can be solved by using a long thin-walled tube about $\frac{5}{16}$ in. dia. for a $\frac{3}{4}$ in. scale engine, and fitting the whistle under the footplate just inside the valance edging. A pipe is then carried to the whistle from a valve on top of the backhead.

A simple design of whistle which will give a reasonably deep note suitable for a Great Western model is shown in Fig. 109. For a $\frac{3}{4}$ in. or 1 in. scale model, the whistle tube might be made $\frac{3}{4}$ in. O.D. and thin-walled. The pipe from the operating valve may be about $\frac{3}{32}$ in. O.D., as a large volume of steam is not required. The whistle tube is first made fairly long and a tuning plunger fitted to the outer end. This might consist of a cork or rubber plug attached to a rod and arranged so that it can be slid up and down the tube while the tone and pitch of the whistle is tried out under actual service conditions, i.e. using the full working pressure of the boiler. When the desired note has been obtained, and this may involve some alteration to the size of the whistle opening, the effective length of the tube is marked off and a permanent metal end fitted to the tube.

Wherever the whistle is fitted, it is important to remember that the opening must be arranged at the bottom of the whistle, and the outer end of the whistle tube set very slightly higher than the pipe end, so that if any water condenses in the tube, it can run out through the opening.

A very deep-toned whistle, suitable for L.M.S. Stanier models, can be made by using a short whistle tube of the type described above, and fitting to it a soundbox. The soundbox can be made of tube, of length approximately equal to its diameter, the diameter being about three times the diameter of the whistle. The soundbox is arranged on top of the whistle tube, with an inter-connecting hole of diameter

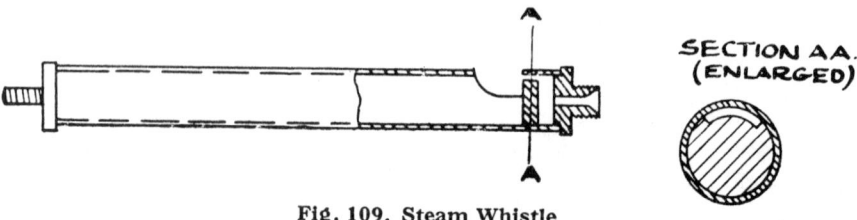

Fig. 109. Steam Whistle

BOILER FITTINGS 135

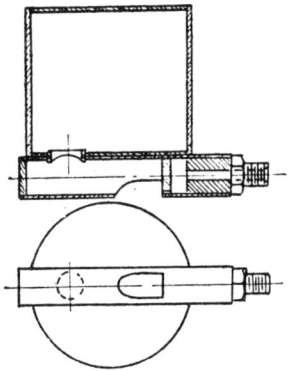

Fig. 110. Deep-note whistle

somewhat less than the diameter of the whistle so that the jet of steam is blown straight across this interconnecting hole. The exact size of the various components is best determined by experiment, using steam from the locomotive's own boiler.

An added touch of realism can be obtained, when using one of these "outsize" whistles, by fitting a scale size dummy whistle in the usual position on the boiler, and running a very small diameter pipe from the whistle valve to the dummy. Thus when the whistle valve is operated, a fine jet of steam will issue from the dummy whistle.

Turrets and Whistle Valves

A "turret" or "manifold" is a combination fitting arranged on the top of the firebox and usually just inside the cab with branches to supply steam to various fittings such as the steam blower, the pressure gauge, injectors, steam brake, etc. The reason for this is not only convenience in arranging the various pipes, valves, etc. but to ensure that all these accessories receive dry steam. Opportunity is generally taken to incorporate the whistle valve in this fitting. The simplest form consists of a rustless steel ball, inside the body of one of the branches of the turret, which can be pushed off its seating for blowing the whistle, by means of a small pin and lever. For additional security, a compression spring is located on the other side of the ball to ensure its seating correctly when the whistle is not in use.

The steam valves themselves are often placed in the turret for supplying steam to injectors, steam brakes, etc. Apart from its value in supplying dry steam, a turret saves having to drill and tap a large number of holes in the boiler.

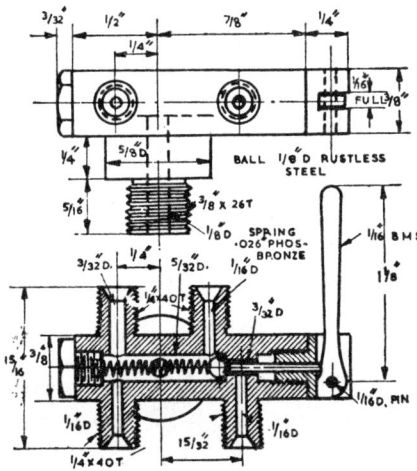

Fig. 111. A Steam Turret and Whistle Valve

136 MODEL STEAM LOCOMOTIVE CONSTRUCTION

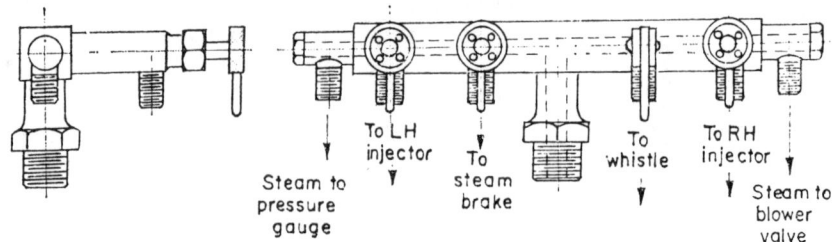

Fig. 112. Manifold incorporating Whistle Valve

Blow-Down Valves

All locomotive-type boilers should be fitted with at least one, and preferably two, blow-down valves. These are located on each side of the firebox immediately above the foundation ring at the lowest point possible. Where the layout of driving or coupled wheels permits, a good plan is to provide a large opening, circular or rectangular, in the mainframes on both sides of the locomotive, through which the

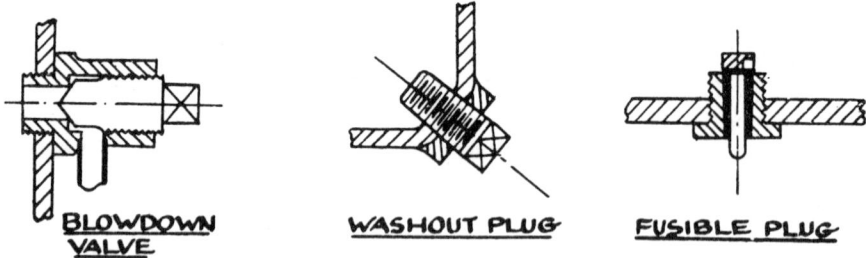

Fig. 113

blow-down valves can be screwed into the firebox. They can then be operated immediately after a run without difficulty.

Unless only distilled water is used in the boiler (an inconvenient and expensive business) solid matter from the water will gradually become deposited all over the inside of the boiler, but particularly around the lower part of the firebox and on the foundation ring, where circulation is sluggish. This trouble applies particularly in districts where the water is hard; but if the blow-down valves are used after the completion of every run, such deposits will be much slower in forming, and the boiler will remain in good condition for longer periods between removals from the frames for proper cleaning.

In large model boilers, washout plugs should also be provided, in the corners of the firebox; bosses for these may be welded on, or silver-soldered, in order to give greater depth of thread. The plugs themselves may have a standard taper thread, though a parallel coarse thread can also be used.

Fusible Plugs

Fusible plugs are always fitted to full-size locomotive boilers, and should be fitted to all model boilers which are riveted and soft-soldered, as they protect the crown of the firebox in the event of the feed water failing. Brazed boilers in which soft-solder has been used over stayheads and nuts should also be fitted with at least one fusible plug.

Most fusible plugs for model boilers consist of a copper rivet soft-soldered into a screwed plug which is put into the crown of the firebox from the inside, being arranged near the front end of the firebox. If the firebox plate is on the thin side, the plug should be screwed into a bush which is previously silver-soldered to the plate. The head of the copper rivet may be so shaped that if the solder melts through the overheating of the firebox, the rivet itself is not blown completely through the plug, but enough steam is allowed to pass to warn the driver and to release the pressure.

Boiler Expansion Joints

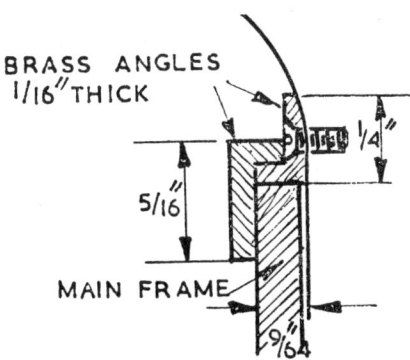

Fig. 114. Boiler Expansion Joint

Boilers are normally held down rigidly at the smokebox end, the smokebox being bolted securely to the saddle and the latter to the mainframes. This means that at the firebox end, the boiler must be allowed to move longitudinally to allow for expansion and contraction.

A typical expansion joint is shown in Fig. 114. This is made from two lengths of brass angle on each side of the firebox. The upper angle is screwed to the firebox with countersunk screws, these being put in with a smear of plumbers' jointing on the threads to prevent any chance of leakage. The lower angle is held to the mainframe by hexagon head screws into tapped holes in the latter, and holds the upper angle firmly down on to the top edge of the frame, while allowing the firebox to move longitudinally.

Chimneys and Domes

The chimneys and dome covers fitted to model locomotives are generally made from gunmetal castings, though brass rod may be used for the smallest gauges.

A chucking spigot may or may not be provided on the casting; (in my experience, if a spigot *is* provided, it is usually too short to be any use!) but it is not usually difficult to chuck the chimney externally just firmly enough to enable the inside to be bored. After boring, the underside may be hand filed to fit the smokebox, but a more accurate method is to fly-cut the underside in the lathe.

Before fly-cutting, a brass mandrel can be turned up, a push fit into the bore of the casting, leaving about 2 in. above the top of the casting. Two flats are now filed on the extension part of the mandrel, the chimney is soft-soldered to it, and the mandrel clamped under the lathe tool-holder at centre height. The cutter, held in the three-jaw chuck, and supported additionally by the tailstock, is set out to describe a circle equal to the diameter of the smokebox, Light cuts should be taken, the saddle being moved longitudinally, and the cutter revolved at a medium speed.

After the underside has been attended to, the brass mandrel is unsoldered from the casting, and the outer part of the mandrel turned circular again. The chimney is then mounted on the mandrel once more and the outside and top finished to shape. If the model engineer is expert in the use of hand tools, these would of course be used to finish the external shape of the chimney, although it is perfectly possible to use the slide rest in the orthodox fashion. A tool similar to a parting tool should be ground up, but with both corners well radiused. By turning both the top-slide and the cross-slide handles at the same time, the required shape can be produced, the chimney being then finished off with round needle files (held in wooden handles for safety's sake) and emery cloth cut in narrow strips.

Chimneys are generally made a tight push fit over the inner liner or petticoat pipe and require no further fixing except in very large models, where very small hexagon screws may be used around the base, put into tapped holes in the smokebox.

Dome covers should for preference have a good spigot on the top, so that the underside may be fly-cut to match the boiler, and the inside of the casting bored in order that the cover may be made a push fit over the inner dome. A brass mandrel can then be fitted by drilling right through the dome casting, the mandrel being turned with a small spigot on the end to suit this hole. It is soft-soldered to the dome, which can then be turned and finished off in the usual way. After melting off the brass mandrel, the small hole left in the top of the dome is used to take a single hexagon-head screw, which holds the cover down on the inner dome.

CHAPTER THIRTEEN

Lubrication, Pumps, Injectors, Brakes

Cylinder Lubrication

The principal types of cylinder lubricator in use on model locomotives are the hydrostatic, with or without sight-feed, and the mechanical.

The simple displacement lubricator is seldom used today on locomotives larger than Gauge 1. The chief reason for this is the general use of superheated steam. With saturated steam, the failure of the lubrication system for a short period is not a very serious matter, but with high temperature superheated steam, the effect might well be disastrous, especially where gunmetal cylinders with soft packing are in use.

In the displacement lubricator, the steam is arranged to condense on the surface of the oil; the water so formed, being heavier than oil, sinks to the bottom of the container. The oil thus rises until it reaches the level of the outlet, when it flows into the steam chest. But the action of this type of lubricator is seldom regular, in addition it sometimes "gulps" oil into the cylinders on the regulator being closed, due to the sudden drop in pressure in the steam pipes and steam chests. A displacement

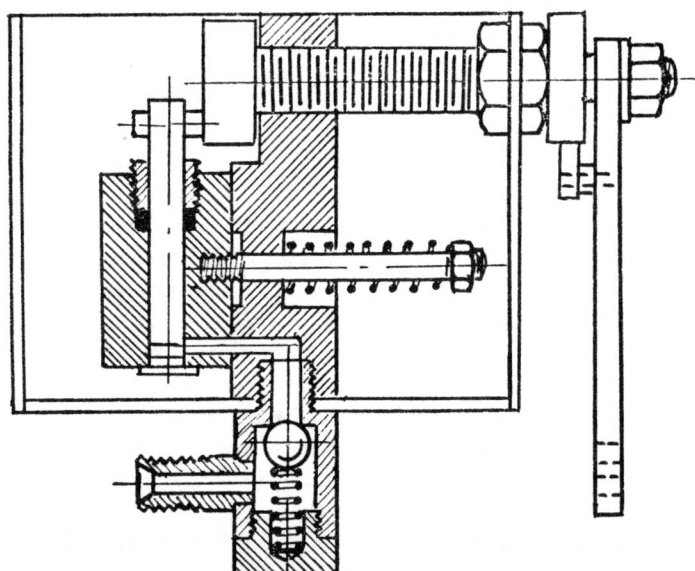

Fig. 115. "LBSC" Type Mechanical Lubricator

lubricator should not be placed too close to the cylinders, in order that it may keep cool in service; it should be fitted with a separate inlet pipe for the steam, and outlet pipe for the oil, and a small pin valve for adjustment. It should also have a drain valve at the bottom of the container, to allow the condensed water to escape.

The sight-feed lubricator was perfected by the old Great Western Railway, and although this type of lubricator is based on the displacement principle, the details are much more elaborate. The steam is taken from a turret on the top of the backhead. The regulator handle is provided with an extension connected to a controlling valve, which is so arranged that oil is admitted to the cylinders just before the regulator allows the steam to reach them. The steam for the lubricator is taken from a small cock on the turret, from which two coiled pipes act as a condenser on the inside of the cab roof; the pipes then lead to a two-way cock on the top of the lubricator. The oil rises and flows to the sight-feed control valves. The oil for the regulator flows through a small pipe forwards to the smokebox. The oil supply for the cylinders flows through small pipes to the controlling valve mentioned previously, and is picked up by the steam from the cock on the turret in this valve, from which it is carried forward to the cylinders.

Matters are so arranged that when the locomotive fitted with the Swindon sight-feed lubricator is coasting, little steam and oil is fed to the cylinders. When the regulator is fully closed against its stops, the lubricator feeds a few more drops of oil and then stops altogether; thus a small quantity of oil remains in the pipes ready to be fed to the cylinders when the engine is started again.

Model lubricators made on the above principle have been successfully made in sizes down to $\frac{3}{4}$ in. scale.

In spite of the success of the sight-feed lubricator in full-size practice, the mechanical lubricator is now almost universal on British Railways, and is equally popular in models. Two main types are in use, the oscillating cylinder type, and the Wakefield type.

Locomotives up to $\frac{3}{4}$ in. scale are generally fitted with a mechanical lubricator having a single cylinder and ram, but on engines of larger scale, it is desirable to fit a lubricator having two or three cylinders, each supplying oil to a separate (traction) cylinder.

One advantage of the mechanical type of lubricator is that the amount of oil fed to the cylinders is roughly proportional to the speed of the locomotive; even so, when a model is working on a short "up and down" track, it generally requires rather more oil than when running on a continuous track, and therefore some means of varying the output of the lubricator while the engine is in steam is desirable. One method of adjusting the output is by means of a simple by-pass arrangement. A needle valve of very fine bore is used, the spindle having a fine thread to allow of accurate adjustment. Another method is to arrange for the stroke of the oil pump to be varied, or for the effective stroke in relation to the oil inlet to be altered.

Mechanical lubricators should be fitted with two check or non-return valves, one being arranged on the lubricator itself, the other being fitted to the steam pipe or steam chest. Where possible, the oil delivery should be made against the flow of the steam from the superheaters, as this helps to break up the oil into fine particles.

LUBRICATION, PUMPS, INJECTORS, BRAKES

Small ball-type check valves are suitable, the ball being kept on its seating by a light compression spring. The spring should not be allowed to bear directly on the ball or it may have a tendency to push the ball slightly to one side. A suitable oil check valve is shown in Fig. 116A.

It is a good plan to fit a slightly stronger spring to the check valve on the lubricator itself than to the delivery check valve as the latter is always subjected to the full steam pressure (when the regulator is open).

It might be thought that two spring-loaded check valves would be rather a severe load for the lubricator to overcome, in addition to the steam pressure. However, this is not so. Tests have shown that mechanical lubricators of the types described, given reasonable workmanship, can deliver oil at pressures as high as 400 to 500 lbs. per square inch.

Mechanical lubricators seldom fail in service. When they do, the trouble is nearly always due to the check valve or valves not seating properly. Of course, care must be taken to ensure that the oil used is absolutely clean and of a suitable grade. A graphited oil should not be used in these small lubricators, but a proper grade of steam cylinder oil such as Shell Valvata or a similar grade by a well known maker.

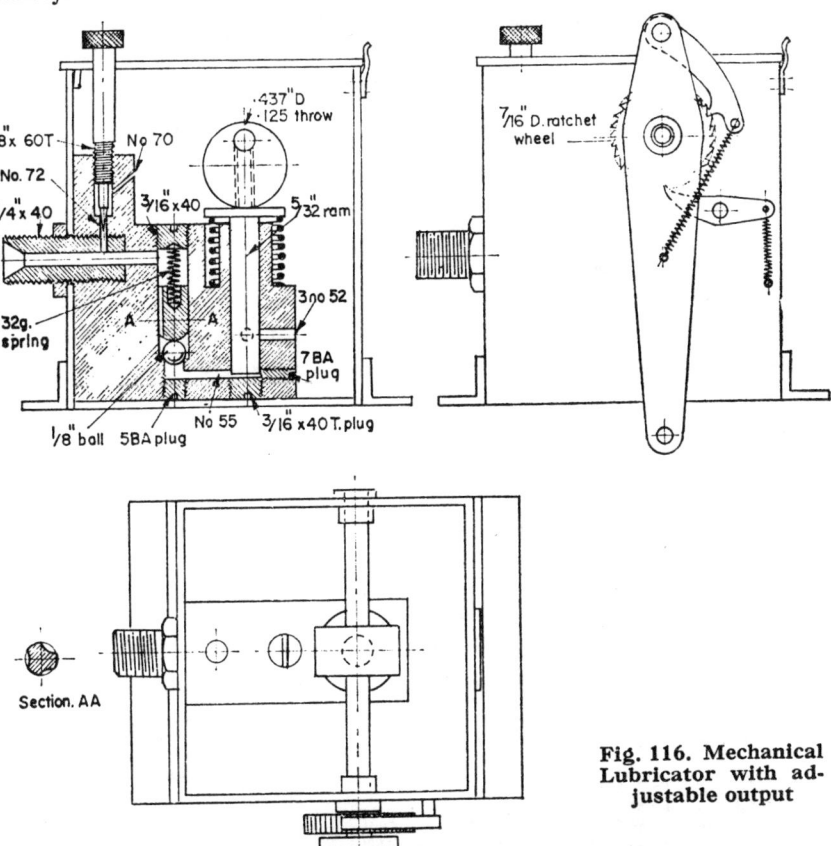

Fig. 116. Mechanical Lubricator with adjustable output

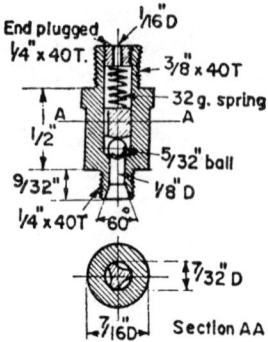

Fig. 116a. Oil check valve for use with lubricator Fig. 116

It has been the custom for some time to fit the mechanical type of lubricator between the frames just ahead of the smokebox. Although this position ensures that the lubricator will be out of sight, and therefore the outward appearance of the model locomotive is not spoilt by the out-of-scale size of the oil container, my opinion is that this position is a very bad one. For one thing, it is very difficult to prevent dust and ashes from the smokebox getting into the oil container when the tubes are being swept, or even when the smokebox door is only opened for adjustments. It is also difficult to reach the driving and ratchet mechanism for cleaning and adjustment, while if the lubricator is fitted with a needle valve or some other method of altering the quantity of oil supplied, this too is difficult to reach.

Probably the best position for a lubricator from the point of view of maintenance and adjustment is that generally adopted on the full-size engine, i.e. on the platform just behind the cylinders. While this position may offend advocates of strictly scale appearance, at least in the smaller gauges, the advantage of easy maintenance, cleanliness, and also the ease with which the driving mechanism may be fitted up, may outweigh the disadvantage mentioned.

When lubricators are fitted between the mainframes, the drive is generally taken from an eccentric and strap mounted on a suitable coupled axle. The drive is also often taken from some convenient point on inside valve gears. Lubricators mounted on the platform are usually driven from the expansion link of a Walshaerts' valve gear, or from a lug attached to the radius rod or eccentric rod. The drive has even been taken from the main crosshead, by means of a reducing linkage, while in models such as Great Western prototypes with outside cylinders and inside valve gear, the drive may very conveniently be taken from the valve crosshead.

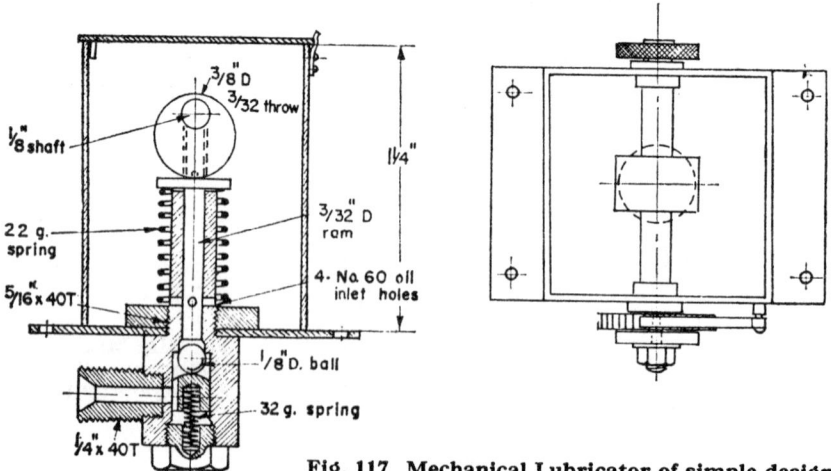

Fig. 117 Mechanical Lubricator of simple design

General Lubrication

All bearings and rubbing or sliding surfaces of the model steam locomotive should have adequate lubrication. Even in ¼ in. scale models, the bosses of coupling and connecting rods, and some of the larger valve gear levers and links may be provided with proper oil boxes, the latter generally having a fine hole at the bottom of the oil reservoir communicating with the pin itself, while on models of 1 in. scale and above, the lubrication arrangements may follow full-size practice more closely.

The lubrication of driving and coupled and bogie axleboxes and their respective horns should not be left to chance. Where space permits, an oil recess may be provided underneath the axle journal and proper felt pads fitted. Oil boxes can be mounted on the platform, on splashers, on the front of side tanks, or on the insides of cab side-sheets. Inside the oil boxes, small trimmings can be fitted. Trimmings for small models should not be made from worsted as the strands are too coarse for the purpose. A better material to use is fine silk covered electric wire; this is twisted up tightly, and bent into the shape of a hairpin, the shorter leg of the trimming is then put into the oil box, and the longer leg fed down a small thin-walled copper pipe, to the axlebox or horn as required.

For models above 1½ inch. scale, a proper mechanical system may be considered, the lubricator being similar to those already described for cylinder lubrication.

Feed Pumps

Water feed pumps are not often used nowadays in full-size practice, their place having been taken by injectors. For model locomotives, however, they have certain

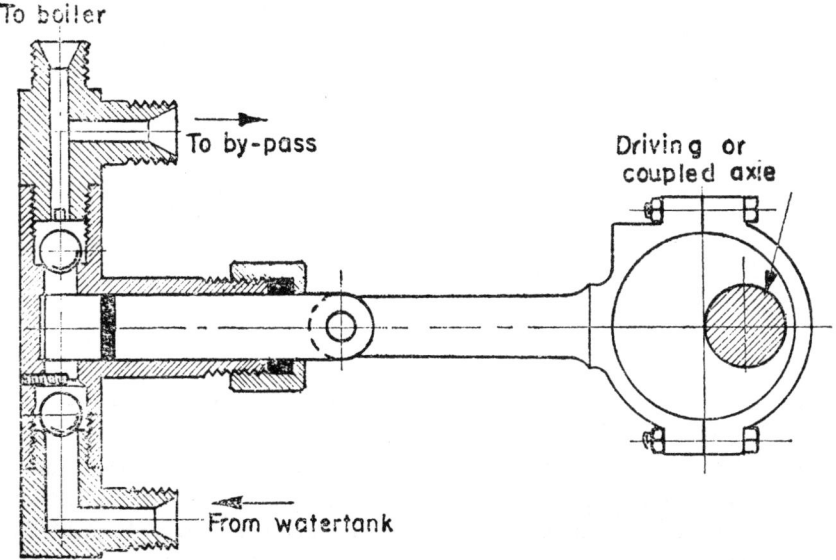

Fig. 118. An axle-driven feed pump

advantages; on continuous running the rate of feed can be adjusted by means of a simple by-pass arrangement to keep the water-level in the boiler practically constant.

Most pumps for small scale locomotives are mounted between the frames, the pump body being either cast integral with a suitable frame stay, or a separate pump body is bolted to a cast frame stay. The pump ram is usually driven by an eccentric mounted on one of the driving or coupled axles as convenient. The eccentric rod should be as long as possible, to avoid unnecessary angularity which causes wear on the gland or end of the pump barrel. The ram too should be made of reasonable length. Another method of driving this type of pump is to arrange for the eccentric rod to drive on to a link suspended from some suitable point on the mainframes above the pump, and to fit a short link connecting the eccentric rod to the ram.

On locomotives above $\frac{3}{4}$ in. scale, it is advisable to use two pumps, set at 180 deg. to one another, rather than a single large pump. This will be found to equalise the thrust of the rams to some extent, eliminating jerkiness in running.

Where sufficient space is available, the ram may be arranged to work right through between the suction valve and the delivery valve, a method which prevents any

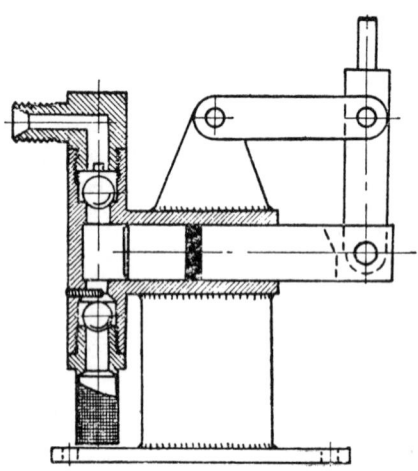

Fig. 119. Tender Hand Pump

possibility of air being trapped in the pump. The valves are generally of the simple ball type, rustless steel or bronze balls being employed, the lift of the balls being positively restricted to about one-sixth of the ball diameter.

Many locomotive men prefer a crosshead pump to an eccentric driven pump, as the drive is direct, and provided the ram is carefully lined up, wear on the gland is negligible. Crosshead pumps may be situated either outside or inside the mainframes, the stroke being of course the stroke of the engine, while the bore may be about one-fifth the diameter of the cylinders. (for a 2-cylinder locomotive)

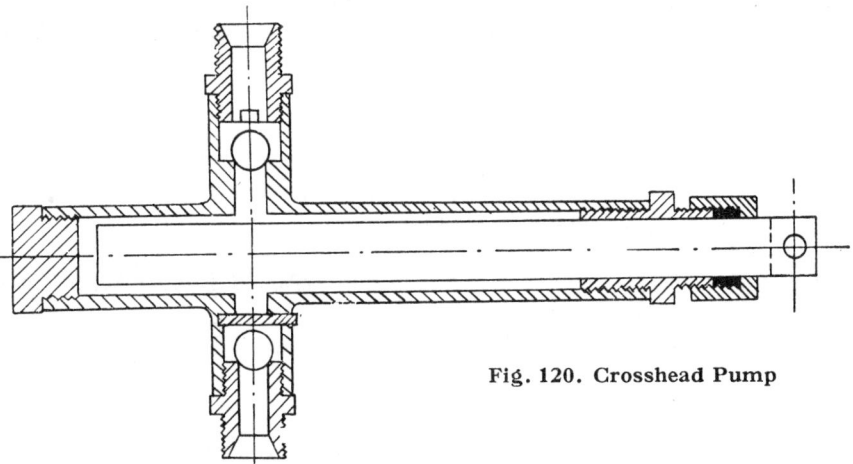

Fig. 120. Crosshead Pump

Where models of G.W.R. engines are concerned, a good plan is to fit the crosshead pump in the position occupied by the vacuum pump in the full-size locomotive; this can usually be done with very little alteration to the external appearance of such a pump.

All feed pumps should be fitted so that they can be removed from the engine for maintenance without too much difficulty. Too often one finds eccentric driven pumps screwed to the frames in such a way that it is impossible to reach the screwheads without dropping the driving and coupled wheels. The position of these fixing screws should be carefully determined on the drawing board so that they are accessible from the outside.

When a model locomotive fitted with the conventional type of feed pump is laid up for some time, it often happens that the ball valves stick to their seats, and the pump fails to function. This is generally due to the furring action which occurs with normal tap water. However the trouble can sometimes be cured without dismantling the pump, by giving the valve box a light but sharp tap with a small hammer. Apart from occasionally cleaning the valves and their seats, the only maintenance required on pumps is the adjustment of the glands (which should have a positive locking device to prevent the nuts slackening back in service), greasing of the pins and oiling of the eccentric straps, and the renewal of the gland packing material, which is usually of the graphited yarn type. At longer intervals, the gland nuts and the pins will require renewal; the ram itself should have quite a long life, especially if made of rustless steel.

It is difficult to specify exact dimensions for water feed pumps for model locomotives as the capacity required depends on the size of the boiler and cylinders, but the following may be taken as a rough guide:

$\frac{1}{2}$ *in. scale.* One pump $\frac{9}{32}$ in.–$\frac{5}{16}$ in. × $\frac{3}{8}$ in. stroke, or Crosshead pump $\frac{1}{8}$ to $\frac{5}{32}$ in. bore.

146   MODEL STEAM LOCOMOTIVE CONSTRUCTION

¾ in. scale.   Small engines: One pump $\frac{5}{16}$ in. × $\frac{7}{16}$ in. stroke.
Large engines: Two pumps $\frac{9}{32}$ in.–$\frac{3}{8}$ in. × $\frac{7}{16}$ in. stroke, or Crosshead pump $\frac{7}{32}$–$\frac{1}{4}$ in. bore.

1 in. scale.   Small engines: Two pumps $\frac{5}{16}$ in.–$\frac{3}{8}$ in. × $\frac{5}{8}$ in. stroke, or Crosshead pump $\frac{5}{16}$ in. bore.
Large engines: Two pumps $\frac{1}{2}$ in.–$\frac{9}{16}$ in. × $\frac{5}{8}$ in. stroke, or Crosshead pump $\frac{3}{8}$ in. bore.

1½ in. scale.   Small engines: Two pumps $\frac{3}{8}$ in.–$\frac{7}{16}$ in. × $\frac{7}{8}$ in. stroke, or Crosshead pump $\frac{7}{16}$ in. bore.
Large engines: Two pumps $\frac{1}{2}$ in.–$\frac{5}{8}$ in. × $\frac{7}{8}$ in. stroke, or Crosshead pump $\frac{1}{2}$ in. bore.

Although suggested sizes of pumps for 1½ in. scale locomotives are given above, for those who prefer pumps even in the larger type of model, a more satisfactory method of boiler feeding would be to use two injectors, one having a slightly lower feeding range than the other.

Suitable pipes for suction, delivery and by-pass for the above pumps would be as follows:

½ in. scale pumps   ⅛ in. dia. 30 s.w.g.
¾ in. scale pumps $\frac{5}{32}$ in. dia. 26 s.w.g. or $\frac{3}{16}$ in. 26 s.w.g.
1 in. scale pumps $\frac{3}{16}$ in. dia. 26 s.w.g. or ^{7} in. 26 s.w.g.
1½ in. scale pumps   ¼ in. dia. 26 or 24 s.w.g. or $\frac{9}{32}$ in. 24 s.w.g.

The water suction pipes from tenders or side tanks to the feed pumps must always be fitted with filters. These should be of large size but of the finest mesh and removeable for cleaning. They are generally made from the fine copper gauze obtainable from motor cycle spares dealers. The by-pass pipe should be direct and not longer than necessary, while the by-pass valve or cock must be of reasonable bore, otherwise there will be unnecessary losses through friction when the pumps are not feeding the boiler.

Steam Feed (Donkey) Pumps

Model locomotives are sometimes fitted with steam feed pumps, commonly called donkey pumps. These are basically miniature steam engines complete with valve gear, lubricator, etc., the pump ram being directly connected to the steam cylinder piston rod. They are usually double acting and may be fitted with one or two cylinders.

Although donkey pumps are most fascinating both to build and to operate, they cannot be regarded as particularly efficient as boiler feeders when compared with a good injector.

LUBRICATION, PUMPS, INJECTORS, BRAKES

Injectors

At one time the model injector was considered a somewhat unreliable item of locomotive equipment. This is certainly not true today, in fact hundreds of satisfactory injectors are now operating on locomotives as small as 2½ in. gauge. In many respects an injector is easier to make and erect than a pump, while the pipework involved is less elaborate.

The main advantages of an injector over a pump are as follows: An injector can be operated equally well while the locomotive is stationary, it can be fitted in a position that is really accessible and can be removed for cleaning or adjustment in a few minutes. An injector is more efficient than a pump, as the feed water put into the boiler is hot and there are no losses due to friction of moving parts.

The only real drawback to an injector is its inability (without complicated additional parts) to handle hot water; thus on small tank engines, they are not always

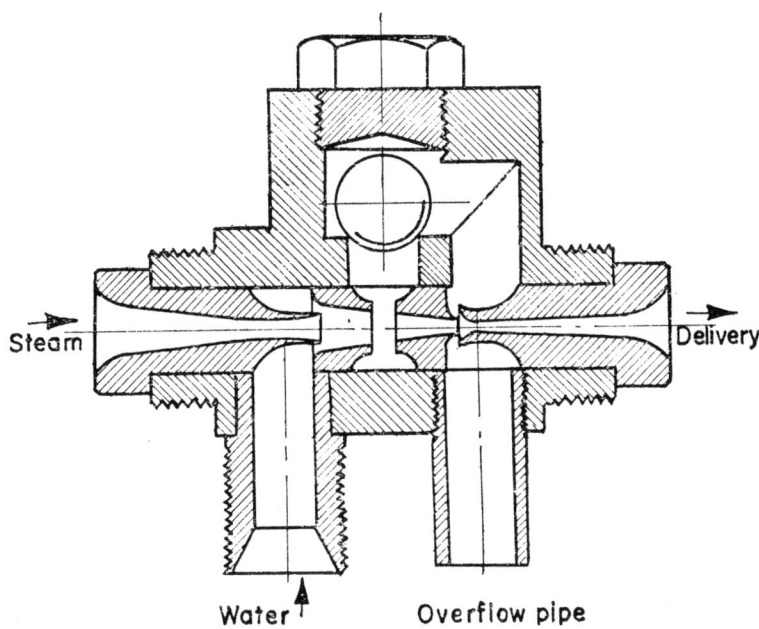

Fig. 121. Injector for Locos ½–1½ in. scale

reliable, unless the water carried in the side tanks is extremely well insulated from the heat of the boiler.

There are three distinct processes in the working of an injector. First the pressure energy of the steam has to be converted into kinetic energy, this then has to be imparted to the feed water, when it is again turned back into pressure energy, the feed water being given a higher pressure than that in the boiler. When an unbroken column of fluid is moving through a closed chamber, its velocity and pressure are interchangeable. Thus if the cross-sectional area of the chamber is increased, the velocity of the fluid passing through it is reduced, and vice versa, though there is always some loss through skin friction, etc. With the lowering of the velocity, the pressure is increased, so that the column of water is able to enter the boiler against the pressure in it.

A typical injector consists of three cones; the steam cone, the combining cone, and the delivery cone, each cone being mounted in line inside the body of the injector. Steam from the boiler is admitted to the steam cone, while the feed water is admitted between the steam and combining cones. A non-return valve is fitted above the combining cone, leading to an overflow pipe.

In the steam cone, the aim is to convert as much as possible of the pressure energy of the steam into kinetic energy. This is done by admitting the steam into a cone which first converges to speed up the flow of the steam, and then diverges, so that the steam is expanded until its pressure is lower than atmospheric.

Both the inside and the outside of the steam cone should be highly polished, where the steam and water make contact with it, and the nozzle should be machined to a knife edge in small injectors. The nozzle should be arranged to protrude into the larger end of the combining cone by an amount equal to the smallest internal diameter of the delivery cone, or slightly less. This last should be qualified by saying that the gap left between the nozzle of the steam cone and the entrance to the combining cone should not be so small that the smallest particle of dirt or foreign matter blocks it up.

Although the combining cone can be made in one piece, the two piece cone is probably more efficient. The angle of the combining cone is not very critical, but about 9 deg. is generally satisfactory.

In some model injectors, a large gap is left between the nozzle of the steam cone and the entrance to the combining cone, and the amount of water fed into the boiler is controlled by throttling the supply from the tender or side tanks. This, however, is bad practice, as an injector should be arranged to work properly with both the steam and water valves fully open. The outlet end of the combining cone should have some of the metal around the actual orifice removed, so as to allow plenty of space for the starting overflow.

The function of the delivery cone is to accept the high velocity column of water and condensed steam from the combining cone, where it is at low pressure, and to slow it down and increase its pressure to a higher figure than that in the boiler. The entry into this cone must be well radiused so as better to receive the water from the combining cone, and this part must also be highly polished for the best performance.

The internal diameter of the delivery cone determines to a large extent the output of the injector. It is therefore convenient to use this dimension as a basis, all other important dimensions being related to it.

The output of a small injector of this type can be obtained approximately from the following formula:

$$\text{Output in ounces per minute} = \frac{d^2}{40}$$

where d is the internal diameter of the throat of the delivery cone in thousandths of an inch.

Although the lifting properties of an injector are not essential in model locomotive work, there are definite advantages in the use of an injector that is capable of lifting, even though it is fitted below the level of the water in the tender or side tanks. Thus any leakage from the check valve on the boiler will pass out of the overflow, and even if the injector becomes overheated, the water besides flowing into the injector through gravity will be picked up by the suction of the lift, and the fitting will be quickly cooled down again. To ensure lifting properties, the first portion of the combining cone must be sufficiently long for it and the steam cone to act as an ejector, so that a partial vacuum is formed in the water space.

The body of a model injector may be cut from solid brass or a brass casting of good quality used. As much of the unwanted metal as possible should be cut away, so that if the injector does get overheated, it will cool down quicker. The external diameter of the various cones, where these fit into the body, should be very carefully turned, the steam and delivery cones being made a nice hand push fit, while the combining cone should be a fairly tight fit. When drilling the cones, a drill somewhat smaller than the minimum diameter of the cone should be put through first, followed by the appropriate reamer.

The necessary reamers can be made from silver steel, using a file in the lathe, the latter being run at a high speed. Using the angles of the cones given in Fig. 122, the following data may be found useful:

6 deg. = $1\frac{1}{4}$ in. per foot. = $\frac{5}{64}$ in. to a point in $\frac{3}{4}$ in. length.
9 deg. = $1\frac{7}{8}$ in. per foot. = $\frac{5}{32}$ in. to a point in 1 in. length
13 deg. = $2\frac{3}{4}$ in. per foot. = $\frac{5}{32}$ in. to a point in $\frac{11}{16}$ in. length.

The above figures are a close approximation, but quite accurate enough for the purpose. When filing the taper, the whole length should not be filed at once, but a short length filed first to a greater angle and the file gradually worked back, finishing with a dead smooth flat file of greater width than the length of the taper. When filing the flat, a start should be made at the thick end, and only very light pressure used. Heating for both hardening and tempering should only be done indirectly. If the flame were to be directed on to the end of the taper, the latter would be quickly damaged.

Fitting up injectors

An injector should, as mentioned previously, be mounted below the level of the tender or side tanks, where it will keep cool and be readily accessible. The overflow pipe must be short and arranged so that it can be easily seen by the driver. The steam pipe should not be too small in the bore otherwise there will be a loss of pressure at the steam cone. The steam is collected from a high position on the boiler, such as the turret or manifold, and the steam valve used should have a good bore and be reasonably quick-acting. The water valve also should be of good bore and quick-acting, and it is most important that it be fitted with a gland, so that no air shall be drawn in with the water.

A fine filter, as fine as can be obtained, is an essential fitting in the tender or side tanks, as the most common cause of small injectors failing is the clogging of the fine cones due to foreign matter in the water.

The delivery pipe to the boiler should be fairly direct and not too short, while the check valve may be given rather more "ball-lift" than is used for pumps. It is also an advantage to mount the delivery check valve directly on the injector, and fit an additional check valve a short distance from the actual point of entry of the water into the boiler. In this way the nuisance of "fur" in the valve can be minimised.

Suitable steam and delivery pipes for small injectors are as follows:

For injectors with delivery cones .014 in.–·019 in.—$\frac{1}{8}$ in. O.D. thin-walled.
For injectors with delivery cones ·020 in.–·023 in.—$\frac{5}{32}$ in. O.D. thin-walled.
For injectors with delivery cones ·024 in.–·036 in.—$\frac{3}{16}$ in. O.D. thin-walled.

Injectors fitted to tank locomotives are not generally so reliable as on tender locomotives as it is difficult to keep the water in the side tanks sufficiently cool. To avoid this trouble, the side tanks must be very thoroughly lagged, and a separate water tank, also lagged, fitted in the bunker under the coal space, the water for the injector being collected from this.

Further, a very large bore water cock should be fitted to the bottom of the bunker water tank, and large diameter balance pipes fitted between the side tanks and the bunker tank. Then if the water does get too hot for the injector to function properly, it can be quickly drained out, and the tanks refilled.

When trying out a new injector, if it is found that hot water comes out from the overflow, but does not go into the boiler, it is probable that it would do so if the pressure was raised. Thus the fault may be corrected by either increasing the size of the steam cone or by advancing the latter further into the combining cone.

If on the other hand, when first turning on the steam supply, one gets hot water, but on further opening the steam valve, this does not go into the boiler, but gives instead a mixed spray of water and steam, the trouble can probably be corrected by either reducing the size of the steam cone, or by withdrawing it slightly from the body of the injector. Once the injector is feeding correctly, it will generally continue to do so even if the boiler pressure drops to say half its normal figure. The knocking-off point can usually be delayed by partly closing the water valve.

Should the injector fail through dirt in the cones, the usual sign of this would be for steam plus a little water to be blown out from the overflow.

Injectors should be removed frequently for cleaning, and in this connection it should be remembered that if the cones are made of brass, they should be treated with care, as the application of hard steel wire, etc., to clear the cones could very easily score the polished surfaces, resulting in loss of performance.

Referring to Fig. 122 For working pressures around 100 lbs.
Where A is the basic diameter:

B = A × 3/2   G = J × 1/10
C = A   H = A × 7/2
D = A × 5/4   J = A × 14
E = A × 15   K = A × 18
F = J × 2/5

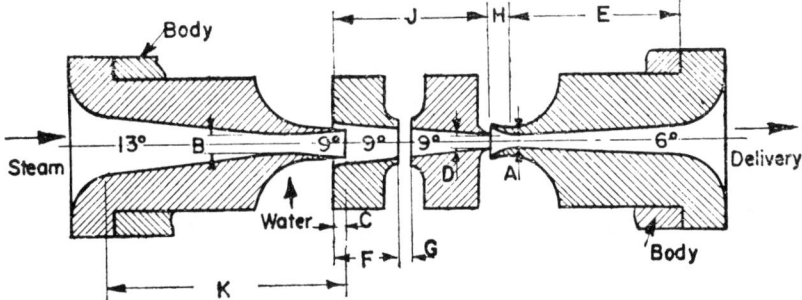

Fig. 122. Proportions of Cones for Injector Fig. 121

For any given injector, increasing the diameter of the steam cone, without altering the diameter of the other cones, will make the injector suitable for a lower pressure. Decreasing the diameter of the steam cone will make the injector suitable for higher pressure.

While the actual angle of the diverging part of the steam cone need not be altered for different working pressures, the higher the pressure, the greater the ratio between the area of the throat of this cone and the area of its exit.

Locomotive Brakes

On model locomotives below 1 in. scale, brakes are fitted merely for appearance as the weight of the engine is so much less than the weight of the average train that if the brakes were used the result would be the locking of the wheels, resulting in the engine sliding along the rails and probably wearing flats on the tyres.

When driving small locomotives, therefore, the driver is well advised to rely upon brakes fitted to his passenger car, where they can be strongly built without difficulty. Hand brakes, however, are very useful on the locomotive itself, in case the latter may be left unattended on the track at any time.

On locomotives of 1½ in. scale and above, the steam brake is on the whole quite satisfactory although sometimes rather slow in action due to condensation of the steam in a cold brake cylinder. For the most reliable results on large scale models, a simplified form of the Westinghouse compressed air brake may be used. This can also be fitted to the train for continuous braking.

The Steam Brake

In the steam brake, the brake blocks are actuated by means of a steam cylinder located between the frames, generally below the driver's footplate. Steam is taken from a suitable high point in the boiler via a quick-acting driver's valve in the cab. The brake blocks are strongly hung from the mainframes and the cross rods connecting each pair of hangers may be flat beams with their ends turned to form pins on which the hangers are pivoted.

For a non-compensated brake system, central pull rods are sometimes used, attached to each beam by forked joints with adjustable turnbuckles between each fork. In a compensated system, the pull rods are duplicated and pull against short compensating levers, these levers being connected by a short link to the adjacent brake beam and to the next pull rod at their other end. In this way, the actual force applied to each of the brake blocks of the locomotive is approximately equal.

The steam cylinder is generally fitted with a packed piston, similar to the traction cylinders, but not more than half the diameter of the latter, and an automatic drain valve should be fitted just above the head of the piston. This valve remains shut under steam pressure, but when steam is cut off, condensation creates a vacuum and the pressure of the atmosphere opens the valve. Alternatively, a very light spring may be arranged underneath the valve, to lift it off its seat when the steam is shut off.

Steam brake cylinders should be of fairly light construction and situated, whenever possible, close to the ashpan. In this way, the cylinders can be kept hot, and the trouble of condensation reduced to a minimum.

In the smaller scales, it is important to be able to remove the grate and ashpan of the model locomotive without delay in the event of emergency. With the normal arrangement of brake rigging, this is often impossible. It is, however, generally possible to dispense with the brake beam which lies immediately underneath the ashpan of the locomotive. In this case, the pull rods are run close behind the driving and coupled wheels and just below the mainframes; the hangers which are now left without a cross beam may be connected to short links brazed to the pull rods. In this way, all the space below the ashpan is left clear, so that instant removal of the grate is possible.

Vacuum Brakes

The vacuum brake is controlled by the pressure of the atmosphere on one side of a piston in a brake cylinder of considerably larger size than that used in a steam brake. The other side of the piston is kept at a pressure below atmospheric, which pressure may be anything between 15 and 21 in. of vacuum, the latter figure being the normal standard maintained.

As a guide it may be said that 20 ins. of vacuum gives a theoretical pressure on the piston of the vacuum cylinder of about 9·5 lbs. per sq. in. but in practice the effective pressure available in a model cylinder of the diaphragm type is more likely to be around 6 lbs. per sq. in., due to losses in the return spring and from the rigidity of

LUBRICATION, PUMPS, INJECTORS, BRAKES 153

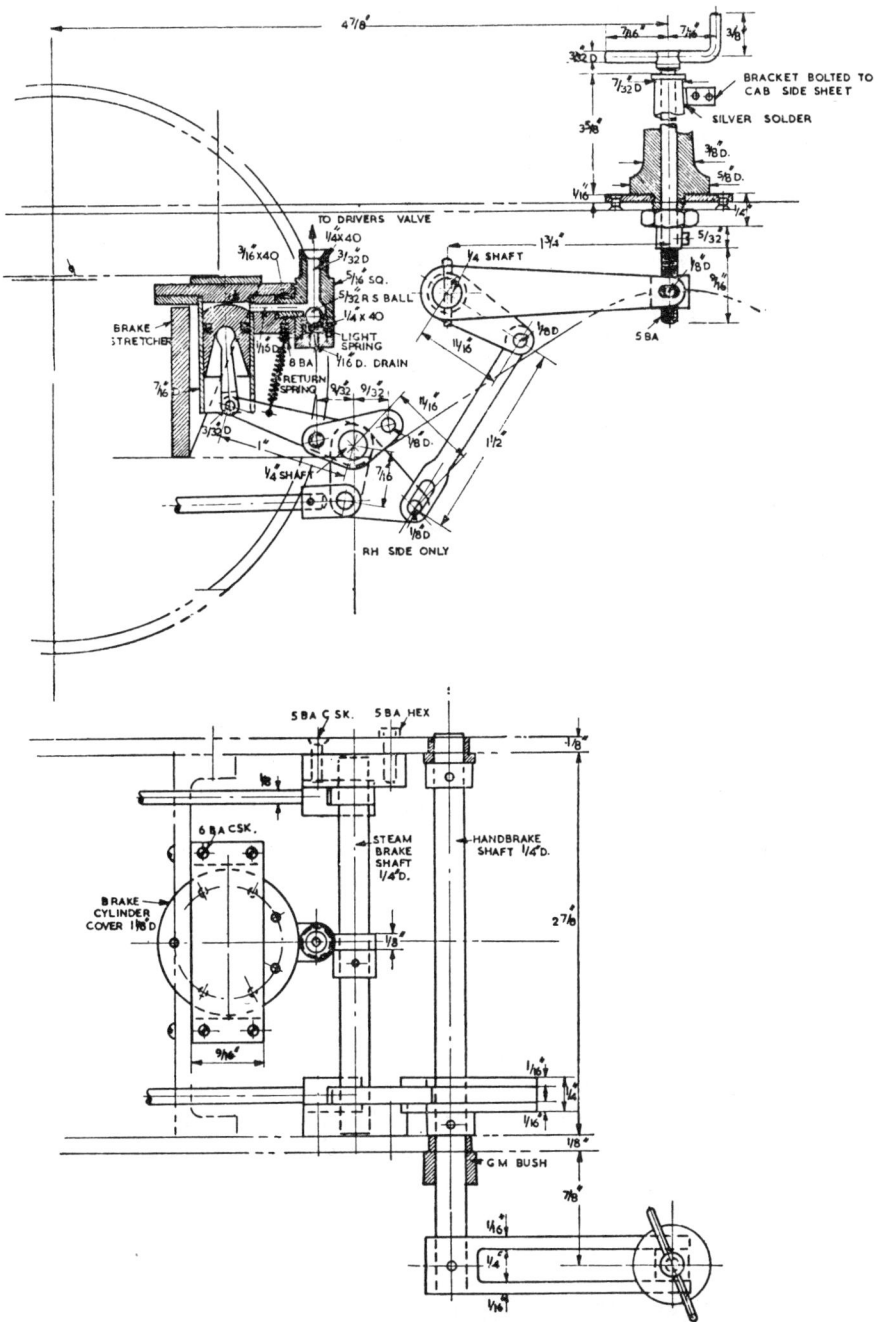

Fig. 123. Locomotive Steam and Hand Brakes

the diaphragm itself. Thus the effective pressure obtainable from a brake cylinder 3 in. diameter is only about 42 lbs. A driver's valve and an ejector to create the vacuum are fitted in the cab, steam being drawn from the manifold or other convenient point on top of the firebox, and the exhaust carried to the smokebox.

For model purposes, the "simple" vacuum brake is probably advisable. In this system, on steam being admitted to the ejector by means of the driver's valve, air

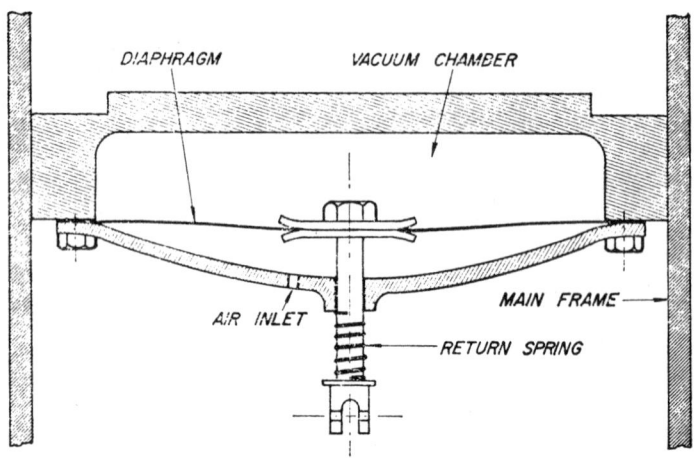

Fig. 124. A Vacuum Brake Cylinder

is evacuated from the train pipe system and the brakes applied. In the "automatic" vacuum brake, the vacuum is maintained in the train pipe throughout the period in which the train is in motion. This system is too wasteful of steam to be suitable for small scale models.

Air Brakes

Where continuous brakes are required on models of $1\frac{1}{2}$ in. scale upwards, a simple form of the compressed air brake should be considered.

In this system, an air pump, directly coupled to a steam cylinder, compresses air which is then stored in a brake reservoir on the locomotive. A brake cylinder, which can be much smaller than that used with the vacuum brake, is fitted to the locomotive and to each of the vehicles of the train. On opening the driver's valve, the compressed air operating on the pistons in the brake cylinders applies the brakes almost instantaneously.

An air pump governor is normally fitted, attached to the steam pipe leading from the locomotive boiler to the steam cylinder, and so arranged that when the pressure in the air reservoir reaches a pre-determined figure, the steam supply to the pump is automatically cut off.

CHAPTER FOURTEEN

Plutework, Tenders, Tanks and Fittings

Locomotive Superstructures

In full-size practice, locomotive superstructures are mainly built up from mild steel sheets from $\frac{1}{8}$ in. to $\frac{1}{4}$ in. thick, bolted, riveted or welded to angle, tee or channel sections. Very little wood is to be found, though it was often used for the footplate upon which the driver and the fireman worked, and on some of the older engines, wood was used for buffer beams, brake blocks, and cab roofs.

Steel is also very satisfactory for the footplates, platforms, cab sides, etc., of the larger scales of model locomotives, being very strong, not too difficult to work and low in price. Brass is used to a very large extent in the smaller gauges up to $\frac{3}{4}$ in. scale, and has the advantage of being non-rusting and easier to solder, especially where beadings and fine details have to be fitted. Nickel-silver has also been used in models, especially in the smaller gauges, it has all the advantages of brass and is also somewhat stronger; its high price however will deter most enthusiasts from using this metal to any extent.

Where side tanks or tender tanks are required to carry water, the use of brass is to be recommended, although in the larger scales, steel can be used for the outer plates, the actual water tanks being of thinner brass or copper sheet and fitted inside with asbestos or felt lagging between the plates. Where this form of construction is adopted, the inside of the steel plates must be carefully painted to prevent rusting.

Generally speaking 22 s.w.g. material will be found strong enough for most of the superstructure of Gauge "1" engines, 20 s.w.g. for $\frac{1}{2}$ in. scale models, 18 s.w.g. for $\frac{3}{4}$ in. scale, 16 s.w.g. or $\frac{1}{16}$ in. for 1 in. scale, and 13 s.w.g. or $\frac{3}{32}$ in. for $1\frac{1}{2}$ in. scale locomotives. Where mild steel is used, $\frac{1}{16}$ in. sheet is strong enough for all upper works except possibly tender floors where the tender is used to carry the weight of the driver.

The footplate or platform edging or "hanging bar" is generally made from hard brass angle, which may be screwed, or screwed and soft-soldered, or rivetted to the footplating. Where curved sections are required, especially the ornamental ends which butt up against the buffer and drag beams, sheet material is generally employed, this being blended into the angle on the straight portions.

The cab front or spectacle plate of the locomotive may be made in two pieces, the division being made on the vertical centre-line. This will be found convenient should it become necessary to remove the boiler at any time, It is usual to mount the spectacle plate on top of the firebox cleading rather than attempt to butt the lagging and cleading accurately up against the former. The spectacle plate of tank engines can sometimes be made in one piece as this may be built up from the level of the top of the tanks rather than from footplate level as in tender engines.

Cab roofs are often cut away quite considerably, even in tender locomotives, to give better access to the firedoor and backhead fittings. This is a pity as the appearance of the model is spoilt. However a good solution to the problem is to fit a large sliding hatchway in the cab roof which can be slid forward, leaving a U-shaped gap while actually driving. Tank locomotives call for special treatment in this respect; on the larger tank engines the whole of the back of the cab and possibly the upper part of the bunker can be made removeable for driving. On models of very small tanks, contractor's engines, etc., the fuel is often carried in a special compartment in the front of the passenger car carrying the driver, the back of the bunker being left completely open for easy firing.

Water Tanks

The side tanks of tank locomotives should be made to hold water and wherever possible, an additional water tank should be fitted below the bunker coal space. The three tanks are connected by large diameter balance pipes, so that they may be quickly filled through the one manhole. The connection between the tanks may be made by unions or by flanged joints, but in the smaller scales, the use of rubber tubes may be considered. These are quite satisfactory in service and very quick to dismantle. Air vents are fitted to each side tank, together with the usual details such as lifting lugs or rings, and fire-iron racks.

On all model locomotives up to 1 in. scale, a hand pump should be fitted to one of the side tanks for use in the event of emergency. This pump should be fitted at such a height that an extension handle may be coupled to it through a slot in the top of the tank, the slot having a cover plate which is put into position when the pump is not being used. The suction pipe of the hand pump is arranged to draw water from the bottom of the tank through the usual gauze filter.

On side tanks above $\frac{1}{2}$ in. scale, anti-surge plates may be fitted to reduce the surge of the water when the locomotive is accelerating or braking.

If it is desired to fit injectors to tank locomotives, every endeavour should be made to insulate the tanks from the heat of the boiler. The water for the injector should in any case be drawn from the bunker tank if fitted.

Locomotive details

To give a proper finish to the edges of cabs, tank and tender sides, etc., half-round brass wire from $\frac{3}{64}$ in. dia. may be used. The glazing of cab spectacles and side windows may be achieved with perspex sheet, upwards of $\frac{1}{16}$ in. thick, a thin "window-frame" of brass sheet being arranged on the inside, the two being held in place by small roundhead screws put through the frame and the perspex into tapped holes in the cab sides, the screws being filed off flush afterwards.

Footsteps can be built up from sheet steel and brass angles, the former being used for the hanging plate for strength. As nothing looks worse on a model locomotive than steps hanging down at all angles, it is a good plan to provide additional stiffening at the back of the plate. A passable imitation of the chequered footstep may be achieved by squeezing the step in the vice jaws (assuming these to be of the usual serrated type).

Handrails on model steam locomotives are generally made somewhat over scale for the sake of strength, but this should not be overdone or the appearance of the model will suffer. The handrails on full-size locomotives vary in size from $1\frac{1}{8}$ in. diameter to $1\frac{1}{2}$ in. diameter, and No. 15 s.w.g. will be found to look about right for a $\frac{3}{4}$ in. scale model, or $\frac{3}{32}$ in. to $\frac{1}{8}$ in. for 1 in. scale. The handrail knobs, which may be made from nickel-silver, or from brass, nickel plated, should not be screwed directly into the boiler where this can be avoided; the cleading, where fitted, may be locally strengthened by a short strip of thicker metal on the inside and the knobs screwed into this.

Smokebox Saddles

In most model locomotives, the smokebox saddle is a strong casting in gunmetal or cast iron as in addition to supporting the front end of the boiler, it acts as a main frame stretcher at an important point, usually between or adjacent to the cylinders. To carry the weight of the boiler better, the saddle may be provided with edges on each side bearing upon the top edges of the mainframes.

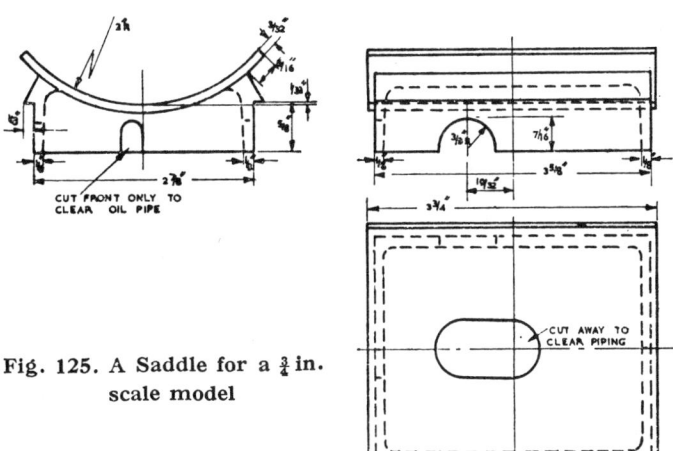

Fig. 125. A Saddle for a $\frac{3}{4}$ in. scale model

If the steam and exhaust pipes pass through the base of the saddle, it is important to make the necessary holes quite air-tight. This can be done by kneading asbestos sheet with water into a putty and pressing this all around the pipes.

The saddle is generally fixed to the smokebox by a row of small hexagon-headed screws along the side flanges, and the whole held down to the mainframes by means of screws put through clearing holes in the frames, into tapped holes in the saddle. The position of these holes must be carefully chosen so that the screws can be removed without disturbing outside cylinders.

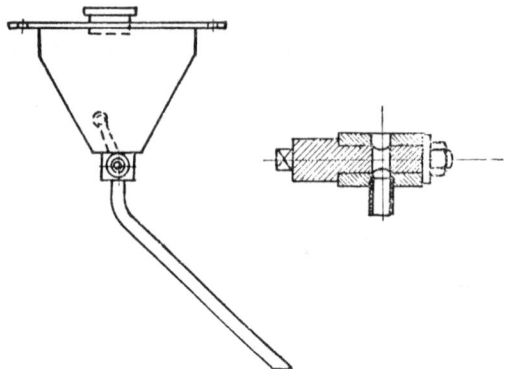

Fig. 126a. Sandbox and Valve for gravity feed

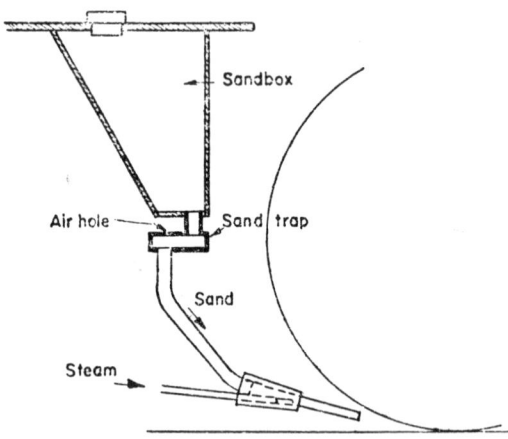

Fig. 126b. Steam sanding gear

Sanding Gear

Working sanding gear is sometimes fitted to models of $\frac{3}{4}$ in. scale and above; in fact it is quite possible to make sanding gear work even in $\frac{1}{2}$ in. scale. In the experience of many knowledgeable model engineers, sanding equipment is of rather doubtful value. The motion work of small model locomotives is so close to track level that it is very difficult to prevent the sand from eventually finding its way on to the bearings, axleboxes, etc., with disastrous results.

There is no doubt that the proper application of sand to the rails does assist the locomotive in starting, or in working on a heavy grade, but it is sometimes forgotten that a sanded rail can cause considerable drag on the wheels of the train, especially where heavy passenger trucks with rigid axles are in use on curved track.

A gravity sanding gear may be built up using sandboxes of the usual shape and fitting them with sand valves underneath of the usual "plug-cock" type; the bore of the valves should be of reasonable size, and a short lever on the valves can be connected to an operating lever in the cab.

If a steam sanding gear is required, a sand "trap" should be made up, (see Fig. 126B) the trap being fitted immediately below the sandbox. The sand trap is provided with an air hole, and the pipes connecting the trap with sandbox, and also the pipes carrying the sand to the railhead may be about $\frac{1}{8}$ in. dia. and thin-walled, for engines of $\frac{3}{4}$ in. and 1 in. scale. Into the pipe leading from the trap to the railhead, a fine steam pipe is introduced. The latter pipe may be about $\frac{1}{16}$ in. diameter outside, and fitted with a fine jet so that too much steam is not used. In use, the sand flows down into the trap, but will not pass any further until steam is applied; the sudden jet of steam, when the main steam valve in the cab is opened, causes a rush of air down the end of the sandpipe, and this draws the sand down from the trap.

In both gravity and steam sanding gears, it is most important that the sand be very fine, and kept quite dry, otherwise the equipment will fail in service.

Boiler Lagging and Cleading

The boilers of all steam models above $\frac{1}{2}$ in. scale should be properly lagged. This should be done before the boiler is finally fitted to the frames. For small models, asbestos string may be used, wrapped tightly around the boiler barrel, while the firebox top and sides may be covered with thin asbestos sheet. Felt is sometimes used, and this can be held in place by binding with fine iron wire. In either case, the lagging material is then covered by the cleading, which can be made from hard brass sheet. 30 s.w.g. sheet is about right for $\frac{1}{2}$ in. scale models, 28 s.w.g. for $\frac{3}{4}$ in. scale, and 26 s.w.g. for 1 in. scale. A good plan, before cutting the cleading sheet to size, is to make up patterns from stout paper or thin cardboard, the necessary holes for safety valves, manifolds, etc., being cut out in the pattern, and the brass sheet then cut to match the pattern.

Boiler bands should be about $\frac{5}{32}$ in. × 26 s.w.g. for $\frac{3}{4}$ in. scale models, and about $\frac{7}{32}$ in. × 24 or 22 s.w.g. for 1 in. scale. While rustless steel is the ideal material for boiler bands, nickel-silver is a good substitute, and even brass, though not so strong, can be used. To strengthen the ends of the boiler bands to take the securing bolts, a short piece of somewhat thicker material can be riveted or silver-soldered to each end of the band. Steel screws and nuts are then used to pull the ends of the bands in tight.

The boiler bands over the firebox may be fixed at their ends by small brass screws put into tapped holes in the firebox wrapper. These should be put in with plumbers' jointing on the threads to ensure that there will be no leakage.

Tenders

A locomotive tender is designed to carry the fuel and water required by the engine, and as far as British prototypes are concerned will almost certainly run on six or eight wheels, though a few older type locomotive tenders had only four wheels.

Nearly all six-wheel tenders have the frames outside the wheels, while the eight-wheelers may have outside frames and a rigid wheelbase as in the ex-L.N.E.R. "Pacifics", inside frames as in some Drummond tenders, or outside-framed bogies as on the ex-S.R. "Lord Nelsons". Many American locomotives were supplied with tenders which were mounted on six-wheel bogies.

The frames of tenders with rigid wheelbases are generally made in a similar manner to locomotive mainframes, being angled to the buffer and drag beams. The wheels and axles may need a little end-play, especially if sharp curves are to be negotiated, in which case the end-play of the centre axle should be made greater than that of the outer axles. Where bogies are used, the axles should only have enough end-play to allow of free running.

Tender springs, which are generally situated above the axleboxes and below foot-plate level, may be either solid castings, the actual spring being a coil spring concealed in a recess in the casting, or built up from spring steel or phosphor-bronze leaves. A built-up or laminated spring may be made less stiff by slotting out every leaf except the top and bottom ones, or by packing out between each leaf.

As tenders used with locomotives of $1\frac{1}{4}$ in. scale and above are generally used for carrying the driver, the frames of these should be made of stout material, well braced between the buffer beams, and the springs can be made of spring steel of the same scale thickness as the prototype. Ball races could be used with advantage in the axleboxes, but if plain bronze bearings are adopted, these should not be less than ⅝ in. diameter (or preferably 11/16 in.) and not shorter than 1⅛ in., these dimensions being for a 1½ in. scale tender.

A problem often met with in tender construction is the fouling of the buffer shanks or spindles by the ends of the frames. One method of avoiding this trouble is shown in Fig. 127 (b).

The interior of the model tender may be built up in a similar way to the full-size tender, though considerably simplified. The front coal plate may require modification in the interest of good access to the cab, it being remembered that the driver is shovelling forwards in filling his shovel, whereas the fireman of the full-size locomotive is filling his shovel in a backward direction.

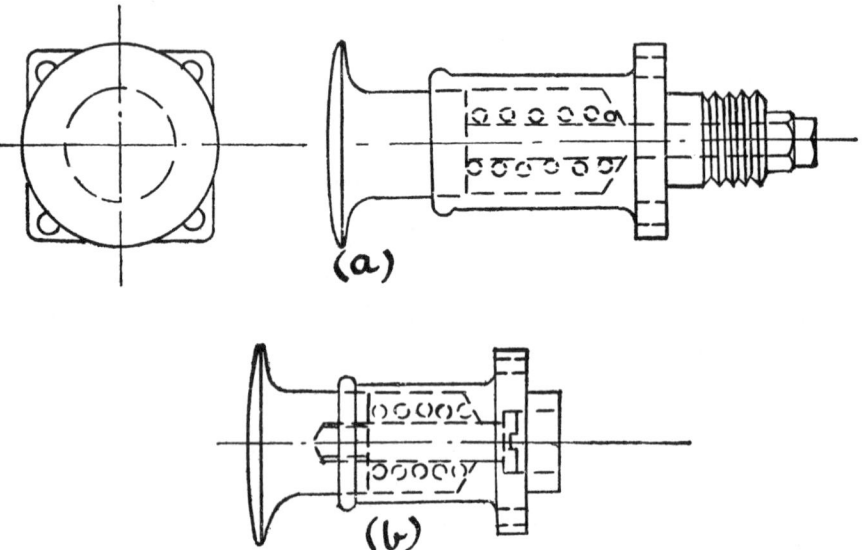

Fig. 127. Locomotive and Tender Buffers

The top of the water tank may be made removeable so as to give access to a hand pump, which is nearly always fitted in case of emergency, and to the suction filters required for the pumps and/or injectors. The filler or manhole should be made rather larger than the scale equivalent, so that the tender can be filled with water more quickly. The water pick-up dome is sometimes used as a filler cap as this is usually considerably larger than the filler itself (on the prototype tender). An additional filter may be fitted under the water filler, though this does tend to slow down the rate of filling even if made of large diameter.

The by-pass from the pump or pumps, where fitted, can be brought into the tender tank from underneath and then upwards towards the manhole. This enables the driver to see at a glance whether the pumps are working properly.

At the front end of the tender, there are usually two vertical columns wit handles, which in full-size practice are used to control the hand brakes and the water pick-up scoop. As the latter is not required in a model (except for a scale glass-case type of model), it is generally used as a control valve for the water supply to the injectors. The water pipe from the tender hand pump to the locomotive should be fitted with a union having a coarse thread, the pipe having two or three coils in it, underneath the tender, to provide the necessary flexibility.

Engine to Tender Coupling

An engine to tender coupling for a passenger hauling locomotive must be substantial, the pin on the locomotive being made a fixture, while the pin on the tender should be quickly removeable but so arranged that it cannot work loose in service otherwise a nasty accident could result.

If flexibility is desired, the amount of movement allowed between engine and tender should not be too great or trouble may arise from the various water pipes, etc. Spring buffers are sometimes fitted, the sockets of these being fitted to the tender drag beam, the heads of the buffers bearing direct on the locomotive beam.

Buffers

Locomotive buffers may have parallel or conical stocks, the former being more usual in modern engines. The stocks may be iron or gunmetal castings, in which case the small footstep which is often fitted can be made integral with the casting. Buffer heads are nearly always made from mild steel, and may be either round or oval. Oval heads must of course be prevented from turning either by the end of the shank being of square section, this working in a square cut in the stock, or a key and keyway may be used in the stock.

The springs in the buffers fitted to the front end of the locomotive may be such that about one-third of the weight of the engine would be required to close the head right up. Those fitted to the rear or tender buffers may be a little lighter. Rubber buffers are sometimes used, placed inside the buffer proper, or a combination of steel coil spring and rubber buffer may be used with success.

Couplings

While screw couplings give a most realistic finish to a model locomotive, they should not be used for "live" passenger hauling except in the very largest scales; a strong single link can be fitted to the hook on the passenger car, and this made to engage the hook on the locomotive.

Difficulty is often encountered in bending up the links of screw couplings. One method in common use is to turn the links from mild steel rod of large enough section to form the eyes, then bend the link on a simple jig consisting of a pin of suitable diameter pressed into a plate, with two levers on each side pivoted at one end so as to bend the ends of the workpiece inwards to the centre-line.

The drawhook is generally made from mild steel, the hook itself being well rounded and tapered in plan towards the outer end. The shank, where it passes through the

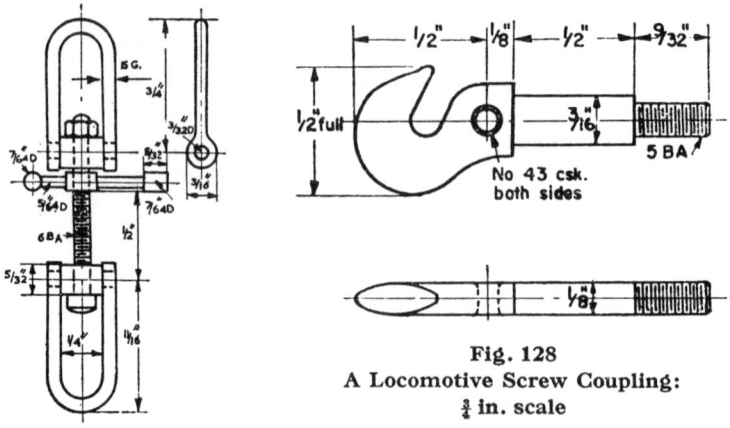

Fig. 128
A Locomotive Screw Coupling:
¾ in. scale

buffer beam, can either be of square or rectangular section, to prevent turning. For operation on sharp curves, the slot in the beam can be radiused on either side.

When plain three-link couplings are being made, the ends of the links should always be brazed, otherwise they may be pulled open in service.

Brake Pipes

Even if proper automatic brakes are not fitted, a model locomotive looks better with a vacuum or Westinghouse brake pipe fitted to the buffer beam. A dummy pipe can be bent up from brass rod, and rubber tubing used for the hose, the hose clips being made from brass or german-silver wire.

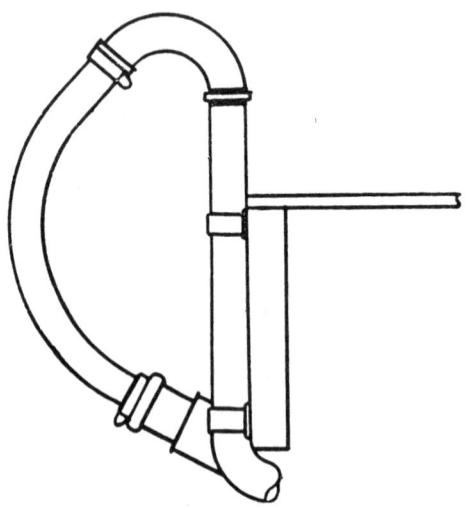

Fig. 129. Vacuum Brake Pipe

CHAPTER FIFTEEN

Fuels, Raising Steam, and Driving

Welsh steam coal is generally regarded as the ideal solid fuel for use in model locomotives, This is a good coal because not only is its steam raising capacity high, but it burns with practically no smoke, provided the boiler is made as it should be, and leaves practically no tarry residue and little ash.

Anthracite is also a good fuel, though it requires rather a strong blast to maintain it at the correct temperature. Many drivers use a mixture of Welsh steam coal and anthracite, in proportions which vary between 1 : 1 and 2 of the former to 1 of the latter.

The coal chosen should be carefully sifted and broken up to size according to the scale of the locomotive. For Gauge O and 1 models, the coal may be the size of peas, for $2\frac{1}{2}$ in. gauge models about the size of broad beans, for $\frac{3}{4}$ in. scale, a little larger, and so on. Charcoal is normally only used for raising steam, while ordinary house coal should never be used in model boilers. Some of the "patent" fuels may be considered, such as Phurnod, Coalite, etc., when Welsh steam coal is not available.

Difficulty in obtaining Welsh steam coal is often encountered by the individual model engineer. Most local coal merchants are prepared to order it specially, though the quantity involved usually means that a high price is asked. Help is often forthcoming from the Secretary of the nearest Model Engineering Society but, in the last resort, the National Coal Board will generally supply the address of a merchant able and willing to supply.

Oil Firing

Some model engineers prefer oil-firing to solid fuel. There are various types of burners available, using paraffin, and these work on the principle of the atomising of the fuel by means of a jet of steam from the boiler or by means of a pressure jet; the oil reservoir, which is fitted with a non-return valve, is pumped up with air to a pressure of anything between 15 and 40 lbs per square in., according to the type of burner.

Fig. 130 shows a vaporising type of oil burner designed by Mr. Edgar T. Westbury. This is of the diffused flame type and burns almost silently using either petrol or paraffin.

The Blakeney burner, Fig 131, is of the pressure atomising type, using steam or air pressure, according to the diameter of the nozzles used.

In all types of oil burners, a lot of noise does not mean that the flame being emitted is a very hot one; on the contrary, it may indicate that too much air is being consumed

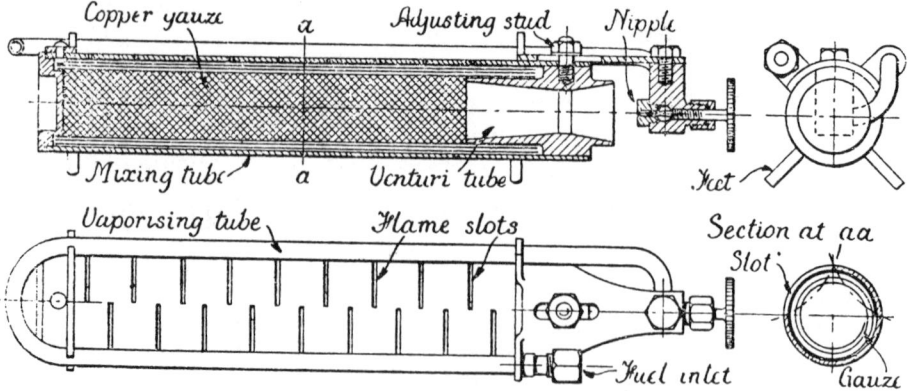

Fig. 130. Diffused-flame Oil Burner

in proportion to the fuel burnt. The presence of smoke usually indicates an insufficient supply of air.

Simple oil burners can be quickly made up using the standard Primus nipples. These are cheap to purchase and prickers can also be obtained to match. All parts should be made of brass and brazed. The only really essential requirement in the ordinary oil burner is that the vaporising tube should be made hot and kept hot.

The fuel container for an oil burner must be designed in a similar manner to a boiler as it has to stand considerable pressure. The cylindrical shape is therefore convenient, and the flat ends should be well stayed. A cycle valve can be used, but the valve must be quite air-tight or the pressure will drop very quickly.

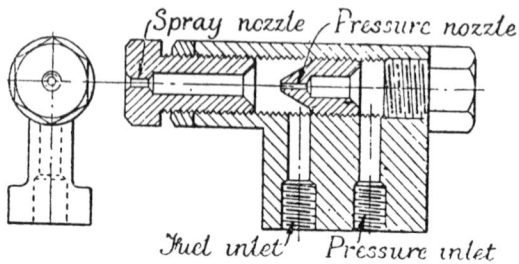

Fig. 131. Blakeney Pressure Vaporising Burner

Raising Steam

Before steam can be raised in a model locomotive fired by solid fuel, an induced draught up the chimney must be provided. There are several ways of providing this draught. One method is to use the locomotive's own blower, air being pumped into the boiler via a non-return valve; the air can be provided by a footpump or compressor. Another method is to fit an extension chimney into the engines' own chimney and to create a draught by means of a compressor or rotary blower or by means of a suction fan.

FUELS, RAISING STEAM, AND DRIVING

If a compressor is used for this purpose, an air reservoir must be provided between the compressor and the jet in the extension chimney. A rotary blower, which can be driven by an electric motor of about ¼ h.p., does not need an air reservoir, but the jet in the extension chimney may be of considerably larger bore as a rotary blower supplies a larger quantity of air at a lower pressure than a compressor.

The usual method of lighting the furnace in small locomotives is to use charcoal, broken up into small pieces and soaked previously in paraffin. The firebars are covered by a layer of the soaked charcoal and the external blower started. A match can then be thrown in and the firedoor closed. If the charcoal does not light immediately, a further teaspoon or two of paraffin can be put in. When the charcoal is properly alight, more charcoal can be fed in until a reasonable depth of fire is built

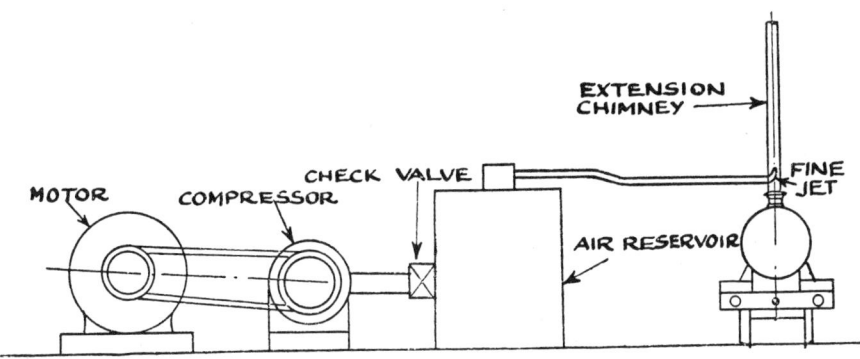

Fig. 132. Steam-raising Equipment

up, when coal can be fed, a little at a time, until a good depth is burning nicely; by this time there should be enough steam in the boiler to work the locomotive's own blower, so that the external auxiliary blower can now be removed.

Another method for lighting the fire is to use cotton-waste soaked in methylated spirit. As methylated spirit is highly volatile, the cotton-waste must be kept in an air-tight container until it is required for use. The soaked waste is placed on the firebars, a lighted match is thrown in, and charcoal added immediately.

Some model engineers use wood chippings to start their fire. These must of course be quite dry, and as soon as they are thoroughly alight, charcoal is fed in, and finally coal as before.

Preparation for the run

When there is enough steam in the model locomotive boiler to work the engine's own blower, it should not be long before the working pressure is reached. Any undue delay here should be investigated. It may be due to a leak in the smokebox, thus destroying the effect of the blower, or it may be that the blower jet has not been properly lined up with the petticoat pipe.

On reaching working pressure, the blower should be turned down a little, so that the various fittings can be tested, without excessive blowing-off from the safety valves.

Blowing-off can also be checked by opening the firehole door. The safety valves themselves should now be checked. If two valves are fitted, one will normally be set to blow off at a slightly higher pressure than the other, it will therefore be more likely to stick in service.

The injectors, if any, should next be tested. If these do not work immediately, the water supply can be checked, while it should be noticed whether the injectors themselves are cool. The water level must be kept under close scrutiny, remembering that the actual level of water in the boiler is always a little lower than shown on the gauge. Operation of the water gauge blowdown valve will ensure a clean glass in the water gauge. The lubricators should be filled with suitable steam cylinder oil, or heavy grade lubricating oil as appropriate, and the rachet gear on the oil pumps examined and tested.

If a steam brake is fitted to the locomotive, this can also be tested at this stage. Before any train is attached to the engine, the cylinder drain cocks should be opened, and the locomotive moved slowly up and down the track with the regulator very slightly opened. This will warm up the cylinders, and clear them of condensed water. At the same time the action of the pumps, if any, may be checked by opening the by-pass valves, and observing the return pipes.

Driving

The driving of the model locomotive follows the same principles as are observed in full-size practice. To start the engine, the reversing gear is put into full forward gear, the blower is closed, and the regulator opened slightly. If the engine wheels take hold, the train will move off smoothly, but if, as so often happens, the engine slips at the start, the regulator must be promptly closed and a more gradual opening tried. As the train gathers way, the regulator may be gradually opened up, and the reversing gear brought back a notch or two according to the weight of the train, the gradient of the track, etc.

The water gauge should be watched, and if the engine is fitted with pumps, the by-pass may be adjusted so that the water level in the boiler is kept as near as possible constant. Where injectors are in use, these should be put on immediately the locomotive is about to blow off, and when the top of the fire is showing bright.

As for firing, the general principle should be that immediately the safety valves show signs of lifting, further coal should be added so that unnecessary waste of steam is avoided. If this method still allows of frequent blowing off, due perhaps to a light load, the firehole door can be left open or partly open, and the fire kept to a smaller size. Coal should in any case be fed little and often, rather than a lot at infrequent intervals. The blower is only used when the locomotive is stationary.

While the train is running, a watch must be kept on the cylinder lubrication. When oil is being fed regularly to the cylinders, a certain amount will be thrown out by the blast and the top of the chimney will have an oily appearance. In addition there will probably be a slight seepage of oil from the piston rod and valve rod glands. On the other hand, an interruption in the oil supply will be noticed by a dry appearance around the top of the chimney and later by a different note from the pistons. If this is suspected, the locomotive should be stopped immediately, and the trouble rectified.

When it is desired to bring an engine to a stop, the regulator should be smartly closed in good time, the blower opened slightly, and the brakes applied as required.

Feed-water

Although many model engineers run their locomotives on ordinary tap water, where rain water is available in sufficient quantity this will be found a considerable advantage as the interior of the boiler keeps cleaner, especially in districts where the water is hard. The regular use of the blow-down valves will help a great deal to remove deposits, while the boiler should be taken off the frames at frequent intervals for proper cleaning.

After the run

As soon as a model locomotive is taken out of service, the ashpan and grate should be removed, and the boiler blown down. The smokebox door may then be opened and the ashes cleaned out, taking great care that these do not fall on to the lubricator or its ratchet mechanism. The tubes and flues can be swept out (suitable brushes can usually be obtained from model suppliers), and any cinders choking the flues or superheater elements carefully dislodged.

While the engine is still warm, it should be thoroughly cleaned down with oily rags, and the motion examined and oiled. If it is desired to pack the locomotive in a crate or box for transport, this should never be done until it is quite cold, otherwise condensation will occur and rusting will quickly set in.

A little care taken over the maintenance of the model steam locomotive will be amply repaid. An engine which has been well designed and carefully built, and driven only in a railway-like manner, should give years of service and pleasure to its owner and to all who follow this most fascinating hobby.

Index

	Page		Page
Adams bogie	41	Boilers, taper barrel	111
Adhesive weight	12	water-tube	109
Air brakes	154	Boring cylinders	57
Allan's link motion	87	Brake pipes	162
Anti-vacuum valves	133	Brakes	151
Anthracite	163	Brazing equipment	112
Articulated locomotives	10	Brick arches	120
Ashpans	122	Buffer beams	21
Atlantic locomotives	7	Buffers	161
Auxiliary blowers	164	Burners	164
Axleboxes	24	By-passes	146
Axle-driven pumps	143		
Axles	33	Cab fittings	125–136
		Cabs	155
Back-set	97	Caulking	118
Baker valve gear	103	Charcoal	163
Ball bearings	25	Check valves	130
Beading	156	Chimneys	137
Belpaire fireboxes	111	Cleading	159
Big ends	72–76	Coals	163
Bissel trucks	45	Combination levers	95
Blakeney Burner	164	Combustion chambers	16
Blast pipes	18	Compounding	18
orifices	18	Conjugated valve gears	104
Blow-down valves	136	Connecting rod big ends	73–76
Blower jets	133	small ends	72
valves	132	Connecting rods	72–76
Blowers	132	Consolidation locomotives	9
Bogies, Adams	41	Coupling rods	70
bar-framed	43	Couplings	161
swing-link	42	Crank axles	37
Boiler brazing	114–118	Crankpins	38
caulking	118	Cranks-return	101
flues	16, 116	Crossheads	63
joints	112	Crownstays	119
stays	118	Curved slides	91
testing	120	Curves for track	3
tube fitting	116	Cut-off	55–57
tubes	16, 116	Cutting ports	58
Boilers, coal-fired	111	Cylinders, inside	52
stayless	120	lining-up	62

	Page		Page
Cylinders, materials for piston-valve	54	Garratt locomotives	10
outside	50	Gauge glasses	125
poppet-valve	54	Gauges, loading	3
size of	54	standard	3
slide valve	56	Gear connecting rods	103
		Glands	61
Details	156	Gooch's valve gear	86
Die blocks	81	Goods engines	9
slip	83	Grates	122
Displacement lubricators	139	Gresley valve gear	104
Domes	137	Gudgeon pins	65
Donkey pumps	146	Guide bars	66
Drag beams	21		
Drain cocks	62	Hackworth valve gear	92
Drawhooks	161	Hand pumps	144
Driver's valve	152	Handrails	157
Driving	166	Heating surface	15
		Hornblocks	23
Eccentric rods	78, 102	Hydraulic tests	120
straps	77		
Eccentrics	77	Injectors	147
Effort, tractive	12	Inside admission	93
Exhaust clearance	57	cylinders	52
ports	57		
Expansion brackets	137	Jigs for quartering wheels	36
links	81–85, 96–100	Joints in boilers	112, 114
Expansion joints	137	Joy's valve gear	88–91
Express engines	6		
		Keat's angle plates	57
Feed pumps	143	Keying wheels	36
water	167		
Fireboxes	115	Lagging	159
Firedoors	121	Laminated springs	27
Firegrates	122	Lap of valves	55–56
Fire lighting	164	Lap and Lead movement	96
Firing	165	Lapping cylinders	58
Flash steam boilers	19	Launch-type links	81
Flues	16	Lead of valves	55
Footplates	155	Leaf springs	27
Footsteps	156	Leaks in boilers	118
Four-coupled engines	7	Lift of valves	130
Frames	20	Link motions	79–87
Free-lance designs	11	Links, expansion	81–85, 96–100
Fuels	163	Loading gauges	5
Fusible plugs	137		

INDEX

	Page
Locomotive types	6–11
Loco-type links	80
Lubrication	139
Lubricators, displacement	139
mechanical	140–142
Mainframes	20
Mallet locomotives	10
Manifolds	135
Marine-type big ends	73
Methylated spirit	165
Mikado locomotives	9
Mixed-traffic locomotives	8
Mogul locomotives	8
Motion brackets	69
plates	67
Needle roller bearings	102
Non-return valves	130
Oil burners	163
firing	163
Outside connecting rods	72
cylinders	50
Pacific locomotives	6
Packing	61
Paraffin	165
Passageways, cylinder	57
Petrol	163
Petticoat pipes	18, 124
Piston rings	59
valves	50, 60
Pistons	59
Platework	155
Pony trucks	45
Pop safety valves	129
Poppet valves	50
valve gear	106
Ports, cutting	58
steam and exhaust	54
Pressure, working	14
gauges	131
Pumps, axle-driven	143

	Page
Pumps, hand	144
oil	140
steam	146
Quartering wheels	35
Radial axleboxes	48
valve gears	88–103
Radius rods	94
Raising steam	164
Ramsbottom safety valves	129
Regulators	126
Relief valves	62
Return cranks	101
Reversing gears	108
Roller bearings	25, 73
Saddles	157
Safety valves	128
Sanding gear	158
Scales and gauges	1
Setting valves	85, 102, 108
Side-control springs	45
Side tanks	156
Silver solders	114
Single-wheelers	7
Slidebars	66
Slide valves	55, 60
Slip-eccentric gear	79
Small ends	72
Smokebox doors	124
Smokeboxes	123
Snifting valves	133
Solders	114
Spokes, wheel	30
Springs	27
Stays	118
Steam brake	151
Steam chests	60
lap	55
ports	54
pressures	14
raising	164
tests	120
whistles	134

	Page
Stephenson's gear	79–85
Stretchers	22
Studded glands	61
Superheater flues	16, 125
elements	125
Superheating	17
Superstructures	155
Swing-link bogies	42
Tank locomotives	10
Taper barrels	111
Tenders	159
Testing boilers	120
Top feeds	130, 131
Tractive effort	12
Trimmings	143
Turning wheels	30
Turrets	135
Tyre dimensions	4
Tyres, steel	29

	Page
Vacuum brakes	152
Valve gears	79–107
travel	57
Valves, piston	50, 60
poppet	54
Valves, slide	55, 60
Walschaerts' valve gear	93–102
Washout plugs	136
Water gauges	125
tanks	156
tests	120
Water-tube boilers	109
Welding	112
Wheel turning	30
Wheels, dimensions of	4
keys for	36
patterns for	30
tyres for	29
Whistle valves	135
Whistles, steam	134